Living at the Edge

SACRAMENT AND SOLIDARITY IN LEADERSHIP

PENNY JAMIESON

MOWBRAY

This book is dedicated with warmest affection to

Philip Gaze,

who with patience and humour has given me so much,
including the following:

I hallow his name wholesomely, changed from what I once was
before the charge of my children was wholly mine, before the
mitre touched my brows with something darker than age, to
assuage their need, comfort, console, cherish, lest if they perish,
I too be cast from the place with my peers.

Charles Williams, 1939

Mowbray
A Cassell imprint
Wellington House,
125 Strand, London WC2R 0BB
PO Box 605, Herndon, VA 20172

© Penny Jamieson 1997

First published 1997

British Library Cataloguing-in-Publication Data
A catalogue record for this book is available from the British Library.

ISBN 0–264–67439–1

Typeset by Keystroke, Jacaranda Lodge, Wolverhampton
Printed and bound in Great Britain by
Biddles Ltd, Guildford and King's Lynn

Living at the Edge

Contents

Acknowledgements   vii

Introduction   1

1   The context of power   8

2   Power in the church   22

3   Discerning   33

4   Caring   53

5   Holding   71

6   Ethics   85

7   The abuse of power   106

8   Authority   125

9   Searching   149

10   Relationships   164

11   Praying   177

Notes   196

Acknowledgements

A book like this owes much to many. By its very nature, it derives its life from a complex web of many, many friendships, fuelled by long and intense discussion. I have been a magpie, gathering treasures from all around me and I am grateful to all who have formed that web. I also wish to thank those who have helped me, who by nature has little tolerance for detail, do the careful work that has enabled this book take published form, in particular Pat Sandle, Tony Fitchett, Erice Fairbrother, Noeline Maffey and Ian Jamieson.

Extracts from poems by Eileen Duggan on pp. 85, 106, 125 and 177 are taken from Eileen Duggan, *Selected Poems*, ed. Peter Whiteford (Victoria University Press, 1994). Reproduced by permission.

Extracts from poems by Robin Hyde on pp. 1, 8, 22, 33, 53, 71, 149 and 164 are taken from Robin Hyde, *Selected Poems*, ed. Lydia Wevers (Oxford University Press, 1984). Reproduced with permission of Derek Challis.

Introduction

████████████
████████████

PINE-STICKS FOR A FIRE

When I am weighted down with fame
And wealthy past desire,
I shall spend every copper on
Pine-sticks for a fire.
    From Robin Hyde, 'Written in Cold'

Archbishop Ramsey is reported to have said of the work of a bishop that the job itself forces one to do theology; it forces one to reflect on power and freedom, grace, faithfulness and failure.[1] And a lot more beside.

I had in the course of my life as a Christian and as a human being reflected often and deeply on these concepts. But despite the intense sense of this call being God's call to the church, a call experienced world-wide, the whirlwind of episcopacy into which I was thrown in 1990 has, of necessity, thrown all these questions of faith, freedom, grace and faithfulness – and also failure – into sharp relief. The life of a bishop is full of ironies, frustrations and institutional quagmires, and somehow they, first and last, have to be held together within the fracturedness of my own spirit. It is only from those depths that I have anything at all to offer the church.

Despite the continuity of my inner life, there was little external continuity for me when I was ordained bishop. I was in fact thoroughly disoriented at every level of my being. In part, the turmoil that I experienced was due to being taken by surprise. I honestly had not expected ever to be a bishop. I do not think most of my male colleagues have been especially ambitious in this regard; but for them it was within the realms of both possibility and desire. For me, it was beyond the reach of imagination. All too often, it would seem, our vision, the exact shape and nature of vocation as we perceive it, is tempered by the available possibilities. God's vision is larger.

I cannot pretend therefore that I was ready and waiting for this call; indeed I was quite resistant, and this was contrary to my earlier experience. When I had sought ordination as a priest, the then Bishop of Wellington,[2] a cautious man, was very hesitant; it took me a long time to persuade the church of the validity of my call. When the church wanted to make me a bishop, it took the church some time to convince me. I am a reluctant prophet.

When, almost immediately following my ordination to the episcopate, I found myself thrown into a maelstrom of confusion, anger and at times downright rebellion, it was that strange Spirit-driven relationship between prayer, experience and theological reflection that provided, often in uneasy and imbalanced proportions, the framework for my return to sanity and to the acceptance and the appreciation, even the enjoyment, of my vocation.

I think that ordination always changes people – that is what the Holy Spirit is about – but for me it has been a sea-change. My consecration precipitated me into a realm of activity, publicity and spiritual turmoil for which, despite my best efforts, I was totally unprepared. The ordinal itself is quite terrifying in the expectations that it gives rise to, but these pale into insignificance against the expectations that people had of me. I scarcely knew who or what I was.

I began a long and painful struggle, always, to my amazement, from the inside of faith, to find the match between the expectations of the church, people and sacrament, and myself: what was the real shape of episcopacy for me? There were some moments of severe doubt; but God knew what God was getting, even if, as it sometimes seemed, no one else did.

I searched long and hard for the key to matching my interior life with my exterior life; specifically to matching the interior life of my spirit, all that I was and all that I longed to be for the God I had been called to serve, with the exterior life, in which all my relationships with friends, family, passing acquaintance and unknown stranger had shifted.

I knew too that to search relentlessly for this match between my interior life and the demands of the job was central to the task that I had been set. For without that fundamental harmony my spirit would have died and I would have little of depth to offer; I simply could not believe that was the will of the God who had called me.

I realized too that this was essential as well to the proper conduct of my office. For, despite all the institutional trappings of episcopacy, the basic task of a bishop is very personal; in fact it is through the construct of personal relationships bridging the gap between the demands of public functioning and the arena of personal piety that a clear and robust relationship with God flourishes. It is to make personal, through conflict and misunderstanding, the kind of unity of self-understanding that enables the church to move beyond preoccupation with its own squabbles, and to hold in focus something of the vision of God's intentions.

It is personal because the basic building brick is trust, which can never be achieved by bureaucracy; it is trying to interpret people to each other, especially at the points when they are inclined to tell each other to go to hell. And all the time the bishop is not beyond the issues, but right there entangled in the middle of them, trying to locate a robust theology of the church, articulating it repeatedly, both publicly and in prayer.

Such a venture depends critically on the degree to which the exterior realities find a place in the life of the spirit. There is the continual blocking-out of reality, the distancing of the view from the earth, that is a necessary consequence of life on a pedestal. I have found the necessity to 'lie low', to listen carefully with an ear close to the ground. There is continual public suspicion which demands that I subject my work to a willing suspicion of my own. There is continual public vulnerability which cries out for an open and receptive place in the heart.

These pages contain some of these reflections. Inevitably they focus sharply on the issue of power, for the sudden elevation to institutional power was the most noticeable shift for me on becoming a bishop. But freedom, grace, faithfulness and failure are also interwoven.

This will not be a comprehensive walk through episcopacy; there have been many of these lately as the self-understanding of the church grows somewhat dim in the face of so many changes. Such studies locate episcopacy within the life of the church across space and across time, for loss of confidence leads the church to identify its authority sources more absolutely in the past, either in magisterial pronounce-ment or in Scripture. This writing is rather a teasing-out of experience, episcopacy from the inside. For sure, this is my experience as a woman; but the longer I am in this job, and the more I get to know of other bishops, the more I suspect that we have much in common. It is a personal experience, with no validity beyond the fact that it is the experience I own, and, despite the undoubted fact that my irritations and limitations show through, it is genuinely a celebration.

My experience is not given for me alone; I have on numerous occasions discussed the issues that are opened up in these pages with women friends, often at length, at times rapidly, always with a mixture of affection and sharp intensity as the reality beneath reality is touched on and we search for the solidarity we long for. And such explorations are always open to the hurt they can so easily cause; for women and power do not mix comfortably together, and my location is that of no one else – at the edge, so to speak. Such talk, though often intolerably painful, is pure gold; it has the quality of prayer from the depth of my being; this is the only place where reconciliation is possible.

For to be a woman in Christian leadership today, especially to be in the high-profile position of a bishop, is to carry numerous symbolic associations in a society that is still fundamentally divided along gender lines. It is to be opening up, through the hints and glimpses given by the symbols, a radical potential; one which, though existing in the present, is constantly pushing the constraints of institutionalism and tradition. And there is not one of us who has not felt the temptation to snuggle into the mystique of these and indulge in premature temporizing. But radical potential is the gift that Jesus gives us.

Central to all these concerns is a critical suspicion of power, the topic of the hour! Over the years the church has suffered from the power of others; it has sought power, it has used power, it has shared power, it has abused power, it has rationalized power and it has denied power. Always there has been a mystique about power. Is this because the inside of power is, necessarily, known only to a few, or is it, within Christian circles, because it is strongly linked to the call of God and to the interpretation of God's will for the church?

The central paradox of our faith is that the power of God is most truly revealed in the weakness of God, and, at the same time, that power is unlimited, uncontrollable, prodigal even and can never be definitively located in any individual or structure. There is more than enough for all who would hold out their hands to receive. But this is not what we mean when we address the contemporary preoccupation with power. Such preoccupation is undoubtedly a measure of the unfaithfulness of the church.

It is, however, significant that contemporary comments on the nature of episcopacy have not addressed this issue. Episcopacy is, all but 100 per cent, a male world, just that and only that in the eyes of many men. The Christian church is so imbued with the normativity of male experience that female experience is excluded; in fact, it is simply not noticed, and the participation of women makes little difference,[3] is not a focus for analysis or comment. The invisibility of women is thus sadly confirmed, just as is the male sense of ownership of the church.

But issues of institutional power are inevitably thrown sharply into focus when women, historically and structurally the ones over whom power was held, assume power within areas customarily reserved for men. Indeed, if the requests to speak or write that come to me are any indication, the mix of women and power is a source of almost endless fascination – and nowhere more so than within church circles. Perhaps this is because the conjunction of women and power in the church is still a novelty, despite the fact that within the Anglican Communion women have been ordained for more than twenty years. The issue appears to have come to a real crunch since women have been ordained as bishops.

As we will see, for women who have wrestled with both the theoretical and liberational challenges of the feminist movement over the past thirty years or so, the issue of the power that has origins and impulse in the spiritual realm is particularly significant. It is an interest that is by no means confined to Christian women. This 'second-wave' feminism, which grew out of the primary energy and insight of Christian women,[4] has consistently acknowledged that for women to resist only the externals of the structures of power is to ignore the internal hold that these structures have on the consciousness of women; feminist responses have included seeking alternative definitions of God, alternative gods and designer gods.

The Christian church has consistently, through both story and symbol, reinforced the structures of male leadership, and is seen by many women not as liberating, but as enslaving, of both the social potential and the spirit of women. So questions arise about the gender of God, about the language we use of God, and about the possibility and desirability of God. This has from time to time indeed been my experience and these questions have been my questions too. I live within the feminist critique of Christian theology and ecclesial practice, but it is the Christian tradition and the pattern of Christian worship that has led me to God. I have found within Christian insights on the Spirit, on incarnation, on creation, on the Trinity and on the one God who is the overflowing source of life, fragments of wisdom and divine insight that I have come to cherish and that continue to amaze me. I have found the reality of the God that is mystery beyond all imagining and all language. However, there are times when it is indeed hard to hold these twin polarities of the Christian faith and feminist insights together. Often, indeed, the bridge is too wide.[5]

So the reflections in these pages are therefore both spiritual and ecclesial theology; spiritual because they come from the at-times agonizing experience of prayer at the depth of my being, and ecclesial as that prayer wrestles with the undeniable reality of the considerable institutional power of a bishop, and with some of the very difficult and unattractive aspects of our church life. These days, a lot of people run away when they confront these realities; not an option for a bishop. In fact, I reckon that one of the radical calls of a bishop is to love the church, continually, robustly and realistically – whatever.

This book is not an apologia for women bishops; it is not my purpose to persuade those people, priests, prelates and provinces that have reservations about the wisdom and theological orthodoxy of the ordination of women to the episcopate, of the desirability of such a move. Rather, this is an exploration of the issues and tensions raised by such an ordination, a theological reflection on them as part of the postmodern critique of power. It is not a book from the church for the church, for it seeks to engage beyond the church, as the church does not exist in isolation from the questions of our times. This is a book that pushes at the edges and, possibly, glimpses beyond the horizon.

Becoming a bishop was not the first time my life had changed markedly, but, while faith has frequently wavered, it is very deeply embedded in my being and is the context in which I instinctually live. I have learnt over many years to practise what I have come to call 'reflective spirituality'. I outline this further in the last chapter. In the process of getting to grips with the realities, spiritual and ecclesial, of the tensions inherent in being a woman bishop, I have learnt considerably more about this. This book is essentially the product of such reflective spirituality, which grew through so many tears and prayers and laughter.

I am what God has made me, in the beginning and from the beginning – no more, no less. Specifically, I am one of many New Zealanders whose lives and imaginative strength are drawn from opposite sides of the world. I spent the first 22 years of my life in England; now I stand as a pakeha (of European origin) New Zealander. I am one of the *tau-iwi*, the people who came later to this country,[6] a fact which has, over the many years I have been here, honed my taste for observation and given me a deep appreciation of the spiritual value of 'living at the edge'. I am a woman, and I write from the perspective of the dominant culture in Aotearoa/New Zealand.

In so many ways, the Diocese of Dunedin has been an excellent place for a woman bishop to explore episcopacy. It is about as far south as the Anglican Communion stretches, and I have been able to get on with the job, without undue self-consciousness and away from the curious eyes of the rest of the communion.

For some years now, I have spent my holidays and reflective time at a small settlement on the North Otago coast. Beautiful but remote, it is for me a place of freedom and release. It has become a powerful symbol of what it means to 'live at the edge'. It was there that I wrote this book, which is essentially about the dynamics that occur when the edges of a particularly strong patriarchal institution are pushed and the vision of what God's church could be is expanded; as such, it is an exploration of episcopacy that is both reaching out, stretching out, and is being stretched. At its best, this is Christian leadership that is both holy and whole, both sacrament and solidarity.

The lines of verse that precede each of these reflections are from two New Zealand women poets whose work has long intrigued me, Robin Hyde and Eileen Duggan. For me, a dabbler poet, they both seek, with a deep affinity for the individuality and the particularity of this country, to plumb the depths, to touch a spirituality that could speak beyond these shores and beyond the constricting languages of doctrine and polemic. They explore the boundaries of the spirit and offer fresh insight and possibilities. These are my hopes for this book.

Much of what I say on these pages will be 'pine-sticks for a fire' – they will offer comfort to some, some they will warm, overheat perhaps; they will throw light on some issues, but they will burn out. These are thoughts of our time; God's future remains as mysterious as ever.

1

The context of power

AFFRONTING GRAVE ORDER

Is it for me to dare, whilst others dream.
Pity, my God, on all bewildered fools
Who must affront grave order, steadfast rules
Mellowed by centuries!
                    From Robin Hyde, 'Joan of Arc'

Much of our fascination about power derives from interest in and analysis of the major shifts in power and the distribution of power that have occurred in recent years. No organization, no institution has remained unaffected by these. They have raised such questions as: what is the nature of power? where is it located? are there any alternatives? what are the implications of our understandings of power for people and communities who have hitherto seen themselves as powerless?

The fragmentation of power

The shifts in power and in the distribution of power that have occurred in recent decades have called into question the seemingly monolithic structure of power, and consequently have also questioned the understandings of truth which have supported the structures of power in the past. This questioning has profoundly affected both the self-perceived and the externally perceived reality of the church.

Power is fragmenting. Since that mighty symbol of power the Berlin Wall collapsed in 1989, the world has seen challenges to totalitarian regimes that it would not have believed possible, in the old Soviet Union, in Eastern Europe, in South Africa and in many other countries where indigenous and minority peoples are asserting their rights. People are seeking local and ethnic identity and governance.

The fall of the most obvious symbols of power, the totalitarian regimes of nation states, is the heaviest; and the consequence has often been the resumption of ancient ethnic hostilities. The Christian venture has known such fragmentation throughout its history, from well before the first major split between East and West, through the Reformation, to the present day which is noted for the proliferation of sects. There is, as well, fragmentation within sects and denominations as people explore their perceptions and understandings of religious reality and group together with kindred spirits. Far from any common basis of theology or ecclesiology we now have many kings in many castles, many bishops in many palaces, and some in lesser dwellings.

But this is not a cause for further warfare, for religious leaders appear to be sufficient to and content with their own domains of power. The gospel we preach points to the Kingdom of God. If we believe that ours is authentic, why take notice of any other?

Gospel alternatives to power

There is a built-in feature of the gospel that contributes to the fracturing of power. The gospel of Jesus Christ preaches liberation from the social conditions and structures that oppress and bind (Luke 4.16–20). Jesus was particularly hard on institutional religion, and proclaimed that he was the alternative. We are a faith with our own built-in critique and protection against the unwarranted accumulation of power, so there is a real sense in which Christianity will never rest authentically on unquestioned structures of power. The divisions of our history testify to the effectiveness of this critique.

The theology of liberation[1] explicitly linked the continuing action of God and the call of Christ to liberate the victims of society with the plight of those who were suffering under totalitarian regimes in South America. It is both a theology and an ethic of confronting the world. With liberation theology went a sophisticated and careful analysis of the way in which the structures of power are forged and the ways in which they can oppress. It was not long before the principles of liberation theology began to be applied to other groups that started to become aware of their oppression. This was the birth of 'Black theology' in the United States[2] and also of feminist theology. And there were others. The churches, and Christian theology, began to see the rise of multiple voices claiming liberation.

The fragmenting of society and of the church led to considerable philosophical speculation on the nature and location of power. This has contributed to Christian theological reflections on power. It is these that I explore in this chapter.

Challenging power with power

The dilemma faced by those who would challenge power with power
has long been clear: we become what we hate. Foucault put it this way:
'To even imagine another system is to extend our participation in the
present system.'[3]

This dilemma is seen most sharply in revolutionary situations where
those who have long struggled against repressive rule are triumphant
and themselves become the rulers. All too often in history, in biblical
times and very recently, we have seen those who assume leadership
rapidly becoming tyrants themselves. In a number of countries in
Eastern Europe and the former Soviet Union, which in the last few
years have discarded communist regimes, there has been within a year
a further revolution to overthrow the leader who has himself become
dictatorial. The Christian position is that oppression should not be
replaced with oppression. Indeed at the heart of the Christian faith is
the call to establish justice, a justice which oppresses no one.

The focus is particularly sharp when a woman gains a position
that is identified as one of power, and carries with her all the ideals
about transforming the nature of power. It is all too tempting for her to
abandon her memories of her own struggle and suffering and, rejoicing
in her own achievement, adopt the ways and means of those who have
always been powerful, and embark on the oppression of others. So
Moses becomes Pharaoh and the Virgin Mary becomes the Mother
Superior.

The inevitability of power

It would seem that our idealism runs away with us, and we fail to
have due regard for the raw fact of the human impossibility of doing
without power. Foucault, locating power within the body, whether
physical or politic, points out that 'for each move by one adversary,
there is an answering one by another'.[4]

Foucault suggests relocating the starting-point for power. Rather
than beginning at the centre or the top, as a hierarchical structure
would indicate, one should look within the community and undertake
an *ascending* analysis of power. Such an analysis not only depends on
the internal dynamics of the community, but, Foucault indicates,
should start with the 'infinitesimal mechanisms' which each have their
own story, the exchanges and relations between individuals.

This is a much finer analysis, but the conclusions that Foucault
draws are noticeably global; he frequently uses language which argues

that power 'pervades the entire social body', or is 'omnipresent'. Thus all of social life comes to be a network of power relations – relations which should properly be analysed not at the level of large-scale social structures but rather at very local, individual levels. In practice, and in brief, power is everywhere and so, ultimately, nowhere. This is extraordinarily diffusive; it is also a profoundly pessimistic position; not only because it confirms the inevitability of power, but also because it points to the endless fragmentation of power. Is humankind really destined to this pattern of endless challenge, fragmentation and struggle?

Responses to power

An analysis of power that focuses on the location of power paints a grim picture. When power is relocated within all parts of the body, it is not seen as a personal attribute, but as an attribute of the structure in which the individual is placed, and the focus shifts to the quality of relationships.

This not only diffuses the negative image of power, but also holds the seeds of redemption. This is evident in Foucault's comment on the fact that in Western societies, since medieval times, institutional power has been seen as repression:

> I believe that this is a wholly negative, narrow, skeletal conception of power . . . If power were never anything but repressive, if it never did anything but to say no, do you really think one would be brought to obey it? What makes power hold good, what makes it accepted, is simply the fact that it doesn't weigh on us like a force that says no, but that it traverses and produces things, it induces pleasure, forms knowledge, produces discourse. It needs to be seen as a productive network which runs through the whole social body, much more than as a negative instance whose function is repression.[5]

In short, power with consent has the potential to foster identity and community and to be both productive and creative with positive results, as opposed to the inertia of negativity.

There is something of the same ambiguity in the responses to the power of God of some Christians and post-Christians, including those women for whom Christianity as practised in the churches has been an oppressive experience. I am not referring to the issue of inclusive language, for the problem is much greater. Institutional power is authoritative, 'top-down', has absolute autonomy, is self-sufficient, independent and separate, and utterly unaccountable. Such a model is associated primarily with the conventional 'Father' image of God.

But where such power is seen as a productive network that runs through the whole body of the church, is seen as cohesive, relational, necessary and acknowledged, and responsible in its turn for the life of the community, then we can see why, despite its negative attributes, it persists. Such a model of power derives support and energy from the theology of the mutuality of the Trinity, where the three persons exist in interdependence and find their mutuality in each other. It supports solidarity.

Power and the structures of power

When power is seen as a function of structure, it becomes possible for the individual who holds the power on behalf of the community, who in many cases stands at the top of a hierarchy, to work in a way that enables the members of the community to acknowledge their own power and their stake in the power-holder. Foucault has here identified one of the reasons for the fascination of power – the twin responses of need and pleasure on one the hand and of resentment, even fear, on the other.

The perception of power as residing in the community, in the body, finds a ready parallel in the Christian image of the church as the Body of Christ, with Christ as its head, which cannot function without the health of the component parts. This image focuses on the whole, and sees the holder and symbol of power as only existing in relation to the whole. But the well-established practice of locating power within the individual, the head, persists. The community may well participate in the structures of power; but in popular thinking, power and its exercise are seen as personal attributes, and since it is individuals who stand at the pinnacles of hierarchies it is the use or abuse of power by individuals that comes under both philosophical and personal scrutiny.

However, such an account, for good or ill, only allows for abstract individuals, not real women with ideals, attempting to respond to the community and the context of their power. Foucault's theory may underestimate the fact that certain institutions, structures, histories and rhetoric are constituted as individuals, and this is an effect and consequence of power. It is natural then for individuals seeking leadership for their community to seek an individual in whom to locate the power enabling that leadership to function.

Feminist responses

Feminism derives its founding identity and its existence from a presumption of powerlessness. It has drawn energy from confrontation and challenge. However, the feminist position depends on a gendered analysis of power. In feminist terms, power, the traditional mark of patriarchy, is itself to be questioned; hence the ambivalence of feminism about power.

Foucault's analysis of power has been welcomed by feminists who seek the further dismantling of the monolithic power structures marked by and equated with patriarchy. But such dismantling has also been sharply criticized by many feminists who say that Foucault's perception of the diffuse nature of power amounts to a refusal both to believe in and to grasp power. They feel that this leaves feminism with no standpoint from which to engage in emancipatory politics, and so nothing to strive for.[6] Many see this as an assumption of powerlessness which can become entirely oppositional and purely negative, relying on exposing and denouncing power rather than transforming the structures and ethos that have enabled such dominating power structures to evolve.

Because Foucault's analysis locates power within the relationships between individuals who constitute the community, it brings an uncertainty which can lead to the ultimate fragmentation of society into individuals standing alone. Picking up on these implications, many women strongly resist the validity of universalist statements and so are uncertain even about the validity of asserting gender as a universal category. This uncertainty extends, as well, not only to race but to any other category. Such a reaction makes feminist discourse hard to grasp.

One possible response to such theoretical fragmentation is a huge celebration of difference, which goes along with a will to resist the assumption of any kind of power – in themselves, in their groups, and in others. This response is strongly associated with opposition to institutionalism of any kind, formal or informal, and is the philosophical underpinning of much of the critique of the church raised by women.

Feminist analysis is primarily critique; it has not seen power as an instrument of community empowering, but rather as the operation of a system from which women are excluded. To this system are attached all the negative characteristics Foucault ascribes to repression: it is silencing, juridical and negative, with the force of prohibition and domination. The reaction against this has generally sought to implement the process of diffusion through techniques of power-sharing. In many ways this simply perpetuates the negative view of power when held by an individual on behalf of the community.

The situation is in fact very difficult. We should not underestimate the extent to which the structures and institutions in which women are beginning to take leadership have been formed and shaped by conceptions of leadership that derive from a long history of authoritarian, monarchical and patriarchal practice. There is real difficulty in creating alternatives. In every situation of historical power imbalance, the ruling class, race and gender construct the material and social relations in which all members of the society must participate. Such structures cannot be dismissed as simply false or misguided; they are very powerfully persistent and, as we have seen, quite intractable.[7]

The dilemma has been frustrating for women. For such fragmentation lacks, by definition, a common vision, and denies to women offering leadership within the women's movement the right to articulate such a vision as would inspire and draw others on – this is a very basic function of leadership. Furthermore, such fragmentation contributes to the tendency among women to avoid divisive issues which might threaten the unity of the group and could render it impotent. Brennan locates this dilemma in the fragmentalism that characterizes current analyses of and responses to power:

> Post-structuralism defines all knowledges, whether feminist or patriarchal, as 'situated' ones, operating from competing interests. This gets away from the notion that there can be ultimate resolution to the question of difference that has so troubled feminism. Instead of a common vision it encourages the cultivation of local allegiances and particular interests in order to dismantle the notion of universal models, 'which however benign they may appear, work ultimately to confirm the old power structures'.[8]

Feminist theory has wrestled with the impotence of this position. One response has been that of the French philosopher and feminist Luce Irigaray, who asserts the connection between women's absence of identity and the male divinity of patriarchy, and who observed that 'the divine provides a possibility for the fulfilment of the subject which must of necessity be gendered'.[9] Perceiving the way in which male-constructed religious systems have supported and encouraged male power structures, she says: 'If he (man) has no existence in his gender, he lacks his relation to the infinite and, in fact, to finiteness. To avoid finiteness, man has sought out a unique male God, God has been created out of man's gender.'[10] She then describes the significance of spiritual independence for women:

> Divinity is what we need to become free, autonomous, sovereign.
> No human subjectivity, no human society, has ever been established
> without the help of the divine . . . If women have no God, they are
> unable either to communicate or commune with one another. They
> need, we need, an infinite if they are to share a little.[11]

This is certainly a position that would reclaim power for women and
one which many women have explored, albeit less theoretically and
more ritualistically. The connection between spiritual and temporal
power is well attested in the history of the world's religions, and the
nexus of spirituality and power remains fascinating and absorbing for
women, both in theory and in practice.

However, the vision proposed by Irigaray leads directly to the issue
of competing gods, and also brings the struggle for gender equity and
justice right into the discussion of the nature of God. In pointing so
clearly to the constructed nature of the male god, and in proposing a
similar construct for a 'feminine divine', Irigaray reduces Godness to
gender-support only. God has always been more than this – more mystery, more power, more vulnerability than is humanly conceivable.
The challenge to all men and women who claim vision, relationship
and support from God is to relinquish ownership and control of God.
It may be that this is too much to ask; but I am quietly optimistic. The
dilemma of power remains, and swings between twin poles: on the
one hand, acceptance of the diffused nature of power and hence of its
vulnerability; and, on the other, the need for a measure of power,
including divine power, to promote vision, equity and social justice.
Both have their place within Christian spiritual theology and ethics.

The power of powerlessness

This is indeed complex. In many ways the diffusion of energy and
power can be seen as a voluntary assumption of powerlessness, a kind
of secular parallel to a spirituality of vulnerability. Such powerlessness, however, though founded on a respect for the difference of others, is also a strongly critical stance that focuses less on the reform of
the wrong use of power and more on transforming the very nature of
power itself.

Such a focus has its difficulties. I have seen people who question the
necessity of power seeking to shed any traces of power they might
have: thinking that in order to champion the oppressed, they must
scramble to identify downwards. In the process they give up their
responsibilities for using the power and resources that they do have.

Moreover, this posture is not always as meek and powerless as it would make out. For such voluntarily appropriated powerlessness tends to adopt a position of 'official knowledge' with regard to what the oppressed are seeking, and thereby reinforces the relations of domination in our society and our institutions by insisting that those who have been marginalized remain at the margins. This is a dynamic that knows no boundaries, that operates within the politics of gender, race, class or whatever.

An analysis of power that focuses on its diffusion and fragmentation essentially makes the struggle for empowerment harder for any group of marginalized people, for it invites them to place more regard on the particularities and rights of other groups, especially those with whom they share marginalization, than on seeking their common vision, identity and purpose. An example of this has been the genuine desire of many pakeha women who, from their own experience of marginalization, find common cause with the struggle for justice by Maori, and the quest for just relations between Maori and pakeha. Because the issues, though similar, differ significantly (see Chapter 2) this can give rise to real tension. The feminist cause cannot be pursued at the expense of the racism struggle, for Maori too are marginalized – the agendas are very mixed.

Similarly, if we place the emphasis on both the heterogeneity and the specificity of each situation, we focus primarily on how individuals experience and exercise power; hierarchical structures, with a single individual at the pinnacle, become the first target of the critique of power, at the expense of an analysis of social structures which empowers group action. In churches, women can all too easily expend all their energy in the critique of those in leadership, such as bishops, and so exhaust any transformational energy they might have had.

Christian justice eschews such a response, for the cause of justice needs to use power to overcome power. It needs an account that will enable and facilitate social transformation, and it regards effective resistance as more significant than the transformation of the nature of power itself. It is thus as vulnerable to the misuse of power as any marauding army of the past has ever been.

Incarnational power

The tensions between universal power and localized power are well known within the Christian story. The at times seemingly arbitrary or irrelevant exercise of the power of God in the Hebrew Testament is transfigured in the gospel experiences into the God who became through the incarnation truly localized and particularized. God became a Jew, suffering under the cruelties of Roman domination, and enduring the death the Romans reserved for those who challenged their power. God was with the Jewish people, not as a philosophical idea or a set of commandments delivered with all the pomp of divine authority, but as a person, who knew them, understood them, loved them, and in doing so drew the threads between the particularities of their own suffering and the universal love of God. It was a profound act of solidarity.

The Christian claim is that the relationship established by Jesus the Christ is not limited to that place and time, but is accessible to all, at every place and every time. This is not a shift back into the easy and distant universalism of the God of the Hebrew Scriptures; it is God incarnate, localized in every human situation, whenever people are open to that relationship, which is every bit as particular and loving as it was in gospel days. I used to have a book, lent so often that it got lost, of pictures of Christ crucified – as a clown, a wounded soldier, a beggar, a king, a woman, a child and so on. It is a profoundly moving book, and a vivid reminder that the power of God is most truly found, not in the structures of power, or in the analysis of power, but in God's willingness to come to us, in relationships. A verse I have often turned back to for Good Friday addresses puts it movingly:

> All we want in Christ, we shall find in Christ.
> If we want little, we shall find little.
> If we want much, we shall find much;
> but if, in utter helplessness, we cast our all on Christ,
> He will be to us the whole treasury of God.[12]

This truly has the capacity to empower.

The structure of power within the church

Human institutions always need some structure. Much of the history of the Christian church can be read as the struggle to find the form of structure that authentically embodies the gospel experience of Jesus the Christ. The intensity and continuing nature of that struggle is convincing testimony to both the difficulty of the task and the constant challenge that God in Christ issues in each place and time.

The hierarchical systems of the church clearly stand within this analysis and critique of structural power. The Christian church has a long-established rhetoric by which it articulates its understanding of the power it gives to its leaders, and so there are many questions that Christian thought and spirituality would wish to address to the post-modernist analysis of power. Some of the questions would undoubtedly mask the reality of our own practice; like most people and institutions, we are very good at not seeing what we do not wish to see. However, it is also true that Christian understanding of power, deriving as it does from the cross, can still mount a strong critique of more worldly notions of power. It is all quite clear in the Gospels:

> 'You know that those who are regarded as rulers of the Gentiles lord it over them. Not so with you. Instead, whoever wants to become great among you must be your servant, and whoever wants to be first must be a slave of all. For even the Son of Man did not come to be served, but to serve, and to give his life as a ransom for many.' (Mark 10.41–45)

Bonhoeffer, writing from his prison cell, expressed this most poignantly: 'Before God and with God we live without God. God lets himself be pushed out of the world onto the cross. He is weak and powerless in the world, and that is precisely the way, the only way in which he is with us and helps us.'[13] This critique, developed over the Christian centuries, is deep within Christian spiritual understanding of power and has informed our theological understanding of our own patterns of leadership, of episcopacy. I shall look at some of these now, and in the further chapters of this book develop a contemporary comment on their practice.

In the first place, when the church makes a bishop it ordains a *person* to that office. It is quite clearly an individual who is called and who is ordained by the action of the Spirit in the sacrament of ordination. The act of ordination is the assent of the church to that call and to the person who holds that office. It represents an individual acting in community and taking on the role that the community requests. This action from below is particularly evident in those churches, like the Anglican Church in New Zealand, in which each diocese elects its own bishop. The single individual placed at the pinnacle of the hierarchy is neither dissociated from the community nor an abstraction on whom power is laid.

The individual in question is, like other members of the community, one who is also called to serve and to live in divine obedience. But this calling is in itself no guarantee that such power will always be exercised with perfect discretion. Indeed both history and our knowledge of human nature would suggest that this could not be the case; but our God is one who lives close to us and the challenges God offers are always very close, so those in power are given the grace to respond with clear self-awareness and can make a new start.

Christians in leadership can never place all the blame for their failings onto the structure, and neither do they need to. As St Augustine said at his ordination, 'For you I am a bishop, but with you I am a Christian . . . As then I am more pleased to be redeemed with you than I am to be set over you, I shall, as the Lord commanded, be more completely your servant.'[14]

Foucault, writing from a post-modernist perspective, and, quite inadvertently, reflecting this theme of servanthood, suggests an ascending analysis of power; one which starts from 'infinitesimal mechanisms'. Although diffusive, and extraordinarily narrow in its preoccupation with power as the basic relationship between beings, this does bear some similarity to the Anglican concept of dispersed authority, in which the authority at the centre is both diffused throughout the structures and is also dependent on those structures for its very existence. This is the calling of Christian leadership to servanthood.

Dispersed authority can result in many different centres of power. A recent report on the administration of cathedrals in the Church of England points to the many different centres of influence within the church: Lambeth Palace, the bishops, the Church Commissioners and General Synod, individual dioceses, cathedrals, parishes and so on.[15] In New Zealand, the structure that holds the seven pakeha dioceses of our church together is currently not very strong; the dioceses are largely independent units. This is not always easy for those who would negotiate with us. It would seem to be close to Foucault's ideal that power should be everywhere and so ultimately nowhere, but for many it is more like a nightmare.

Yet such dispersed authority is deeply rooted in Anglican self-identity. Bishop John Howe said that within Anglicanism 'authority moves towards the centre and not from it'. But there are a number of indications throughout the present-day Anglican Communion that, whereas the centre of authority is primarily to be located at the centre of the structure, the general drift of credible authority (see Chapter 8) is largely centrifugal, towards the edge. This raises some serious questions for women who would exercise episcopal leadership.

The tension between relational authority and hierarchical authority is clearly seen when the bishop is in synod. The system of synodical government, which was put into place in this country at the time of the first constitution (1857) by George Augustus Selwyn, first Bishop of New Zealand, formalized the relationship of the episcopate with the houses of laity and clergy. The bishop is called to lead the church, with the church, constantly discerning the mind of the church, so that the church might move only at a pace which is within the ability of the whole body to follow.

These three points – the personal sacramentalization of the bishop, the directionality of authority, and the place of the bishop in synod – are the sacramental and structural ways in which the church has sought to understand, to own and to profit by, the authority it places on those it calls to be bishops. They are clearly not foolproof safeguards against either the actual or the perceived abuse of that power. The structural place of the bishop is very strongly defined, and in that respect the bishop is often perceived as less than a person, both by those for whom he/she is bishop and by the bishop him/herself. The natural tendency of authority appears to be to centralize, despite the rhetoric to the contrary; and whereas the synodical process defines the role of the 'bishop in synod', it would be unreal to pretend that the bishop does not have considerable influence in and of her/himself.

The rhetoric that Christians employ to articulate their understanding of the power invested in their leaders the bishops is often very moving. Ted Scott speaks of the 'authority of love incarnate ... leading to change, to transformation and renewal'.[16] It is really great stuff – but many Christian women have seen the authority of love incarnate as belonging only to the person of Jesus Christ, and we have come to be quite wary of people who claim divinity in the exercise of their own authority. There is in fact a real gap between the reality of structural authority and the idealism of the church. Women are particularly aware of this, for if love is promoted as a substitute for justice, it becomes the enemy of justice.

This book explores life lived within this gap between rhetoric and practice. It is a gap I am very acutely and personally aware of. As I proceed, I shall weave the strands that bind women in leadership positions, whether they operate in secular or sacred territory. I shall take some aspects of a bishop's 'job description' and turn them inside out to explore their nature in my experience. I want to explore these aspects as they have formed part of my own experience in ministry as a bishop, and to identify both what I owe to the tradition of the church and the points at which I have had to rethink accepted formulae. As such it will be a reflection on both the difficulties and the opportunities, and on how these interface with a life of prayer.

And ambiguity is at the heart of it, for my life is essentially an experience of incredible delight. In my best moments I have a strong sense of the completeness that comes when we follow where God calls; but there is also a sense of divine discomfort as I seek to work out the way of authenticity for the church which has called me at this time, and for myself as the one who is called.

Because there are so few women bishops, the dialogue, the tension between us and our vocation, our identity, our vision, our particularity and the tradition onto which we have become (perhaps rather tenuously) grafted, is all the more noticeable. It is my belief that this tension is a gift. For women in Christian leadership can be a source of radical potential. But it is a potential that can only be realized when it is centred in the heart of God.

2

Power in the church

━━━━━

> It was not to govern others you came this way,
> And the echoes prophesy, lean in the streets of fame;
> It was for rhythms of dust, defeat and chilling delay,
> And through fires without flame.
>
> From Robin Hyde, 'Interlude'

In November 1994, the Auckland-based glossy magazine *North and South* published an article on women and power. I was quite surprised to find that I was one of six New Zealand women featured in the article. Each of the six had achieved or been given her significant power by one or other of the established, historically male-dominated institutions of this country. The most obvious reason for my surprise was the fact that the church was considered a powerful enough institution to give power to one of the six most powerful women in the country. This is a very secular society; while the church is respected, it is not currently a significant influence.

But the church, particularly in its bishops, still retains much of the ceremonial pomp and circumstance and regalia of ancient monarchies, when bishops competed with kings for temporal power and kings competed with bishops for spiritual overlordship. It is all very romantic and all a long time ago, and not very relevant or convincing in present-day New Zealand. And these images are particularly startling for Christian women because the images of power (at least of 'power over') with which episcopacy is invested are so ambiguous, if not alienating.

The article clearly revealed the fascination of the present age with power, and particularly with the changing face of power as it is worn by an increasing number of women in so many different settings. It is almost as if two incongruous concepts, 'female' and 'power', are colliding and challenging our assumptions both about who controls and orders our lives, and also about the most intimate and basic of human relationships, that between a man and a woman.

Such simplistic conjunctions always deal in generalizations, pulling on the archetypes of the makeup of humankind. There has always been fascination with power – who has it, how they came about it, how it is used or misused, how it can change the course of history and how it can be challenged. Part of that fascination, I believe, derives from the potential that power has to hurt. Place this alongside the stereotypical perception of the gentleness of women and there is the sense that this is a situation which, if not lacking in credibility, then is certainly packed with an unknown potential.

A story

For me it all began with the electoral synod held in November 1989 to elect the seventh Bishop of Dunedin. This synod was unusual in a number of respects. In the first place, the diocese had very diligently set about compiling portfolios of references and information about people who might be nominated at the synod. In the second place, among the 23 potential nominees were three women. It was the first time that *any* women had been considered for nomination by an electoral synod in our church.

That my name was among those three is now history; the story of that synod, its concerns and its deliberations must be told by someone who had firsthand experience. For my part, I can only say that I knew it was time that women's names were put forward at the electoral synods of our church; and I thought, naively so it would seem, that there was safety in numbers. How wrong I was!

At that time the canons of our church required that the nomination of the synod be submitted to the Standing Committees of all our dioceses; if a majority assented to the proposal, then the Archbishop, having obtained the assent of the nominee, would announce the identity of the bishop-elect. It was a process that normally took less than a week; in this case it took nearly two weeks as the church began to come to grips with what had happened.

I was grateful for that two weeks; it gave me some opportunity to consider my response. For I was indeed taken by surprise. My immediate thoughts were practical and pragmatic, and were for the people I was closest to, my family, for it would clearly affect them considerably, not least of all because it would entail moving to Dunedin from Wellington, where I had lived for 25 years.

It also precipitated a tortuous process of discernment: I was concerned to discover whether the proceedings and the result of the electoral synod had any of the marks of the activity of the Holy Spirit, or was it the random action of some will-o'-the-wisp? I set about one of the most complex and most rushed processes of discernment of my whole life. In general terms I began to sense a continuity between the decision of the synod and what the diocese thought it was looking for; some congruences began to emerge, for the diocese, for myself and for my family. And so I said yes.

It was only after my election was announced that I began to have any idea as to how it was perceived by other people; my own deliberations had been entirely personal and spiritual. There was an enormous response, and a dominant theme was the conviction that God was doing a 'new thing'. Suddenly I was struck by the public face of episcopacy, and I was truly amazed. There was massive pleasure – coming from all quarters, from all church communities, not just my own, and also from the secular community.

It was clearly seen as an enormous triumph, not for me personally, for I had been but a passive player in the process, but for women in general, whatever their walk of life. There was a sense that I could, and would, be a bishop for women, within and outside the church; a sense that anything was possible.

At the same time I discerned some ambiguity in it all. Was the sense of triumph, of achievement, because a woman had gained a position that was defined, at least historically, as one of the most powerful that society has created? Or was it because a woman had broken the stranglehold that men have held on the episcopal leadership of a church which is undoubtedly one of the most patriarchal institutions in the history of Western society? Either way, I quickly realized that these perceptions of the power of the office, and in particular of the power of having a woman in that position, would be one of the most dominant factors with which I would have to come to terms. I began to tremble.

So reflection on that power – what it meant to those who had laid it upon me, what it did to them and for them, what it did to and for the work of Christ, and also what it did to me – has become a constant current of my prayer. The strands that bind me in identification with women of power in secular fields show me that I am clearly not alone in this. Indeed, that *North and South* article, mentioned at the beginning of this chapter, suggests that there is a clear if somewhat awed fascination with what it all might mean. These reflections form the deeper substance of this book.

An ambivalent place

The ambivalence of the position of a newly elected woman bishop reflects the ambiguity that many women experience in the assumption and exercise of formal power. Such formal power is always within structures that are historical and patriarchal and from which, by definition, women have been excluded. Such an assertion is sometimes countered by reminding us that women have undoubtedly wielded much power in informal and often domestic situations, and they still do. Women have also, we are reminded, held spiritual power, in the Christian and other religious traditions. Spiritual power is the power to influence others through one's own being – by example, by kindness, by wisdom, by love, above all through prayer. Institutional power, it is said, has to do with ambition and exercising control, while spiritual power, on the other hand, has to do with surrendering control. Institutional power is a matter of externals; spiritual power is a matter of what is within.

But these are not the zones of women's ambivalence about power. The sphere of domestic power is the home; and of spiritual power, the interior life of the soul. Clearly their possession by women is but little challenge to public institutional power. It is the possession of formal, institutional power that raises questions about the central adult role for women. No longer in New Zealand society is this seen as exclusively domestic and private.

Much of the ambivalence that women feel comes from the need for security. The root of this need is the dependency, whether on state or partner, that child-rearing brings. If men are strong, so the argument runs, women and children will be safe. This need is reinforced by generations of social conditioning, and it is easy to translate it into the quest for security within church structures, a security that is often declared to be watertight when leadership resides with men.

So while women might recognize and deplore their position of powerlessness, they also by biology and social conditioning tend to know their need for security. This, for many women – and men – produces ambivalence about the expressive and formal assumption of power by women within male systems. But it is not only women's cynicism and uncertainty about their own power that keeps them from using it. The problem is also that when women realize that they are not at the mercy of historical events, but can in fact determine them, they lose many of the traditional identity markers of femininity that feel right and comfortable.

As women we have to deal with this ambivalence both within society and within ourselves. In general terms, women tend to be anxious when they assert themselves; men are relieved and reassured by acting tough, and often appear to have a self-satisfied sense of having done their duty. Women neither historically or personally have grown accustomed to the expectation of assuming power. When I was elected as a bishop, I had not anticipated such an event; all my latent ambivalence about power rose to the surface. And my own ambivalence mirrored that of so many women; perhaps that was the underlying reason for all the fascination that my election attracted.

This ambivalence is further complicated for women who have chosen to live within the heart of Christian spirituality. There is much within traditional Christian teaching and practice that is quite clearly excluding of women in leadership positions. In the early months of my episcopacy I received several letters, all of them from overseas, requesting that I explain my position in relation to certain well-known and carefully selected passages of the Epistles to the satisfaction of the writer, or resign.

Deeper and perhaps more damaging are the many strong injunctions on women to serve, in humble and lowly manner, and to do so uncomplainingly. Vulnerability is a much-lauded virtue, for women; some of the force of this comes from biblical injunctions such as the Beatitudes. These can be very difficult, for, when interpreted as commands issued from within a hierarchical structure, they take the delight and energy that the Christian woman experiences in following the call of Christ and then, by simplistic reference to his spiritual teaching, place a very rigid barrier between that call and a woman's freely given response.

I would not be the first to point out that when a woman responds to the call to ordination it is frequently seen as a failure to be content with a life of service and as an inappropriate seeking after power; but when a man responds to the call to exercise leadership through the ordained ministry it is called 'responding to the call to serve'.

These can be profound and at times troubling questions for Christian women who are called to exercise leadership. At root they are spiritual issues: what happens to the conscience of the woman who dares to be different? how does the interior match the exterior? As a bishop, I have been no more immune from these ambivalences than has any other ordained woman, but I have observed both as a bishop and as a spiritual director that women ordained into a church that is accustomed to and accepting of the ministry of women have a much simpler time of it. Some things do get easier. Nonetheless, I think that one of the major tasks of women in Christian leadership is to develop an authentic spirituality of strength. I shall draw this out further later in this book.

The messages that women in power receive are decidedly ambiguous; this has been especially noticeable lately with regard to women politicians. On the one hand they are frequently criticized as not strong enough, and not tough enough to offer the leadership that their position demands; on the other hand, the same critics will spend a disproportionate time passing comments on such issues as hair style and dress, comments that clearly detract from the perceived stature and strength of the woman. Helen Clark, the present leader of the Labour opposition in New Zealand, said recently that the thing women politicians dread most is not being taken seriously.

Clearly what is regarded as 'strong' or 'tough' is primarily defined by men, and in such a way that few women can measure up. The question is one of changing stereotypes and developing new norms. The challenge to women in Christian leadership is not to eschew strength, but to reorient and redefine it, authentically and appropriately, with a firm foundation in Christian tradition and spirituality. I am sure that when we do this we will find that the vaunted 'new thing' is not so new at all, but has rather been buried beneath centuries of male definition. The exploration of this redefinition is a sub-text running through this book.

Gender, racism and power

The juncture of racism and sexism produces a further ambiguity for women who would move into positions of leadership and power, for both are among the oppressions that compete with each other for consideration, and raise the challenge of the responsible and altruistic use of power.

Most feminist analysis, both Christian and secular, derives from the perspective and experience of white women living in Western-style societies; as such it is not only a theology deriving from the experience of marginalization and oppression, it also can be and has been oppressive itself.[1] When the structures of such societies are considered in isolation, the feminist analysis of the position of women as marginalized and oppressed is acceptable. But where there are other racial and ethnic populations within a society, a structural analysis shows that white women are ranked among the white population which is in so many cases the dominant social grouping. They must accept that they are part of the oppressive structures of society. This is certainly the position of pakeha women in Aotearoa/New Zealand in relation to Maori, the indigenous people of our country.

The intersections of structural analysis in this situation place pakeha women in a most ambiguous and interesting position. In relation to pakeha men, we are on the underside of the power structures of society; but, in relation to Maori women, we take our place with the dominant pakeha population of our country. Maori are an indigenous minority with little political power in the only country in the world which they can call home. They are, in Aotearoa/New Zealand, *tangata whenua*, the 'people of the land', yet persistently, in both the political and Christian history of this country, they have been exploited: they have been defeated in war, their lands have been confiscated or bought for a song by cheats, their health, education and employment rates show the tendency of those in government not to notice the particularity of their needs, and the numbers of Maori in prison are disproportionately high. Such racism is a continuing sore in this country.

Recent years have seen a strong rise in Maori ethnic consciousness and sense of identity; there has also been increased pressure to right the wrongs that occurred in the earlier years of colonization and to restore justice. There has been in effect a call to honour them as the *tangata whenua*, and to respect them as partners in the Treaty of Waitangi of which they, together with the representatives of the British Crown, were signatories in 1840. The changes that the Anglican Church has recently made to our constitution (see Chapter 5) were made to try to give structural effect to the obligation for pakeha and Maori to live together in partnership.

Our revised constitution has brought with it a measure of separation, for now Maori and pakeha are each autonomously responsible for their own mission and ministry; but we do not live apart, we are part of the same society, and there are times when our values come into conflict. This is so with regard to the place of women in Christian leadership. The Maori church, Te Pihopatanga o Aotearoa, has been slow to ordain women as priests; they are a tribal people and the practice is more acceptable in some tribal areas than in others. There is a strong awareness among pakeha women that to struggle for such recognition on behalf of Maori women is to impose our agenda on them and is an irresponsible use of the power that we have by being pakeha. For many Maori women the primary point of oppression (the 'primary emergency'[2]) and of identity is being Maori, not being female; Maori women are forging their own struggle among their own people. On the other hand, many pakeha women, perceiving the marginalization that we share with all Maori, have put much energy into supporting Maori in their struggle to obtain justice, both within the church and in the wider New Zealand society.

The same awareness of Maori oppression was one of the reasons why the Bishop of Aotearoa did not attend my episcopal ordination in 1990. It took Maori until 1928 to achieve the episcopal ordination of one of their number, and it was not until 1978 that the Bishop of Aotearoa gained the status of a diocesan bishop. Some Maori quite naturally felt resentment that a pakeha woman should become a diocesan bishop within twelve years of the first ordinations of women as priests.

There is then, for me, a real sense of oppression and exclusion from collegiality with Maori leadership in our church. I have found this very painful at times; and there have been many within the Diocese of Dunedin who, out of support for me, would fall into the easy reactionism of racism themselves. It has also been challenging, for I remain, by conviction and obedience, bound to pursue our constitution's goals of partnership, so I must in no way let the difficulties that I have experienced form the attitudes and responses of this diocese to Maori issues. Together with other pakeha I am called to use our pakeha-derived power to support and encourage the work of Te Pihopatanga o Aotearoa in this diocese.

These difficulties have, however, become isolated to the official and structural areas of our church's life. There are many Maori, bishops, women and men, with whom I enjoy an easy and confident friendship, who have come to trust my commitment to Maori self-determination. I rejoice in the *awhi* (warmth and affection) that I share with them.

But at a structural level, the tension remains. As one of the most powerful women in our church, I am also on this issue disregarded and isolated among the bishops of our church. In maintaining working relationships through this situation, I have come to appreciate the virtue of courtesy. In experiencing so sharply the tensions of both power and powerlessness, right in my own being, I am continually reminded (and bishops can forget[3]) of the pain of oppression.

The underside of power

The structures of power are essentially relational. As bishop of a diocese, I am in a position of power for those for whom I am bishop, and also in relationship with the other bishops of our church, both within this country and elsewhere within the Anglican Communion. That relationship is structurally defined as one of collegiality. But structures are not everything.

I am frequently asked how I get on as the only woman within the New Zealand House of Bishops. I could have wished that by this time, some six years into my episcopacy, another woman would have been elected. But so far this has not happened. The situation is not a new one for me; I was among the first women ordained in the Diocese of Wellington, and I was frequently the only woman present at clerical gatherings. This is not an uncommon situation for women in secular leadership and management roles, and there are now a good many of these; most make their way within the system that they have become part of. But there can be times of real isolation. It is a place where, as a woman, I am aware of a woman's relative cultural powerlessness; and there would be few women who would say that they can sense the system as being them, or theirs.

There is often an illusion of neutrality; in such environments as the House of Bishops, the question of gender differences is a risky one to raise, for it can draw attention to the isolation of women in a way that embarrasses and shames my male colleagues. And yet such differences must be acknowledged, even when we would not wish to, for there are times when the perceptions of others, for both good and ill, are coloured by the gender of the person exercising leadership, and this cannot be passed over. Social forces operate differently for women than for men. There really is no neutrality.

The possibility of neutrality is further reduced for me when I am with bishops who have not had the experience of exploring collegiality with a woman. In such situations it is the relative social status between us, as it is perceived by my colleagues, that determines the nature of the interaction. To them I am more obviously woman than bishop. Not surprisingly, then, it is their customary way of regarding women that will inform and shape their response to me. So a frequent pattern for them is to begin by trying very hard, but before long old habits reassert themselves, and I notice that I am spoken across or disregarded in the processes of debate. This is a general although not universal pattern, and while I am well equipped with techniques for counteracting this dynamic, I would on reflection have to say that there are times when I am personally and painfully reminded of the lot of most women. It is good for the soul!

Can anything change?

At root, it is a question of how we claim belonging, of whether or not we can assert a position of validity on the inside, even when there are those who would exclude us or deny us the right of belonging. For women exercising leadership in a minority situation there can be no clear answer. For us the boundary is always blurred because we belong on both sides: for me, where the bishops belong is not where the women belong, and vice versa. Our apparent institutional security defines us very ambiguously. The culture of institutions that have been shaped by centuries of patriarchal rule is in fact very resistant to change and very intractable. It takes more than one or even a few women in leadership roles to counter the drag to return to unconsciously assumed norms. Our marked minority status is simply a phase in history that must be lived through before deeper change can occur; I think it will last a long time.

Since women were first ordained in this country in 1977, there have been high hopes placed on us that we would be the ones who would humanize the system and make it more accessible to lay people. Similar expectations have been particularly high in Britain following the 1992 decision to ordain women to the priesthood, probably because of the long wait. It is also an expectation that has been loaded onto women in other professions, most noticeably medicine and law.

But the expectation that women could rapidly humanize an entire institution is unreal. It is patently unfair to heap high expectations on women to change both the culture and the character of established structures when the place that most of them occupy on the scale of power is relatively low. What changes can be effected without significant power? As Elizabeth Bettenhausen says:

> The reform of long-lived institutions is dangerous work, for the temptation to see improvement is nearly irresistible. The temptation is to mistake political temporizing for hope, tokenism for acknowledgement of capability, smiling spite for collegiality, and rhetorical rejection of abuse for an increase of justice.[4]

It is also true that even when significant changes are made, they are frequently gradual, for that is often the style that women adopt; and people tend to forget what things were like before, so that the comparisons become muted and temporizing is all too easy.

There too was the expectation that ordained women, women as priests, celebrating the holy mysteries of God, would be a visual and personal reminder that both men and women are made in the image of God (Genesis 1.27), a point of Scripture that is habitually contradicted by the tradition and language of the church, and thus would be able to make both God more accessible to women and this aspect of the nature of God more noticed by men. For many women and men, the relatively few women who have been ordained have given them glimpses that this could be so, but there is a growing impatience with the resilience of the church to really effective change.

There are other social changes that are occurring in parallel to the rising profile of women, and these too affect outcomes. This has been most evident in rural ministry in this diocese, where women have taken a steadily increasing leadership role in our rural parishes during a time of marked concurrent rural depopulation. They have frequently worked as non-stipendiary priests, and have been as strained in their ministry as ever men were or are.

The fundamental question for women in positions of power is whether the culture of these institutions is so intractable and seductive that they become themselves taken over and remade in an old likeness, taking on the characteristics of those who have held that power before them; or whether authenticity is possible, for it is only from the depth of such authenticity that changes can come.

Ordained women have often felt that by their inability to make significant changes they have let other women down. Women clergy have from time to time felt isolated from the Christian feminist movement, which is evolving and whose critique of the core of Christian theology is becoming much sharper, but which continues somehow to identify with its Christian roots. It is making increasing demands on ordained women, demands they often neither can nor want to meet. It is not uncommon for feminist clergy to feel abandoned by feminist colleagues.

A parallel situation arises in other professions. Women medical practitioners have felt ostracized by the Women's Health Movement because they have failed to effect changes. Again the reasons are twofold: women doctors have not changed the style of medical care because they have not been in power, but it is also true that the political awareness of the Women's Health Movement has risen sharply. So even among women, some sharp divisions between those who are 'professional' and those who are lay can grow very rapidly. But it is a basic reality that those who are outside an institutional structure and working for change will not readily unite with those who find their identity and their mission within.

3

Discerning

WHAT FACE?

Yet this will haunt me, not until I die,
But till our fiery world turns ashen grey
And no known planets people the clear sky . . .
What was the face I turned away this day?
From Robin Hyde, 'Pilate'

Our lives are made up of choices, from the significant to the trivial. Among the significant would be the major life choices we are faced with and the decisions that affect the direction of our working lives; among the more routine are how we spend our time and money, the causes we put our energy into and the people with whom we choose to spend time.

For people in positions of power, particularly for those of us in Christian leadership, the choices we make have the significance of impacting on other people, for they reflect, at every level, the workings of God in this world, the ways in which the church, the Body of Christ, is perceived and the way in which the gospel is presented. Gregory the Great called the failure of a bishop to discern aright 'having a little nose'.[1] This applies as much to our personal and private lives as it does to our public lives, for God is the God of the whole of our being. Our choices matter: 'What was the face I turned away this day?'

So the authenticity of Christian living and Christian ministry depends crucially on our willingness to submit the choices we make to a process of discernment of the will of God, with integrity. It is a critical aspect of the ministry of a bishop, who is called to be the voice of conscience both within the church and within the society in which the local church is placed.[2]

Many people, among them many women, find the whole idea of discernment quite elusive and approach it with a critical suspicion. To many, the word appears as a kind of jargon dragged in to buttress decisions that ought to be open to greater scrutiny, and it is a rhetoric that has undoubtedly been abused by people in power. However, discernment is in truth the practical point of intersection between God and the church. Its roots lie in prayer, both personal and corporate.

Personal prayer is the focus of a later chapter. Here I am looking at three aspects of discernment: first, the context of our discernment and why it is so hard to speak of discernment convincingly; second, some of the principles and processes of corporate discernment that I have found useful in working with the church; and finally, by way of illustration, an arena of discernment that is a particular responsibility of a bishop.

The context of discernment

Discernment is a process of discovering how God's priorities operate in a world in which God is honoured. But contemporary society is an ambiguous place for God, and there are multiple world-views in which our discernment needs to gain credibility. Hence the concept of God's engagement with human affairs is necessarily open to critical suspicion. But our discernment also needs to be credible within the Christian world view.

Christians live in the middle of a mighty gap, the gap between the immensity of God and the singularity of a particular human life and situation. It is the nature and calling of the Christian church to hold to the vision of the Kingdom of God, the place where the conjunction of the perfect love and perfect freedom of the nature of God is realized in human living. That God entered into human living in this perfect love and freedom makes it clear that God wills that humankind should know these within the framework of human living.

But we don't; for now, 'we only see through a glass darkly' (1 Corinthians 13.12). We only catch glimpses and struggle to find images that express our longing and relate to the experience of our humanity, images such as that of the heavenly banquet, which Jesus makes very human in the parable of the wedding feast. But it is the hope we hold and the reason why so many of us hang in with a church that manifestly fails to live up to expectations. We live with that gap, between the longing for all that God promises and its realization.

We call this hope eschatology – the study of the last things. In many respects, theologians, by this very act of naming, almost imply an acceptance of the inevitability that humankind will continue to live in such a way that the gap will endure. But the driving energy behind many a Christian life is the awareness that this gap is not inevitable, that living in acceptance of its inevitability is not how God intends us to live, and that the hints, the glimpses, that we have received through what Jesus has shown us of God can fill us with a kind of divine discontent, even a divine rage. Christians live with a vision of how the world might be if God's Kingdom were to come. Authentic Christian living is characterized by a deep longing.

When we travel the Christian way, we know indeed the magnitude of what God can do with us, we find ourselves again with glimpses of what is possible with God and we long for that possibility to be more widely appreciated; when we have the courage to go deep into that of which we are aware in ourselves, we find ourselves caught up into much more than we can know by ourselves. Who knows what God could do, given half a chance?

It is the job of discernment to try to bridge the gap; to help us to become aware that the choices we make as human beings are of significance to God, and to God's relationship with God's creation. I have found these choices to be particularly significant as a bishop.

Discernment and power

The somewhat off-hand but classic statement of authority 'Do as I say, but not as I do' says a great deal. It points, albeit humorously, to the gap that we all experience in our own lives. Like Christian eschatology, it is the gap between what we hope for and reality; it is the gap between what we would be and what we are.

But it is not only a statement of authority, it is also a disclaimer, a disclaimer of accountability; and as such one of the least subtle ways people in power use to shirk the power, the responsibility, that they do have. However, I have found that it is not as easy as that to be free of accountability. The Christian faith is incarnational; we see God most clearly in the person of Jesus, who, in common humanity with us, was faced with all the complexities of daily living. As 'the Word became Flesh and lived amongst us', so in a very real way what we say *is* what we do, and what we do *is* the message we give.

Authentic ministry requires actions as well as words. And the more public, the higher the profile, the more responsible and the more powerful our ministry is, the more this is true. And for bishops, whose actions are so public, this is quite marked; our actions are the decisions that we make, and the words we speak are the substance of what we do.

It is true that the words we utter, the ways in which we use them to form and to shape our relationships, the decisions that we take, and the way in which those are reached, do have an impact on the spirituality and culture of the church. I was once told by a young woman who had suffered badly from an abuse of clergy power that she wanted me to know the whole story because, she said, 'you are the conscience' of the church.

On a more trivial but nonetheless irritating level, I found that when I became a bishop something of the flippancy of speech which has always been a characteristic of my interaction with people had to be checked, simply because many people tended to take what I said far too seriously and without the humour with which it was intended. Offence was easily taken. I have also had to be careful how I make suggestions; they can be interpreted as instructions by people who only see the role that I occupy, and acted upon often without the further discussion that is often necessary.

I have wondered whether this is an experience that many bishops, depending on personality, may have had; or whether it is a dynamic related to the fact that I am a woman. But certainly the advent of institutional power into my life has radically shifted the importance and significance of what I say, and I have learnt to be very aware of the power that I have, and to be cautious.

Restraints and accountability

So where does the power come from, and to whom are bishops accountable? What are the restraining factors? First there is formal accountability by which the ministry of a bishop is related to the structure, the hierarchy of the church. This accountability is to the General Synod and is acknowledged both in the declarations that bishops sign on accepting office and within the service of ordination for bishops. The question put by the presiding bishop is 'Will you uphold the authority of General Synod and the Constitution of this Church?' and the reply is 'Yes, I will. I am under that authority, and will exercise it in partnership with my sisters and brothers in Christ.'

To many people this seems pretty loose; probably because power and relationships of power are primarily perceived as being between people, not between people and structures, which have always been a more clumsy and less personal means of calling people to account. In general, then, it seems as if bishops have a pretty free rein. Certainly there is no one directly breathing down our necks, and it seems to many that we are beholden to no one.

Obedience to God

This may all seem like a splendid freedom, but a bishop as much as anyone else owes obedience to God. In the ordination service it is expressed as a relationship, one of vitality and empowerment. The question is 'Will you then give glory to God, the holy and blessed Trinity?' and the reply is 'Glory to God on high, God of power and might. You are my God. I can neither add to your glory nor take away from your power. Yet will I wait upon you daily in prayer and praise.' It is essentially the claiming of a relationship, and it is a claim made by all who come to be ordained deacons, priests and bishops.

So, then, *all* Christians, whether or not they are ordained, owe obedience to God. For deacons and priests this obedience is mediated through the structures of the church personally, through the person to whom they are licensed; often that person is the bishop. I first learnt about ecclesiastical obedience when I was a curate. I was being trained for priesthood by a very experienced priest who was nearing retirement, and who had very high expectations. He treated me exactly the same as his other curates; I was told exactly what to do and there was no discussion. It was for me both a shock and a sharp lesson. I struggled to come to terms with this situation, which at first felt thoroughly abusive, but then I realized that it was not; I learnt the extent to which, despite my long struggle to ordination, I carefully guarded my sense of control over my own life. The experience did little for my pride, but it did much for the development of my trust in God.

What does it mean to say we owe obedience to God? Surely many would say that this is simply an excuse for doing what one likes and placing the responsibility elsewhere. Undoubtedly, because of the diffuse, unpredictable and uncontrollable element in divine obedience, the church has sought to institute a layered system of checks, a hierarchy, so that obedience is owed to one higher up in the system. It sometimes seems that we do not trust each other to live in authentic obedience to God.

These days, in this church, the notion of unquestioning obedience to clerical superiors is much less clear than it was when I was a curate. Apart from the fact that the current critique of power makes it quite unacceptable, it is, I believe, preferable that relationships within the church should be founded on mutual respect and the imperative of a common commitment to the gospel. But this does have the effect of eroding a clear line of accountability, and it is less easy these days for bishops to enforce ecclesiastical discipline than in the past.

The obedience owed by a bishop

What about bishops themselves? Formal accountability may lie with the General Synod but, for bishops, obedience is not mediated through any direct and human authority. I was very aware of this when I first became a bishop, because it contrasted very sharply with my previous experience. For the first time in my ordained life I was not subject to the often unwieldy and unresponsive authority structures of the church, mediated by slow-minded bishops. When I first sought ordination as a priest, in the early days of the ordination of women in the Diocese of Wellington, it was a protracted process, and the struggle to get the church to respond to my call to ordination made me very aware of the structures of authority within the church. I had learnt both to act within them and yet to challenge. It is a learning curve that many women travel.

So, while I have always been pretty much a free spirit, I do have a strong sense of the value of the good order of the church and a profound respect for it. I have frequently worked with those on the boundaries of the church and of human society, but I have always, well generally, operated within acceptable bounds. When I became a bishop, this freedom became institutionalized; I realized that now there was no one person above me (for this is not the role of the Archbishop within the New Zealand church – see Chapter 5) to whom I was directly accountable. I was, both structurally and spiritually, directly responsible only to God. This was precisely the point where any skills that I had developed in the art of discernment would become urgently needed, and where, too, if my discernment was not to be sheer manipulation, my dependence on God in prayer had to be real and authentic.

I think that this is why there is so much suspicion of the power of a bishop: he or she appears to sit at the top of the pyramid with no visible constraints but those that are divine. Women, who have been excluded from episcopal circles and other places of power, feel this suspicion particularly acutely. And even to say this lays bare the cynicism of the church, and for this reason it is rarely acknowledged in discussions on the authority of a bishop.

It seems that the sheer presence of a hierarchical structure with no evident accountability for the bishop is very hard for people to understand. Spiritual authority does not seem as reliable as human, and also not as accessible. Sadly, there is plenty of evidence of the abuse of power by clerics who very easily claim the authority of God for actions that are experienced as abusive. It is not only such faithlessness that leads to cynicism; it is also quite a common reaction to the power of others.

Women are often only too painfully aware of the gap between the spiritualizing explanation of the accountability of the bishop and the reality that they have experienced when they have encountered that power head-on. Many of us who are now ordained have been initially told by our bishops that our call to ordination had no divine origin, and that 'in obedience to God' he must decline us. There are also many who are not ordained who have had that experience. The 'I owe obedience to God' line can seem like a less than subtle attempt to evade responsibility.

Such language points to the ease with which bishops are perceived as considering themselves as God. Clearly we are not, but the individualized nature of the authority that we hold explains this perception. The exercise of authority is a continuing balance between openness to the will of God and the temperament and prejudices of the individual. It is not possible from any Christian perspective to discount God, or to relativize God, or make God the equal of one's own desires and prejudices. In all my ministry, I have been profoundly grateful that the prevailing and traditional genderized images of God make it impossible for other people to think that *I* am God, and very difficult for me as well.

The process of discernment

The need for discernment seems to be constant. Some years back the patterns of both society and the church were more clearly established. Conduct tended to follow known conventions and there was less room for disputation. However, these are such rapidly changing times that few existing patterns can be accepted unquestioningly. This means that many situations are 'first time', and there are no precedents. Many decisions have to be made entirely on their presenting facts.

All this raises the question about how the process of discernment is conducted and about how decisions are made. At the beginning of an episcopate, as every new bishop discovers, there are so many decisions to be made so quickly and so many people giving contrary opinions as to what they should be. It can be quite bewildering. Pleasing everyone is not possible, but nonetheless becomes a beguilingly attractive proposition. Another tactic is to do what the last person to speak about the issue has suggested. Both these approaches effectively place the responsibility for what the bishop does or does not do onto other people. Both leave people on the receiving end feeling as if they do not know where the bishop stands on any given issue; both can be very frustrating.

I found that first year a sharp learning experience; I did learn very quickly to take my time, and that basic approach has been valuable ever since. With time I can listen and process, with other people and in my prayer, all that I have heard. I also found out that the manner of decision-making, the process by which decisions are reached, was a significant factor in their effectiveness. I learnt that I needed to make decisions that I could stand by, which could with integrity withstand the inevitable displeasure and the criticism of some of the people who were affected by them.

I learnt also of the dreadful mistakes that I could make if I was too quick off the mark. When someone in a powerful position makes a mistake the damage that is done can be alarmingly far-reaching, and there is little, if any, opportunity to put it right. I also discovered the dangers to my own soul of the abuse of power. It was not a happy time.

So, for me, discernment needs to be slow and prayerful; it needs to be visible and transparent; it needs whenever possible and appropriate to be talked through very carefully – not just with individuals, but with groups of people who both care for my ministry and whom I can trust; for the signs of the Spirit can emerge in group discussion. By this means I ensure that episcopacy is exercised with the church, in solidarity with the Christian community who in turn see that oversight, of which I am both sign and agent, belongs with them as much as it did on the day they elected me to be their bishop.

Discernment within the Body of Christ

We are so used to regarding discernment as the outcome of a one-to-one relationship with God that we have less sense of a community standing in need. All too often we conduct the business of our church as if it were any other business meeting, with little sense of the reality and significance of God's guidance. At times we operate on an explicitly win–lose model, where, following the conventions of parliamentary debate, we seek to defeat the opposition with our prowess in argument. And when we win, we take the credit ourselves and God really does not figure very much in the process. True, we pray at the beginning of a meeting and open the time and the issue to God's guidance, but all too often that is where it stops.

I have come to learn that God is at work throughout the whole body of the church; indeed, following St Paul, we call the church the Body of Christ. I have learnt to expect that a group of people will together be more in touch with the feelings and responses of the church than I am alone, or any other single person. Too, I have learnt that in the interchange of ideas the wisdom of the Spirit can be found. With time and commitment any issue can be held to the mirror of the major features of Christian doctrine, like our call to be a forgiving and reconciling community, or our commitment to share the Good News of Christ, or others, and relevant biblical passages can illuminate the issues at hand. It is an environment in which a variety of skills and insights can be brought to bear, where experts must interact with people who are closer to the pulse of the diocese. The size of the group is only limited by the dynamics of group communication.

It is my conviction that the call to be involved with the business side of the church, with administration, is a ministry; and as with other ministries – of care, of teaching, of reconciliation and justice-making, to name just a few – it is a place where we should and can expect to find God, for our God is the God who cares, who placed Godself into the heart of our lives. Such a God is always and everywhere present to us and in us; it is we who are sometimes absent. The call to serve on boards and councils is also a call to in-depth spirituality, for we are called both to be and to build the church, and we can expect to be summoned, together and as individuals to the quest for holiness. To accept the call to 'be church' is to accept the call to seek God's holiness.

It follows then that, as bishop, I cannot not take *all* decisions at diocesan level. But I do regard myself as responsible for the authenticity of the process by which decisions are reached, and I have learnt to take responsibility for ensuring that decisions are well made, that people have all the relevant information, that we take the time that is necessary, that we listen carefully and pray carefully, that our Christian identity and care is always taken as relevant data, and that the outcome is a win–win solution and is acceptable as widely as possible.

These then are some of the major features, as I see them, of discernment within the Body of Christ. They are essentially touchstones that I have learnt to keep in my head and my heart as I work through issues in the diocese. While I always intend to follow them, I do not always manage it; at times the pressure of the moment or the disruptiveness of others is too great, at times my own anxieties get the better of me and at times I am just simply not as careful as I would wish to be.

Shaping a group

The Anglican Church in New Zealand is committed to synodical government, and the canons and the statutes of our church provide for innumerable committees that allow for a democratic and consultative process. Everything that I am saying about corporate discernment is appropriate for any one of them, but I am here addressing the process of discernment on particular issues, for these are task-oriented groups and the group formed might well have quite a short life.

The process of group formation varies, but generally speaking there is a sense of responding to the obvious. I regard it as my job to check this out, in my prayers and with others. I need to be sure, and so do the other people, that the make-up of the group makes sense to God.

In a small diocese people generally know one another quite well; that is particularly true of the clergy, who can sometimes form what seems to outsiders a somewhat exclusive club. I have found that one of the consequences of power is that people are uneasy about any suggestion of an in-group, who share it, exclusively. So it is critically important that the membership of task-oriented groups be transparent and that there be no holy huddles or secret societies, and no sense of undisclosed political intriguing which would undermine both the spirit and the work of the group before it has a chance to get started. It is also important to vary, as far as is possible, the membership of the groups; this helps to keep us outward looking and in touch with a wider section of the diocese.

Safety

Every group needs to be formed within an environment of care and of safety; the values that the church at large would declare to be Christian have a cherished place within its life. If there is a combative spirit present then people will become uneasy and not be able to contribute as God calls them to, and they will not find in the experience of the group that this is a place where God is present.

Listening and reflecting

Listening in a group-discernment process can be quite complex. It is not simply a question of going round the group and making sure that everyone has the opportunity to make an opening statement, for the agenda is task-oriented, not personal. In general, the best way to begin is to explore fully what the initial situation is with regard to the issue under discussion; to open up the questions; and to try to steer people off making strong statements that have been previously framed and from which it would be hard for them to back down should the discussion take a different turn.

This first stage is the time when those who know less about the issues have an opportunity to ask questions and to get up to speed. It is important to establish an atmosphere that accepts their initial lack of familiarity, for this gives a strong message to everyone that all ideas are acceptable. It is also true that people who come new to a situation often articulate perspectives that those more familiar with it have not thought about. The value of listening is established at this stage.

The talking, the explorations and hence the listening may start off at a fairly superficial level, and this is useful, for it is an easier environment for the set of relationships that will be unique to the life of this group to take shape. After a while people will begin to articulate and to hear the deeper needs of the community gaining expression. They often enter the discussion somewhat tentatively, and there are usually at least some people who find it hard to hear what others say. At this point, I find it necessary to take some initiative in beginning the process of naming and reflecting back to the group what people are saying, so that these thin small voices can be heard. It is possible, but not always easy, to do this in a spirit of serving the group; I use the pronoun 'we' frequently, making it clear that I too am listening and that any contribution I might make is just one among the many.

Gospel insights

In the course of this reflective stage, I generally begin to introduce a wider context for the issue at hand and I begin to ask questions. Who are the people most affected in this situation? What are the underlying values at stake here? How do they either impinge upon or reflect the kind of community that God calls the church to be? – which, I frequently remind people, is why we are all here at all. And, of course, other group members quickly join in with their own contributions.

It is important at this stage to keep concentration, and to keep focused. I have found that it is not helpful to be too quick to propose biblical references, for to have the group divert to opening their Bibles can, at times, subvert this focusing. We become a Bible-study group, and not a Christian group looking at a particular question in the light of their faith which is biblically founded. Sometimes a reference to a particular biblical passage helps, and a Bible is always accessible, but it is often more helpful to draw on our shared familiarity with the Scriptures. There is always something for us there.

I have found that this stage often takes up half-articulated prayers that were offered at the beginning of the meeting, and, where the process works well, it enables a connection to be drawn between those prayers and the actual nitty-gritty of the discussions that are taking place. It allows for an interweaving between our prayer and our corporate life in an open and accessible way.

Some suggestions

At this point the meeting begins to get practical. We begin to make suggestions as to how we approach the question at hand. There is no limitation on the number of suggestions that can be offered; I have always found it helpful to write all of them on a large piece of paper so that everyone can see and they are accessible to the whole group. This declares that each is equally valid, but because there are frequently far more suggestions than can be adopted, it also makes clear the necessity of choosing. Choosing is the heart of the discernment process, and it is what the group have convened to do.

Other factors

Here the agenda stretches out considerably as we look all around us to see what are the implications of any choice we might make. How does it impact on other people, on the concerns of other committees and groups, on decisions that we have made in the past, on what we understand to be the direction in which God is moving the church? As we do this, the range of suggestions that we have in front of us begins to contract.

The cost of change

When the possibilities have narrowed, it is not uncommon for the group to find that they are faced with unpalatable alternatives. It is true that this point was often predictable at the beginning of the meeting, but the careful work that has preceded this conclusion makes it easier for the alternatives to be dealt with.

Rather than focus on the choice too rapidly, I have found that it is useful to introduce into the discussion some consideration of the cost of change, and also, by implication, the cost of not changing. Here we are attempting to be realistic: can we afford to go this way? have we the resources of courage, time, energy, finance and so on, and can we afford not to? It is a discussion that needs to be held in a spirit of real love and acceptance, and an awareness that God does not call us to do the impossible; and that, by the grace of God, we can quite easily live with our inability to do and to be everything.

Generating alternatives

So we may need to generate alternatives, to think laterally. At this point, lateral thinking is not wild dreaming, but very focused; it acts as a critique on the rest of the discussion. It is only when all the alternatives have been considered that the final decision of the meeting becomes both obvious and acceptable.

Decision-making

This is not really a stage, because if all has gone well beforehand a sense of resting before the obvious or the inevitable comes over the group. The process may well not have been peaceful or without disagreement, but the sense of acceptance can be quite satisfying. Here it is important to try and trace, and to name, what the participation of God has been for us, and how this decision will relate to and affect the wider purposes of God in the church.

It is important to tidy up properly: to name the acceptance out loud; to care, without judgement, for any who might feel worsted by the process; to make sure that any responsibilities that people have undertaken are clearly agreed upon and that where the decision will go to from this point is known; to undertake to keep the members of the group informed of its progress. Our closing prayer gathers all this up.

As the leader

My role as the leader of such a group is always ambiguous, but I have learnt to accept that ambiguity. In many ways, I act as a facilitator; I certainly take considerable responsibility for moving the group towards a point of decision-making. But I am never not the bishop. And I have to acknowledge that it is the power I derive from that position that enables me to determine the nature of the process that we follow. It is my job to assist the group members to get in touch with their own religious experience by creating an atmosphere in which they can, at ease, share their faith. I need to call them to search their own hearts for the will of God and for the strength and courage to speak that will, and to follow it as it emerges in the process.

It is also clearly my role as spiritual leader, when the group does not seem to be listening either to the wisdom of the Spirit or to each other, or perhaps even to themselves, to recall them to quiet, prayerful reflection. No matter what the agenda or how heated the topic, no matter how 'secular' the issue, it is up to me to keep the members of the group true to their commitment both to God and to God's church.

But having done that, I need to sit very light to both the process and the result. I need to be able to accept decisions that I might not have thought of and which I might not wish for, and afterwards to enable them to take effect with integrity and commitment. If I feel that this is unlikely, then I do not call a group into being; it is quite frankly unfair and manipulative if, under the guise of democratic process, I am only concerned with getting the result that I want. I need to hear, through the wisdom of the group, the deep need of the community I serve in leadership and to be open to persuasion and change of mind.

For I too need to listen. I need to seek the shared wisdom of the group and I need to seek God. Spiritually, for me, this can be a profound act of 'letting go', of placing my trust in the God who I know dwells in the church. There is an ancient and holy virtue of disinterestedness, which I am only just beginning to explore.

Discerning vocation

The task of discerning vocation is one that is explicitly given to a bishop at ordination. The question put by the presiding bishop runs: 'In selecting, training and ordaining, will you be thorough and discerning?' and the answer: 'God grant me wisdom to care for those ordained.'

In this country, because of the independence of each of the dioceses, the task of discerning vocation is carried out separately in each diocese. Because our dioceses are relatively small our bishops tend to be closely involved in the process, generally in conjunction with a group of examining chaplains, who take part in the selection process and advise the bishop. By this means, the bishop is enabled to listen to the church; and the church, represented by but wider than the bishop, begins the process of owning an ordinand.

Because the bishop must take the final responsibility for the selection of an ordinand, this is an area of a bishop's ministry where the power of the episcopate is most evident for would-be ordinands. For in many ways the relationship between bishop and ordinand is a very personal one, and when it is wished for on one side, but not validated on the other, the sense of rejection can be very acute.

The root of our trust in embarking upon a process of discerning vocation is biblical, and rests upon the assurance that we can be certain that God does call. It is perhaps reassuring to remember the words of the prophet Jeremiah; they pull us back to our basic task. 'Before I formed you in the womb I knew you; before you were born I set you apart' (Jeremiah 1.5). However, there will always be a measure of humble provisionality in our discernment of that call.

God calls us all

The common understanding of vocation is that it simply means what one does for a living, an occupation or career. The secular definition usually implies only income-producing activity. But the religious meaning of the word is broader. The word *vocation* literally means 'calling'. It is derived from the Latin word *vocare* meaning to call – the same word that is at the root of the adjective *vocal*. The religious meaning of vocation, therefore, is what one is called to do, which may or may not coincide with one's occupation, with what one is actually doing.

We speak not only of vocations to art, aerobics and aviation, science or soldiering, but also to celibacy, marriage, the single life, or to home-making or retirement, parenthood or childlessness, gardening or globe-trotting. Anything in fact, any activity or condition at all, no matter how prosaic, that God means for us.

In this sense *vocation* implies a relationship, for if someone is called, someone must be doing the calling. This someone is God. I believe that God calls us human beings – whether sceptics or believers, whether Christian or not – to certain, often very specific activities. Furthermore God relates to us individually, so this calling, the manner of it and the outcome, are utterly individualized. God does not work in package deals, no stereotypes; what God is calling me to do is unlikely to be what God is calling anyone else to do.

Religious vocations

So while there are many vocations, many callings of God, both secular and religious, I am concerned as a bishop with the task of discerning a particular call to live a consecrated life within the formal structures of the church: to be openly and unambiguously a 'God-person'. Generally these days, this means the priesthood, with a consequent sense of being the 'A' team. This notion is of very doubtful spiritual value. We do need to remember that *all* are called to holiness. It could be that some plumbers and schoolteachers are being called to become more reflective plumbers and schoolteachers, living a more open Christian life, as lay partners in ministry; the religious life too is one possibility amongst many.

That God calls women and men, that God continues the work of creation through the creative obedience of men and women to that call, I have no doubt; I have seen it work too often. But the vision of the exact shape and nature of the vocation is frequently tempered by the available possibilities. When I left school, I thought God wanted me to be a nun. It really was the only way a young woman at that time could conceive of living an openly dedicated Christian life. I thank God I was deflected. I would have made a terrible nun! But the finger of God was on me at that time, and it has never left me.

People are similarly limited these days; for many of the people presenting as would-be ordinands, the priesthood is the only option for open and dedicated Christian service. The finger of God is clearly upon them, but the question is 'Where is it pointing to?' It is all too easy to think in stereotypes – and that is not the way God works.

The process

Sometimes it takes a long time for that question to be answered. In my case it took around fifteen years, a north–south switch of hemisphere, and a good many other changes. But it seems to me that time is very important; persistence and a growing sense of the confirmation of call has traditionally been held to be one of the major ways in which the will of God is made clear. The Dunedin group charged with discerning vocation has been asking people who indicate an interest in ordination to spend six months doing some supervised ministry. This is intentional ministry, openly undertaken and named specifically with the exploration of vocation in mind. Such questions are raised as 'Why do I need to be ordained to do this?' and 'Can I see the hand of God at work in this situation?' The community has an opportunity to respond to and validate the call. We find that there are some people who in the course of this process gently pull back from seeking ordination, often finding new purpose in their secular employment. God is a gentle guide in such situations, and their vulnerability is not exposed.

Once a formal application is made, the outcome is much more strongly focused on acceptance or rejection. A strong sense of personal call does not guarantee a personal right to acceptance. Many people become so sure of their call that they seem to leave little room for the process of discernment. It is here that the group responsible for the process has to begin to act as a living organism, sharing wisdom, sensitive to the insights of the Spirit moving among us, aware of the temptation to 'talent spot' clones of ourselves, drawing out different perspectives from among ourselves to connect with the needs and responses of the whole Body of Christ of which we are a microcosm; always aiming to work to complement one another's input and insights. When this is done prayerfully and openly, we find God does give pointers. So this discernment happens in a context of waiting, explicitly of waiting on God.

Once a postulant has been accepted as an ordinand, there is a commitment of three-way mutuality, among God, the church and the ordinand; so regular prayer for each person journeying towards ordination becomes part of the life-flow of the church, as vocation is shaped by response. It is a journey that continues long after ordination;

God's call continues, there are calls within a call, and the challenge to discern that call and to dare to say yes never really lets up.

Non-stipendiary ministry and women and ordination

Discernment requires not only a good process, but also needs to take account of circumstances. For all the move towards greater participation by women in the formal structures of the church, there is still a considerable variation in the position and circumstances of women within our society which means that they bring different skills and make it inappropriate always to look for the same response.

We are still a society that is highly structured on gender lines and a consequence of this is that women find mobility more difficult. They tend therefore to gravitate more readily to the non-stipendiary ministry, which has enabled many women to enter the ordained ministry without undue family disruption.

The development of local ministry has also provided women with opportunities to serve in the ordained ministry. In recent years, this diocese along with others within our church has developed this model of local ministry. This is taking place primarily in our isolated rural areas; it is designed to develop the concept of a church for the local community and run by the local community. Some of these communities have called women from among their number to be priests, not in the sense of exercising leadership in a sole-charge situation, but by working in a team with lay leadership, so that they are free to pursue the specifics of their priesthood, to gather the people of God around the holy table of God, without the burden of being on a pedestal. Their firm sense of location within and of the community of the baptized is a strong sign that priesthood is a gift that belongs to the whole people of God. So the challenge to the local church is to move from being a community that receives ministry to becoming a 'ministering community'.

Women take readily to this type of ministry because they often already have deep roots in their communities and find team relationships familiar territory. Women working as priests in these communities are beginning to develop new patterns of relating between women and men. One of the most exciting and startling things I have had said to me recently came from a man in one of these communities who said that having a woman whom he had known for so long taking a leadership role had made him really feel that Christianity was closer, was for him; it was not just for 'the professionals'. Her ordination had made the gospel more accessible. That is cause for giving thanks.

This is not to say that it is easy for such women to take on ordination as a response to a call from their community. There is always a substantial period of discernment during which both they and the church endeavour to test their vocation. It is not uncommon for this time to be marked by considerable unease and even discomfort, for there have been few who have gone this way before. There is also the discomfort of having been asked, even singled out, with the consequent sense of obligation that many women feel to respond to requests with an automatic yes, the desire to please, even when every ounce of prayer and wisdom points to a no.

While these developments are good for the ministry of the church and provide openings for women to exercise an ordained ministry which would not otherwise be accessible, they have led to a high disproportion of women who do not receive a stipend, or receive only a part stipend for the ministry they offer. While this may suit the circumstances of many of these women, it is questionable whether we are actually achieving the equity that would appear to be implied by the relatively high proportion (now around 25 per cent) of women in our ordained priesthood.[3]

Our processes of discernment work primarily on a one-to-one basis within given policy guidelines. But there are times when wider issues need to be considered. In this case, there are issues of both justice and power here which are not irrelevant to our discernment, and the root question, which continues to puzzle me, is whether justice for an individual and for the community she serves is a right course of action, when it does little to address the issues of genderized power that are still strong in both the church and society.

For, one could well ask, what has changed? Are not these women, as were their grandmothers, kept firmly in a position of dependence, often on their husband, but also by a still patriarchal and increasingly impoverished church? The opposite has also been claimed: that priests without a stipend are in fact independent because they are not dependent on the church for an income. And there is potential here.

But discernment is also God's work. These women and the communities in which they serve are also intentionally exploring a different relationship between ordination and power. They seek to be priests within and for their communities, but not necessarily to equate their priesthood with leadership. I have a strong feeling here that in the ministry these women are offering God is doing a new thing, the dimensions of which we cannot yet see. I value highly the prophetic quality to their ministry.

Responses of women to ordination

Because men and women come from different positions in society they also come with different responses. These relate not only to social positioning, but also to position in time. Women were first ordained to the priesthood in this country at the end of 1977, and the time interval of nearly twenty years between the earliest and the most recent ordinations has produced some very different attitudes.

Carole Grahame's 1994 study[4] on the perceptions of ordained Anglican women in New Zealand suggests that their attitudes have changed over the years since the first ordinations in 1977. She compares the attitudes of women ordained between 1977 and 1980 with those ordained between 1981 and 1990. At the time of selection for ordination, women in the earlier group tended towards a more 'traditional' model of priesthood than did women in the later group. But by the time the survey was taken in 1992, the women of the earlier group had moved towards a less traditional and more feminist model than their more recently ordained sisters. For the record, I was ordained to the diaconate at the end of 1982.

These findings are most interesting, not least because they confirm my own experience, and that is always reassuring. Because we had a very cautious bishop, the Wellington diocese was slow off the mark over the ordination of women. Because I was the only woman ordained over a period of some years, my ordination had the character of the early period, both as regards my own position and through the friends I found in other dioceses. I have strong memories of gatherings of these friends at which we moaned that those ordained later on after us little realized or appreciated the struggle that we had had, and were all too willing to serve uncritically in a church that, given half a chance, would not give women a fair deal. It certainly makes intuitive sense to me that women who have experienced considerable difficulty in having their call to ordination heard are likely to have internalized a feminist position.

The climate of discernment for women

It has not been usual, in my experience as a bishop, for the women who present for ordination to express concern as to how the church will perceive their call; perhaps this is a function of women's having been ordained to the priesthood in New Zealand for a good many years now. There is little doubt, nowadays, that women will get a fair hearing, though there is an awareness that parishes may be reluctant to appoint a woman. There is little of the rhetoric of gender bias around these days, and women do not interpret a refusal as attributable to their gender. Enough women have been ordained to make this manifestly not so.

While I believe this to be a better climate for testing vocation, I do sometimes mourn the loss of any real prophetic sense about many of the women ordinands these days. Carter Heyward has said that one of her understandings of the concept of 'call' is that it means to 'tell our stories and in telling our stories manifest a new reality'.[5] Women in the 1990s seem far more concerned to convince the church of their acceptability, and their vision for ministry can be quite limited. Now that the ministry of women as priests is more or less taken for granted, I think that women, and the church in which we serve, are having to face the fact that any real prophetic value cannot take root in the shallow earth of novelty, but must be deeply grounded, as all prophecy is, in the profound reality of God and of God's call. This is only to the good.

4
Caring

HEALING THE WOUNDED CHILD

And we, who served a meek God and a dying
And unbelieving went to Calvary,
Woke in the nights, to heal that frustrate crying,
Turned back, for such a wounded Child as Thee.
        From Robin Hyde, 'Thine Accursed'

The image

I have not heard any priest or bishop speak about their ministry
without thinking 'He, or she, sounds like a very caring person'. The
development of a 'pastoral heart' is one of the surest signs of a genuine
vocation that I have discovered. The ethic of care is very deeply set
inside our being. Indeed, it is the very root of priesthood. It is also the
best-known characteristic of the Lord whom we are called to follow.
And the prayer of a pastor is very often the prayer that God will enlarge
our hearts.

Care, within the context of the church, is primarily seen as one-to-one
care, personal care – 'pastoral' care as it is often called in church-speak,
to the bewilderment of many non-church people. And all pastors, all
priests and all bishops fail at some time. But not only through personal
error. There are ways in which the very structure of the church, its
ordered hierarchy, establishes relationships of responsibility, and
power can distort and sometimes destroy the pastoral ministry of the
church.

Certainly, caring is the most commonly identifiable Christian
quality and it is what the world expects of us. Whenever I am involved
with a parish who are searching for a new vicar, the first quality that
Boards of Nomination tend to request is *visiting*. Not only do they
want their new vicar to care for them in times of crisis, but they also
want to know that he or she will take the initiative in getting to know

them, their families, their interests and their needs, so that they will know they are loved and cared for. Every new ministry begins with good intentions in this area and with much promise.

The characteristics of a strong caring ministry are then in clear focus, but this ideal is a hard one to live up to. Caring is probably the strongest feature of the church's ministry, and there is much about our practice of it that works extremely well. This chapter looks specifically at the ways in which this ministry interacts with the dynamics of power and of hierarchy within the church and at how these can undermine the caring that we would wish to do; it seeks to place the analysis of care within the context of a society where there is still marked gender imbalance. It will probably seem somewhat negative, because it will focus on what does not work. In this context, power can be a very negative factor.

The image shattered

I know only too well that the caring which we intend is not always perceived as caring by other people; and it is not always easy for people to say that to us, or for us to hear it. As a bishop I have had more letters than I would wish from parishioners who find fault with their vicar over his or her failure to care. Generally it is a failure to visit or to respond in some way to a need. And, I would have to own, I have been the subject of some complaints myself.

The thing that has always struck me about such accounts is the depth of the hurt aroused by the failure to offer care to meet a perceived need. Authority attracts and crystallizes people's deep longings for dependable care, and religious authority entwines this need with God. So it is as if the very essence of ministry is being disowned, as if God's very being is being denied and the authenticity of the church is at stake: 'How could *he*?' 'How could *she*?' A letter I received recently was written on behalf of three people who, the writer said, were all too upset to say anything themselves. The sense of outrage was very strong.

Quite often, when this kind of thing happens, people have no words with which to face the issues and confront the offending cleric themselves, and they have no advocate, sought or unsought. So they quietly – or not so quietly – withdraw from their parish, sometimes to another. Perhaps another priest will pick them up and offer ministry that enables some kind of reconciliation with the church, if not with the priest concerned. But it is also clear to me that very often deep hurts are sustained over many years. It is as if perceived disregard of the call to care cuts very deep into the confidence that people can place in the church, and consequently in God.

I have also been surprised quite often at the seemingly small ways in which lack of care is perceived: 'You came up to me too quickly. It took me by surprise.' 'I tried to share one of my favourite books with him, but he didn't seem to appreciate it.' 'He's always in such a hurry.' They are all seemingly trivial things; but whatever the right or wrong of them, hurt has been caused.

Underneath the image

Now, in many of these situations there are at least two human agendas involved that do not match. An image of priesthood is, for one party, perceived as disregarded, even destroyed; for the other it never existed. For one there is the hierarchic image of the sacrificially caring priest; for the other, the self-image of a fairly ordinary human being, doing his or her best to live up to all the implications of their divine calling. This mismatch affects all clergy, but from my experience it affects women in particular ways; for the expectations that people have about women in positions of Christian leadership are not so well established as are those about men, so the mismatches in perceived image can at times catch both pastor and parishioner in very unexpected ways.

When criticism of pastoral care comes to clergy, and I would include myself in this, it is always taken seriously. The enormous depth of the pain that is experienced in such cases causes, in turn, much soul-searching in the hearts of pastors. In supervision or spiritual direction we may be helped to see the limits of our own responsibility; to see that at times the expectations of others are unreal, or that we are being asked to feed into fantasies that bear little relation to the reality of who we are or what is our calling. At times we may come to realize that we have made a genuine error, to acknowledge that and to find ways of living up to our ideal of ourselves better next time. In essence, if we are enabled to reflect on these situations carefully, honestly and prayerfully, we can come to realize the limits of our humanity, and so draw closer to God. Paradoxically this is the way that God can, in turn, enlarge our hearts.

Caring women in a man's world

The entry of women into the world of ordained pastoral care has raised many issues which it is not easy to be precise about. There are clearly different styles of pastoral care among women, as there are among men. But there is some evidence that women spend more time than men on the delivery of pastoral care.

Indeed, women are very deeply socialized to care for others and they tend to gravitate naturally towards positions calling for skills in pastoral care. Such positions draw on the expertise that many women have developed well, skills of nurturing fostered in the family environment. Some of the early rhetoric that supported the case for the ordination of women to the priesthood drew a comparison between the role of the priest in providing the bread of heaven for God's people through the Eucharist, and the habitual and socially established role of women in feeding their families. It was claimed as a natural extension of that role for women to be priests, nurturing and sustaining the people of God. This reasoning has been worked out in practice, either consciously or unconsciously, in the pastoral ministry of many women priests.

The nurturant aspect of pastoral ministry has a symbolic parallel in the use of parental honorifics to refer to clergy. The practice of calling male clerics 'Father' reflects a long-standing tradition. It is an honoured and honourable tradition that has fulfilled a valuable role in making the priesthood distinctive and recognizable and in making clear the expectations of a quality caring ministry that people can expect from such a person. In New Zealand, women priests have not sought the title 'Mother', and its use has not been expected, but there are provinces within the Anglican Communion where it is used, and, I can only assume, used quite respectably and respectfully.

There would appear to be two reasons why women have, in some places, chosen to use this title, and they intersect with each other. The first arises out of a church culture that is predominantly Anglo-Catholic and where such usage appears to come naturally. The second derives from situations where women have experienced a prolonged and bitter struggle before their ordination was permitted. In such situations it is not uncommon for women to choose to adopt the external symbols of priesthood, such as black shirts with their clerical collars and the honorific 'Mother'. Both of these are ways of both claiming and asserting equality of function and status with their male colleagues, visibly and publicly.

But to my mind this can be a pathway full of traps. The very tradition of the honorific 'Father' and the use of the symbols of dress that reinforce the images of clerical authority have done much to support the patriarchal character of the church against which women have struggled. External symbols are undoubtedly very powerful, but when women adopt them so clearly they do little to broaden the vision and the scope of the church's ministry through their ordination. While inevitably pushing the symbols, they appear to be walking uncritically the path of clerical authority which they have themselves experienced as oppressive. Little wonder then if they are perceived as being potentially as unhelpful, even damaging, as are those whose style they have adopted. It takes time for all of us, the whole church and beyond, to process the baggage that comes to us from the past into new symbols that have the potential to transform.

Dependency and transference

The clear analogy being made when both men and women invite the use of the parental honorifics 'Father' and 'Mother' is one of the church as a family, a family ruled and owned by the parent figure. It is a very powerful image and exists in many churches which are ruled by a powerful parental figure, whether or not the honorifics are used. Such parental expectations in turn invite people seeking and expecting pastoral care to regard their pastor in that parental way, and this can shape the character of the pastoral care they are looking for.

In human terms, we have a right as little children to expect that our parents will meet our every need. We begin life in total dependency and our earliest memories are of those needs being met, somehow. But the meeting of such needs, particularly our very basic needs for nurture, shelter, food and love, does not continue for ever to be exclusively a parental responsibility. Quite simply, we grow up; and we begin not only to look after our own needs, but to establish relationships of mutuality and of trust whereby we offer such care to others and receive it back ourselves. This may occur in the context of a marriage, but not necessarily so, for we can receive all these aspects of care through a variety of adult relationships. And many people, as they move into adulthood, establish adult-charactered relationships with their own parents.

Shifting affections

But we never really leave behind the child within, and adult children who return to their parents' home will often demonstrate childish ways of behaving long since dormant. Similarly, when normally well-functioning adults find themselves in a community led by a father or a mother figure offering pastoral care, they can often find that the child within them stirs; and the feelings and phobias of childhood memories that derive from their experience of being fathered and being mothered are shifted across, transferred from the place of their formation, onto the pastor.

But this is not the natural or the acceptable place for such feelings. The pastor is not a real parent; the demands and expectations, if they are given clear expression, feel quite unreasonable, even impossible. Such transferred feelings and emotions can be both positive and negative, and may come either from positive or negative childish feelings. I have known people who have had a good but unresolved relation with a parent, or sometimes with a sibling, to transfer these unresolved feelings onto a pastor of the same gender as the longed-for parent or sibling, with such a sense of longing for what has been lost that it is akin to a love affair.

Negative transference works similarly. Childhood experiences of cruelty or alienation leave their mark, and because a child is seldom in a position either to challenge or to withdraw, there is rarely opportunity for the damage to be confronted and healed. Such unhealed experiences can lead to real tension between adults, so that the one transferring is always expecting the other to be acting in a cruel, damaging way.

Even if the internal delusions of the one who is transferring are not given direct expression, there is still damage to the quality and the authenticity of the relationship: in the mind of at least one of the participants, it is not what it seems to be. It is not uncommon for a give-away sign to be the energy with which someone expresses their like or dislike; it is often an energy that is totally inappropriate to the relationship.

While the use of the honorifics 'Father' and 'Mother' provide a clear symbolic context for transference to occur, it may also occur when these words are not used. Clergy still carry unambiguous spiritual authority, and gender does not need to be reinforced by language for genderized transference to take place. Clergy, by both profession and nature, may be charismatic personalities; and they often seek, as part of their job, to form authentic and influential relationships with young people. It is little wonder that at times these young people, and older people too, seek escape from the unresolved problems of their parental relationships by transferring onto clergy whom they have come to admire.

Transference has been around for a very long time and, like many other aspects of the ordained ministry, it has taken on a normative character based on the male model of ministry. We are all familiar with the cartoon stereotype of the little old lady, or the horde of little old ladies, who, while they delight 'Father' by doing many little chores to establish their affection and their loyalty, also make his life hell by presuming on his privacy. We may note the pattern at least in our cartoons of blaming the woman, while making her a figure of fun.

Such transference is not neutral, and neither is it not gender-related.

Men in pastoral ministry who set themselves up as 'Father' are, un-intentionally, inviting such a response. And the fact that in many cases it suits them and is useful to them, so that they express thanks and gratitude, only feeds the syndrome. It is then irresponsible to blame the woman and unkind to make her an object of comic concern. There is also the potential, where the relationship is one of blindness and inauthenticity, for further abuse, both physical and spiritual.

It is also inauthentic ministry. Such ministry has the tendency to send messages which, although the sender might not intend them, are nonetheless quite clear to recipients. So a patriarchal style of ministry which attracts positive transference can often be marked by a high level of devotion which, in the context of a worshipping community, can only attract the approval of 'Father'. So 'Father', who has theological justification for being an *alter Christus*, is also standing in the place of God – and that has no theological justification at all. Both parties are spiritually damaged by the distorted relationship. 'Father' is damaged by the fact that his ego is flattered undeservedly and the woman is damaged spiritually because she has got a God-substitute, when she thought she had the real thing. It is cheating. This is, of course, the source of the very deep hurt that many people experience when the one they had looked to for pastoral care is perceived as having let them down. For them, it is indeed as if God has let them down.

The issues are thrown into sharp relief by that sector of the church that chooses to use the honorific 'Father', but the same tendencies towards damaging and inauthentic transference are there in all clergy who adopt a paternalistic style of ministry that, for effectiveness, centres on themselves, and invites personal loyalty and devotion. Women who operate a 'maternalistic' style of ministry are equally at risk of inauthenticity. The invitation, the challenge to all, is to adopt a style of pastoral ministry that enables the positive aspects of such ministry to flourish, but in a context that acknowledges the neediness of many who seek pastoral care, and can offer such care in a manner that respects them as adult.

Transference and gender

Transference is indeed gender-related. We all begin life with both father and mother, even if one of them is distinguished by their absence. Whether we like it or not, gender is such a dominating fea-ture in the way we relate to the world and the way the world relates to us, that it clearly has very great implications for women who enter the ordained ministry and offer pastoral care. I have noticed this very strongly in my own ministry as a priest, and also in the experience of other women for whom it has been my privilege to offer pastoral care as a bishop.

There are many ways women can fall into the trap and operate a similarly inauthentic ministry. But they do have one real advantage over men. Because of the traditionally ascribed male gender of God, when we women dare to offer Christian pastoral care few people mistake us for God!

But transference does still happen, and in my experience it has happened more sharply since I have been a bishop than before, both negatively and positively. I am not sure whether this is because a bishop has a higher profile in the church; or whether the expectations that people have of a bishop are higher than those they have of a priest; or whether the authority that is carried by the symbol of a bishop stirs subliminal feelings of maternal transference, so that I become a particular target for maternal transference. Whatever the reason, I am not uncommonly confronted by abnormally high energy levels in the way people respond to me.

In parish ministry it was easier for people to get to know me and to respond to me for who I am, and to know with some sense of reality what they could expect me to be for them. As bishop, I am more remote, and hence it would seem more of an empty vessel for people's hopes, dreams and phobias to land upon. And so I have experienced people responding to me with great affection and responsiveness, but I have also learnt when to watch their energy levels and to be aware that their responsiveness may have more to do with the particularities of their own past than it does with my own pastoral skill. Similarly there have been times when I have bitterly disappointed people, and have experienced some harsh criticism. In such situations it helps to work out just where the other person is coming from, and what might be the energy source. For whether such criticism is accurate or deserved is not the only point, but the energy levels that drive it can also be significant.

Transference and power

Transference is clearly related to issues of power, but in a very much more subtle and more insidious way than when power is considered as a political concept. This is because it relates more to the sub-structures of our minds, where it intersects with our spirits formed, if not as Jeremiah proclaims in the wombs that bore us, then in the early years of our childhood, and generally beyond our easily accessible memories. Parents of both genders are undoubtedly figures of power in a child's life; they need to be, for the child begins in total dependency and must have someone to take full responsibility for them. So when an adult unknowingly transfers unresolved feelings left over from the parent–child relationship, they will almost invariably be feelings associated, happily or unhappily, with the powerlessness of childhood.

This makes a particular target of transference of anyone who assumes a position of leadership associated with power, most noticeably where that is spiritual power, of nurturing and of leading into the ways of wisdom. It also means that those who so transfer under such circumstances are placing themselves in a position of dependency and hence of some vulnerability. The relationship is a power relationship and is essentially asymmetrical.

But transference can also occur 'downwards'. The pastor can transfer onto a parishioner feelings of longing for the ideal child, the child they never had (for no child is ideal), and can assume proactively, from their position of power, a parenting role. Likewise this can be both negative and positive. It fits into the previously noted pattern of pseudo-family relations when a pastor, male or female, sees a younger parishioner as in some sense their spiritual child, and so invests the relationship with an intensity that is quite inappropriate. A double transference can be a particularly potent mix if the young person, as is not uncommon, is in turn transferring onto the clergy person. It is a dynamic that is not confined to young people.

Transference in a patriarchal society

Transference finds its origins in the whole culture of a patriarchal society, a society in which the father traditionally ruled the family life. It could at times be a wonderfully beneficent society, one in which a deal of extraordinary kindness was at work in providing a good environment for the raising of children. But it could also be an exceedingly cruel culture in which women and children might be badly abused. It was not, and is not, an evenly gendered culture, though it is in many western countries a culture that is being challenged and is under threat.

In such a culture it is not only in families that patriarchal patterns of relating occur. They are also reinforced by the general pattern of relating and of assigning leadership that exists throughout the society, though this is also being challenged by women acquiring positions of leadership in both the religious and the secular world. So challenge is being posed both within families and in the wider social context. This means that for some people there is a double threat involved in the general movement that sees more women, particularly younger women, gaining positions of leadership.

The primary caring role that mothers generally assume leads to the socially determined probability that men will find it more difficult to separate from their mothers than they do from their fathers. Furthermore, the patterns of patriarchy in society at large encourage mothers to see their own security in their sons' success and many, unfortunately but understandably, make a disproportionately high investment in their sons' future. So we find that many men reach adulthood with, at best, feelings of irritation about their mothers and at worst feelings of out-and-out hatred towards their mothers, neither of which are deserved. Abuse of mothers by growing sons is related to these distortions that uneven patterns of parenting produce.

This difficult set of interactions and circumstances makes, I believe, for a higher level of negative transference from men onto women who assume roles of spiritual leadership. But the converse also holds: because of the strong role that mothers play in the rearing and forma-tion of their sons, women clergy can also attract positive transference. Either way, any woman entering pastoral ministry would be wise to be aware of these dynamics.

The damage of transference

There are many reasons why it is well for clergy to be very aware of the potential for damage that transference can cause, not least because it can cut right to the heart of the pastoral relationship and become a major source of spiritual distortion. When we think of God, when we enter into a relationship of prayer with God, we become willingly open to God's taking us out of ourselves, to our moving beyond the limitations and confines of our own lives. There is a sense of the reality engendered by the Other, who, albeit in relation to us, is larger than we are. At its best it is an enormously exhilarating experience. And it is one that many people experience in ordinary human terms when they fall in love – for an active and vibrant prayer relationship with God has all the energy and joy of a full-blown love affair. It is natural, one would hope, for clergy to be the kind of people whom parishioners can respect and look up to; but when this admiration takes the form of transference it can assume, for the person who is experiencing the transference, the nature of a love affair, but an unconscious, distorted and dangerous love affair that has nothing at all to do with God.

I am not suggesting that all pastoral relations are at risk of or distorted by transference. Most are not. For one thing life would be far too unproductively complex if we had to spend excessive time figuring out what were the dynamics of transference in every situation. But it is advisable for us all to be wary of the possibility, for such dynamics can cut to the very heart of the character of our ministry and of the authenticity with which we are able, by the grace of God, to bring people into a closer and deeper walk with God.

However, I am not willing to dismiss all the negativity directed at clergy, whether men or women, as the somewhat mindless operation of negative transference. That would also be a mindless response. Mercifully, the general pattern among adults is to regard each other with mature respect and to act accordingly. I have known many fine relationships, both as priest and bishop, ones in which I have been able to give much, and also ones in which, in some mysterious and God-given way, I have received a very great deal. And I thank God for them all.

Hierarchy and care

Pastoral care is not only a calling and a privilege of individual ministry, it is also a calling and a privilege of the whole church. So the structures, the order of the church, if they are to have any validity at all, must operate for the good of everyone involved; and because, as William Temple is quoted as saying, the church is the only institution that exists for the benefit of non-members, our divine obligation to work in a beneficent and inclusive way is quite clear.

Whenever I have been involved in high-level discussions about the nature of the ordained ministry, and about Anglican ministry in particular, I am struck by participants' ready assumption of the value of the church, their belief that it is universally experienced as good news, and that if such is not the experience of other people then it ought to be. However, as we have seen, this is not necessarily the case. Rather, I think this attitude reflects how hard it is for those at the pinnacle of an organizational structure to hear the voices from below.

The church is essentially a human institution and as such susceptible to all the human errors that one could imagine, however much it may claim divine authority for the nature of its structures. A hierarchical structure may provide the parameters for formal accountability, but this is no guarantee that the care on offer will always be experienced as Good News.

The concept of boundaries is now well established as a way of maintaining a professional standard of care; it will be more fully discussed in the next chapter on the abuse of power. It provides useful guidelines in preventing gross damage being done by those with responsibility for pastoral care, but it does not necessarily ensure that the positive potential of Christian ministry will be realized. There is much about the hierarchical structure of the church, with its built-in resistance to mutuality, that makes this quite difficult.

One-directional care

One of the effects of hierarchy is that it places the component parts in a ranked relationship to each other; it orders them. It is in effect a kind of line management schema. When this is applied to the delivery of pastoral care it implies that there is an ordering of responsibility which somehow determines the direction of pastoral care and which also limits it. So, this argument would run, bishops care for the clergy and the clergy care for the laity. By extension the laity in their turn care for others who may or may not identify with the church.

There are some real strengths in a structure that provides, at least formally, for pastoral care on such a comprehensive basis – no matter that it is humanly impossible for any of us, any part of the structure, to live up to the expectations that it can generate. But there are also a number of problems, all of which spring from the probably unrealistic association of responsibility for pastoral care with the exercise of power, whether as a bishop or a priest.

A hierarchy is essentially a directional structure with different components operating one way, moving either up or down. As the hierarchy of the church is conceived, responsibility for pastoral care operates in a downward direction. This inevitably means that the care that is offered is directly associated with power. While this may well empower the relationship, it also leads to the possibility for the distortion of power to enter the relationship. This can happen in a number of ways: it can create dependency, buying into patriarchal expectations; it can lead to physical and spiritual abuse; or it can create suspicion and mistrust. The true goal of such a relationship of pastoral care should be to free and to facilitate the adult functioning of the recipient, and this can be stymied by the power component.

A more subtle form of abuse can arise from this dynamic. Those on the receiving end of pastoral ministry at times find their own reality is disregarded by the priest or bishop concerned; they are viewed, as it were, through pre-set lenses, and only what the other expects or wants to find is noticed. So it is not uncommon for people to complain that their pastor does not listen, does not see. It is clearly not very efficient pastoral care.

When pastoral care is associated with power, and pastoral ministry moves only in a single, downward direction, mutuality is discouraged. At times, this can produce a severe distortion of the relationship of pastoral care. It implies that one party has everything to offer, and the other can only receive. Whereas in Christian reality we all thrive best in situations where giving and receiving are interwoven. This of course means that the one offering the pastoral care needs to give away a certain measure of both distance and control, and be willing to accept a level of vulnerability – which might well be costly, but is frequently more healing.

A third and related difficulty is that the ordered nature of the pastoral hierarchy suggests that each component of the hierarchy has responsibility only for those in the layer immediately below. In effect this means that, until recently, the bishop has been seen as the *pastor pastorum*, with primary responsibility for the clergy. When, as was the case for so many centuries, both bishops and clergy were male, this system had the clear sub-agenda of male bonding. The combined force of this was thus enormously powerful, and very excluding of lay people. The advent of women into the ordained ministry has broken into this male bonding and gone some way towards weakening it. Though I have to say that it is an extraordinarily enduring characteristic of the ordained ministry.

The range of episcopal care

Hand in hand with this has gone, over the past decade or longer, a growing awareness that the charge that is given to bishops at their ordination is not merely to care for clergy alone, but for the whole church. When a bishop is ordained within the New Zealand church one of the questions that the presiding bishop puts is 'Will you oversee with compassion and patience the people of God entrusted to your care? Will you give encouragement to all, and labour to strengthen the Church's witness and mission?' There are undoubtedly times when the caring ministry of the bishop can conflict with the responsibility for the witness and mission of the whole church. Certainly this is the case when the interests of clergy and laity are not compatible with each other. In New Zealand, bishops are obliged by our canons to take careful account of the wishes and views of a parish when appointing a new incumbent. Clergy who have been used to a system whereby the bishop is in a position to act on their behalf have found this very difficult. The pastoral responsibility of the bishop is for the health and Christian integrity of the whole church. It clearly is a responsibility that can clash with the one-on-one responsibility for the welfare of individual clergy.

Power and pastoral responsibility

I can think of no other organization that attempts to run with this association between power and pastoral responsibility. At its worst it can be quite paralysing, producing situations where decisions cannot be made nor movement effected because people's self-image of being nice to each other would be violated. At its best, though, it can mean that hard decisions can be taken and put into operation without a gratuitous harshness and a rhetoric of annihilation. It is at times an extremely difficult structure to operate within. Nonetheless, it is one that challenges all who participate, particularly the bishop, to live under the vision of God's impossible love for us, constantly and painfully aware of the gap between our eschatology and our experience.

Women clergy have both a reputation and a good track record for being effective in pastoral ministry. In this they are greatly assisted by the fact that, being female, they do not carry the additional symbolism of cultural power that their male colleagues are burdened with. Because women are not numerous among the powerful in our society, they are more readily perceived as identifying with those who feel that their own needs and sorrows are insignificant. Women are a living critique of institutional power. It is therefore, I believe, structurally easier for women to work effectively as pastors within these institutions.

I believe this system to be sustainable, but only when lived with a high degree of courage and honesty, where difficulties and differences are both confronted and named. I have found the call to hold in tension both the pastoral and the juridical responsibilities of my office to be one of the hardest aspects of being a bishop; and, like all bishops, I have had to work out my own tactics of the Spirit for handling this. In essence, I have found, it is a question of discernment, and each time I have had to go back on my knees and try to see the situation through some approximation of the mind and the heart of God. At times it has been right for me simply to name the issue and then 'hold the space', to wait in patience and in prayer. At times I have been led to confront issues head on, but I have learnt not to do this too quickly, for if I do, the personal element in the conflict becomes too hard to handle. I have learnt to take time. The occasions on which I have had the prayerfulness and the patience to follow this strategy and have proceeded slowly and carefully and with good consultation, gradually seeing the shape of the space that God is preparing for me to move in, have led to the decisions with which, in retrospect, I am most comfortable.

When I reflect on what I do – using the opportunities that my experience as a woman offers to me – it seems to me that I am seeking to make space, 'wombspace' if you like, where others can grow and experience the life-giving power of the Spirit. Often I feel that, as in pregnancy, I am 'holding the space': by my attitude and responses, and not least by my prayer, I am, in a non-anxious mode, holding the boundary, defining that space as being unambivalently Christian and as intentionally within the church. This is particularly significant in times of potential controversy: as when one of our priests died of AIDS, or when a promising ordinand went awry and there were calls for instant cancellation of the status of ordinand. One of these needed safe space to die; the other needed safe space to discern the meaning of vocation. In both instances, it seemed to me that providing such space was uniquely both the function and the privilege of the bishop. For *wombspace* is like *sheepfold*; both are images of both enclosure and room for growth. An ancient image of episcopacy is reborn.

I am also aware that when I take time to work out the direction of my response, it is as if I too have been inhabiting wombspace, the wombspace of God; as if I too have been sensing the swirling of the Spirit becoming gradually focused. And then too, like any womb, it can become too cosy, too easy, and I need to seek the grace to move out and do what I have to do.

Therapy and spiritual direction

This discussion reflects the role confusion that surrounds clergy in a culture that no longer knows what to expect of those in the ordained ministry and which has little understanding of the God we serve. Little wonder that so many look to exercising their ministry in the more understood and respected fields of therapy and spiritual direction.

It is common and not undesirable for clergy and others seeking to develop a pastoral ministry to undertake training in the fields of counselling and psychotherapy. Many are well aware of the damage that is possible when people approach them with needs and expectations that cannot be met. Others seek to resolve their role confusion by adopting therapy as their primary work location, and they are only secondarily identified with the Christian enterprise. They have moved with clarity and intention into the realm of secular professionalism.

Christian people who are intentionally seeking help to resolve personal problems are frequently aware that many values of our contemporary society run counter to their Christian convictions and they look for a therapist or counsellor whom they can identify as Christian so that they will not have to defend needlessly their underlying values and convictions. There is considerable value in this.

Other clergy seeking to establish a recognizable place in a confusing world in a specifically Christian ministry are developing experience in spiritual direction. Spiritual direction is a specialized area of pastoral care. There has been a major revival of interest in its practice in recent years. Many more people are seeking to find a spiritual director, and others, both ordained and lay, are seeking training in the art of spiritual direction.

This is pre-eminently a sign that people are taking their own spiritual life, their own relation to God, more seriously and are seeking ways of deepening that relationship, of inviting its significance to inform their lives in a penetrating and transformative way. It is pastoral care that is sought by those who know of it and require it, and is not associated with the general but vague expectation that people have of their parish clergy.

People working in this area frequently bemoan the use of the term spiritual 'director', because it clearly denotes a non-reciprocal relationship, a relationship of power. Other terms such as 'soul friend' have been proposed, and the quest for spiritual guidance is also referred to as 'The Journey'. Both these terms place greater emphasis on the mutuality of the relationship, on the openness of each party to learning from the other, with a consequent deepening of the spiritual life for them both. But the persistence of the term 'spiritual director' is quite remarkable.

Whether therapist or spiritual director, both are variations on the pattern of pastoral relationship that we know so well, where one person in some need – whether serious or not, whether articulated or not – comes to another whom they believe to have the skills and willingness to help. Because there is a measure of vulnerability, the relationships need to be open to all the professional constraints that exist in any professional relationship these days. That is, the needs of the person seeking therapy or direction must be acknowledged as the agenda of the encounter, and this should not be subverted by the needs of the one providing the service. That person must be aware of the dynamics that can subvert this relationship and which clearly mark it as an unequal relationship. These include transference and projection. It should go without saying that the relationship should never become sexualized.

I think that it is important to be clear here, for vulnerability is greatly increased where there is the possibility of denying it is there. Since many of those seeking therapy and spiritual direction are women the potential for damage is greatly increased, and women have at times found that in the relationship their needs can be discounted. They are drawn into a situation that, whether this fact is acknowledged or not, is designed to meet the needs of the therapist or the director, who is in fact in control of the situation but who denies his or her power in the name of mutuality. It has the potential to be a very dangerous situation.

But professional ministry, whether ordained or not, whether of pastor, priest, therapist or spiritual director is not the whole story of pastoral care with the Christian community. This community consists of a vast network of relationships in which faith is shared, both formally and informally. Many deep friendships have been formed on the basis of shared faith, and the sense of mutual delight and exploration can be very effective in deepening our relationships with God. When we are open to the possibilities that God is holding out for us, we can find a gold mine. Relationships of faith shared and explored, of mutual friendship and prayer are the ligaments that bind the Body of Christ, hidden within the body as ligaments are. Within such friendships, problems and questions, personal and social, can be fruitfully explored and new directions found.

And when the door is shut we know that we are not just a file to be carefully replaced in the proper place where it can be found at the next consultation. We know that the prayer and the care continue, we know that the friendship is deepened by mutuality, we know that we matter, as we matter to God, and, too, we are ourselves strengthened by knowing that we can give that message to others.

I sometimes wonder if we have lost the art of friendship. This chapter has attempted to dig beneath the confusion that is associated with a contemporary understanding of the pastoral ministry and to trace the ambiguity in role identification that sets our understanding of ministry. The search for a clear role take us into the area of professionalism, into the territory occupied by the therapist and the spiritual director. But there is a difference: the therapeutic relationship does not aim at truth – it aims at psychological effectiveness, and spiritual directors can fall into this trap too. The ministry of a friend who is a 'soul friend' (see Chapter 11) aims to approximate to and reflect the friendship and affection with which God holds all of humankind. It is a relationship to be enjoyed with mutuality, avoiding the strain that unaware and inappropriate neediness might impose. It may well be ill understood, for increasingly we are tempted to take refuge in the security that we think that the image of 'professionalism' might give us, but I believe that it is still an ideal. It is an ideal that finds its natural place within the body of Christ which is called to be a spiritual community in which spiritual convictions can be embodied, and where healing for wounded and damaged spirits can be found.

5
Holding

■■■■■■

SHELTERING THOSE HEARTS

But rain slides round us now, a fine grey cloud
Like the wraith castle in a fairy tale,
Sheltering those hearts that could not quite prevail . . .
From Robin Hyde, 'The Awakener'

Bishops are called to be a focus of unity. It is a calling that bishops take seriously and refer to often. It can encompass different perspectives, ranging from the unity that we have in Christ, through a measure of doctrinal orthodoxy, to unity within the Christian community. It entails holding the tradition of the church and making it live authentically in the present generation. Essentially, for people in the pews it is about what we belong to, how we belong, how differences are resolved as the church moves through changing times. It is a function that clearly relates to issues of power and control, for unity can be used as an excluding device just as much as it can be used as an including device.

Women are particularly aware, not to say wary, of appeals to unity, for arguments about the need to maintain the unity of the church have been used repeatedly to exclude women from the ordained ministry of the church. But whose unity, one might ask. For it could be, and is, well argued that the exclusion of women from all levels of ordained ministry has in the past been used to ring-fence the concept of unity. And this is a far cry from our Lord's statement in St John's Gospel, 'That they may live together in unity so that the whole world might believe' (John 17.23).

The call to be a focus of unity is an immensely powerful one. It is, in effect, ecclesiastical language for holding the show together and is just what any organization would expect of its managing director. But the job of a bishop, according to church tradition, is not that of a managing director. The church in the development of its self-understanding over the centuries has evolved a rhetoric by which it has justified and maintained its power structures, and it has linked this understanding of its leadership to the truth by which it seeks to live. Foremost amongst these statements of self-understanding is the description of the bishop as an agent and guardian of unity. In the ordinal in the New Zealand Prayer Book the presiding bishop tells the congregation: 'The church looks to [bishops] to promote peace and unity among all God's people and to encourage their obedience to God's word.'

While the Christian church has a strong tradition of promoting unity through means that are primarily pastoral, it is the association of this function of episcopacy with the authority which the bishop holds which has caused so much difficulty. This chapter looks carefully at the issues of power that gather around this concept of unity. In particular it explores the nature of our diversity and the strains that press upon this unity. It finishes by looking at the issues that surround the promotion of unity by pastoral means and at what might be the shape of authentic unity in today's church; it reflects on how we might 'shelter those hearts'.

Structural questions

When we say that the bishop is a focus of unity, it is a very clear statement of the relationship of the person of the bishop to the structure of the church. The bishop, like any leader, has by virtue of character and being a distinctive role in shaping the culture of the church. To be 'a focus of unity' is a structural concept, in that a diocese is defined as the people who are gathered around the person of a bishop, who is in turn in a collegial relationship with the other bishops of the church. In this regard there are direct parallels to the management structure of many secular organizations. At another level it spells out very clearly the responsibility that the bishop bears for the integrity and Christian authenticity of the life of his or her diocese.

The unity that the bishop is required to hold is both institutional and spiritual. The church gives its bishops leadership, and expects them to orchestrate the administration and the decision-making processes for the life of the church. But the call of the bishop is also to spiritual leadership; it is both a call and an empowering that is very evident at ordination with the invocation of the Holy Spirit. As I reflected in an earlier chapter, spiritual power is the power to influence others through one's own being – by example, by kindness, by wisdom, by love, above all through prayer. Whereas institutional power has to do with ambition and control, and is a matter of externals, spiritual power has much to do with surrendering control, and concerns what is within.

They make a powerful combination, and like all such combinations they are potentially dangerous, both for the church and for the one who possesses such power. It is always a temptation to the possessor of institutional power to lose touch with his or her humanity and thereby forsake the path of spiritual power. Not for nothing were monks, so the story goes, warned against those who would make them bishops – *nolo episcopari*.

So the ministry of a bishop is essentially a ministry of being; it is what the bishop is, by ordination and by person and by God, that makes him or her a focus of unity for the whole church. But it is a role that, despite all the theory, is worked out in the detail of dealing with particular questions and especially those that are perceived as strains on unity; it has both a theological and a practical import.

The nature of diversity; the relation between power and truth

The church gives its bishops responsibility for maintaining both institutional and spiritual unity, so there is a very high convergence between doctrinal and structural unity. They reinforce each other. Unity is traditionally seen as a mark of truth[1] and threats to unity are seen as a threat to the ability of the church to be a credible sign of the Kingdom.

The early church saw the significance of the relationship between the structure of power and the structure of doctrine when it established, largely in response to the Gnostics, a clear system of mono-episcopacy. In fact, the equation was drawn between mono-episcopacy and mono-theism: one bishop, one God. And in the face of religious pluralism where there are many religious systems and many doctrinal positions, the rationale for that can be readily seen.[2]

There has always been theological diversity. When Irenaeus was defending the faith against the Gnostics his strategy was to move towards the definition of the canon of the Scriptures. But the Scriptures themselves contain a variety of perspectives and interpretations on the Christ experience. The complexity and struggles of the history of the Christian church reveal the plethora of perspectives on religious truth that have struggled for a place in the sun. This present time is no different.

Philosophically and in practice this is a extraordinarily fragmented age. It is undoubtedly the age of pluralism, both sacred and secular; it is the age of the individual in economy, in conscience and in faith, and this has had a marked effect on the lack of cohesiveness of community life, certainly in this country. We have now made a virtue of this diversity and the quality we value most is tolerance.

Such fragmentation raises some fundamental questions about truth. This is particularly difficult for Christians who seek to articulate convincingly their belief in the truth of the one God. Basically in this diffuse and pluralist society, the question is 'Is there any such thing as truth?' What right have we got to claim to be able to talk about Truth or God? One person's truth is, it would seem, another person's fiction. Indeed, as Christian apologists, we frequently find ourselves not only talking about God as we see God, but, pushed a step further back, we argue for a consideration of the very possibility of God or of Truth. For the very notion of God invites a consideration of a reality that is larger than the experience of any one individual, and one which by definition must be acceptable and convincing to other individuals. This age is very resistant to being persuaded on the basis of someone else's perception of God.

According to much contemporary thought, no absolute knowledge of truth is possible. The post-modernist critique of truth cleared a space, defined a new territory, forced recognition that there is no such thing as a 'God's-eye view' or, as it is sometimes put, a 'view from nowhere',[3] and to ignore the necessity for particularity blinds us to seeing that 'a universal exists only as it is particularized, and that this particularization is always interested'.[4] Tolerance is not only a virtue: it seems it is the only possible response. This represents a clear reaction against the rigid and absolute conceptions of doctrine which have been strongly in place in both the scientific and religious world since the Enlightenment, and which are seen to give an effective monopoly on the exercise of power to the people who have the knowledge, or, in terms emanating from a past age, have the responsibility for defining truth. Such a reaction effectively relativizes truth, which, while enabling freedom, does not support those who claim that truth is to be found within an institution. This is not an easy time in which to be an apologist for the Christian faith.

The impact of diversity on the church

Part of the contemporary structural critique of power within the church relates to the perception that those in power hold knowledge which cements that power: 'Stewards of the mysteries of God' (1 Corinthians 4.1). While the structures of power were the exclusive domain of men, it followed that the structures of truth were similarly defined. In recent years this has been challenged by the rise in lay theological education and the entry by women into the structures of theological truth as they have traditionally been understood. Feminist theology is a critique of many established positions, and it could only flourish when more women entered positions of institutional leadership. Those who expressed anxiety that the ordination of women would lead to doctrinal challenge were quite correct.

So this plurality affects the church in a number of ways. In the first place, there are many people who live profoundly spiritual lives and yet see no need to belong to a Christian community. God is accessible and available in all places and perhaps least of all, at times and to our shame, within the church. So the question 'Why the church?' is raised.

In the second place, within the church there is an ever-increasing variety of spiritualities and perceptions of God that are claiming both acceptance and validity. Among these is feminist theology. It is tempting to define these against a body of doctrine regarded as traditional and therefore as constant, but, in practice, the questions they raise are more complex and diffuse, and tradition itself has been questioning. The current situation of diverse theological perspectives seeking a place within the church certainly at times stretches our understanding of Anglican comprehensiveness.

For a bishop this means that there is, even in a small diocese, an extraordinary diversity, not only to hold together but also to relate to. This diversity manifests itself in a number of ways, many of them quite unremarkable. The last twenty or so years have seen wide diversification of worship styles and as I move around this diocese I have found my spirit expanded almost unbelievably as I am drawn into the presence of God in a huge variety of worshipping situations. When I was a parish priest I was able to shape worship according to the broad parameters of my own spirituality; as a bishop, it is I who must move into the worshipping environments that others shape. I realize that when I was a parish priest I tended at times to be defensive and off-putting about the introduction of worshipping practices that did not fit in with my own spirituality. It was a powerful position.

Church people generally seem to be tolerant of diversity until they are confronted with it personally or in their own parish. A corollary of this is the rise of congregationalism. If people find a spiritual identity within the institutional church at all, it is within their local church, and it becomes increasingly difficult for the diocese to find a single style of worship that truly gathers all our parishes together. For the bishop this diversity means an incredible stretch, and a strong need to relate personally and at depth with as many parishes and people and issues and concerns and needs within the diocese as possible. I have

frequently thanked God that this diocese is small, for this places some
limits on our diversity.

The strains that such diversity brings become most noticeable when
we have had visitors to the diocese who come from one or other clearly
defined arena of the church. They invariably attract protest from the
opposite camp, and there are times when that protest takes the form
of asking me as bishop to exclude the person so disapproved of. It is
almost an attempt to hijack the perceived power of the bishop. I have
had to make it clear that my personal views are irrelevant and that all
visitors should be received with courtesy and respect, but that debate
– open, informed and respectful – is to be encouraged. The church
is larger than any one subset of its doctrine, and I have found that to
point to this range is in effect to point to the largeness of the heart of
God.

Strains on structural unity

Unity is also stretched structurally. Within the last twenty or so years,
the perception that our society consists only of white males has died.
The pluralism of perspectives that has seen the recognition of the
categories of gender, race, age, sexual orientation, whether partnered
or not, and so on, has buried the older world-view. Yet in administrative structure, in personnel, in worship and in doctrine, our churches
have barely begun to respond to this social reality.

The debate is there, even if the response is slow. Post-modernism
has taught us, whether consciously or not, to be aware of the place
where we stand and to be respectful of the fact that that place, that
turangawaewae (a place to stand) might not include, in fact might quite
precisely exclude, others. So we have become more alert to our own
racism and ethnocentrism, and as a church have travelled some way
along the road towards creating a more just society.

Intentional diversification

In 1992 our church passed a new constitution which sought to change
the assimilationist philosophy of the first constitution introduced by
Bishop Selwyn in 1857. The Revised Constitution established three
separate cultural strands within our church, and called these by the
Maori name *tikanga*: Tikanga Maori, Tikanga Pakeha (the successors of
the colonists) and Tikanga Pasifika (the people of the countries of the
Pacific that make up the Diocese of Polynesia). Each of these three

strands in our church takes responsibility for the development of its own ministry and together they define the reality of our church. No longer are we, officially, a colonist church with a strong Maori membership and a missionary diocese in the Pacific. This has had a very significant impact for the other two Tikanga; it has enabled them to claim a measure of autonomy and independence within the life of our church. But Tikanga Pakeha, who are still a large majority, have been slow to relinquish their self-identity as the dominant strand within the church. For many pakeha, the process of power-sharing has been a humiliating experience. We have had to come to grips with the fact that our way of seeing things does not hold all the truth. But humility never did any soul any harm.

The constitutional changes have brought changes in the structure of unity within the church. No longer is each diocese a separate geographical entity, because the Diocese of Aotearoa (Tikanga Maori) runs over the whole country. So the Bishop of Aotearoa has responsibility for Maori mission within all the other dioceses. For pakeha bishops in this country this has meant accepting the existence within our dioceses of a non-territorial jurisdiction.

This has had a profound effect on our sense of the relationship between unity and power. No longer do we seek unity through the structures of control; rather do we seek to shape relationships of respect and mutual encouragement. But old habits die hard

Diversity within the ordained ministry

Awareness of the fact that our identity does not include that of others is behind the practice of diversification within the ordained ministry of the church.

Allowing for cultural differences, the general pattern a quarter of a century ago was that young men were selected for ordination, preferably after they had completed a good first degree, and then, still unmarried, they went to seminary or theological college for three years to train for the priesthood. During their curacies, generally two, they served their obligatory year in deacon's orders and were also 'expected' to make a suitable marriage. So, in their late mid-twenties, or marginally older, and newly married, they were launched into the practice of ministry. This was generally, but not solely, stipendiary parish ministry where, with all that training, we expected them to be competent to do the job by themselves.

There was always some diversity, but now the situation is vastly different. In general this is because the gateway to ordination has been

opened much wider. Not only has the requirement for degree qualifications in theology been challenged as a necessary route, but most
candidates for the priesthood are well over thirty; some have reached
retirement age. They are not all married; some are gay and living
openly in a committed relationship. Many serve in non-stipendiary
positions; and, too, some are women. Some still spend a year as a
deacon, others much less, others much more; and many work in teams
with other ordained people and with lay people.

And their training for ordination varies too. By no means do all
attend theological college: some are trained in regional ordination
training programmes and many make use of distance teaching
facilities. Some are excellently prepared, some markedly less so. And
they serve in a variety of situations: in stipendiary ministry, in non-
stipendiary ministry, as local priests, as 'community-facing' priests, as
attached to worshipping communities and as free floaters, as clergy
couples, as chaplains in hospitals, prisons, schools and universities,
as ministry educators and theological college lecturers, and as any
combination among all of these.

All of this demands extraordinary flexibility of a bishop; I have
found it necessary to be able to respond with care and particularity to
the individual situations of individual priests and also of the communities that they would serve. There are no set patterns any longer;
yet the call is to run a ministry that is identifiably the same ministry,
serving within the same church, and relating, both formally by way of
licence and informally by way of personal understanding and respect,
to the same bishop. It is essentially the call to hold the centre while
letting the edges move. It is not only my heart that needs to be large,
it is also my vision.

Collegiality

Bishops are called by their ordination to maintain collegiality with
other bishops. In practice this means meeting regularly, maintaining
communication, respect and attentiveness to each other. Within the
New Zealand church, the bishops, meeting alone, are not part of the
governing body of our church, however the bishops' meetings are an
informal way in which the questions of one bishop become the questions of the others, thus at least partially enabling the dioceses to move
together and to maintain a consistency, but not an identity, of patterns
of mission and ministry across our dioceses.

In many informal ways bishops look to other bishops for personal
support, and in varying degrees this is offered. In a small country,

where the bishops know each other and there are no major divisions, such a responsiveness is readily achieved. It is also achievable out of a strongly male tendency to develop strong working relationships of power; men find it easier to do this than to form personal friendships. It is a variation on the well-known theme of the old-boys' network and, more politically, of brotherhood. It can be very effective.

The injunction to episcopal collegiality is more than an informal and incidental association between bishops; it is a strong imperative. This dynamic, together with the long history of male bonding, tends to make bishops very accepting of the idiosyncracies and even the failings of their colleagues. There can be a cosiness that is not a ready environment for sharp challenge, for the cost is seen as a breaking of collegiality.

Many women have become wary of the concept of collegiality; many see in it a ready mechanism by which the concerns of women and women themselves can be discounted. It is also a place where the pressure that women bring to bear on the leadership of the church can be resisted. In our neighbouring province of Australia, the maintenance of collegiality is seen by many bishops as an imperative that is stronger than the call to deliver justice to women and to acknowledge their call to ordination. This injustice extends not only to the women who seek ordination, but also to the men and women who want them to be ordained. Further afield, the meeting of the primates, the provincial leaders of the constituent churches of the Anglican communion, failed to tell one of their colleagues who had gone into exile, and resisted appeals from his diocese to return, that he had a primary responsibility to his diocese and should return.

Ordination of women as bishops

It has for some time now been claimed that the ordination of women as both priests and bishops is a threat to the unity of the church. The 1988 Lambeth Report puts the question clearly:

> How will the ordination of women to the episcopate affect the
> episcopal ministry and its relation to the communion or fellowship of
> the Church? The episcopate has long been seen as the focus of unity in
> the Church. Can unity be sustained when a woman is ordained to the
> episcopate? And, if so, what is the nature of that unity?[5]

In order to answer that question, we need to consider the nature of the unity that is preserved if women do *not* enter the ordained ministry. It is essentially a unity that looks in on itself, that is more concerned with keeping what is known and safe than reaching out to embrace the excluded and the new. In that it is the unity between bishops that is held to express the unity of the church, it is a unity that excludes the dioceses that might elect a woman as their bishop, and it would seem to depend in no small measure on the dynamics of male bonding rather than on a concern for the effectiveness of the mission of Christ through the church.

The difficulty lies with those who cannot accept that women can be authentically ordained to the priesthood or the episcopate. When this becomes an excluding difficulty, the connection between power and control is clear. Fortunately the church of God is larger of heart than this questioning would suggest, and the reality of our communion (*koinonia*) with one another has much to sustain it without the rather sharp emphasis on who can 'accept' whom. The final report of the Eames Commission repeated a point made in the first report when it

> encouraged bishops to take every opportunity to emphasize their fundamental agreement on matters of faith, practice and the received understanding of the apostolic ministry to which they all steadfastly adhere. The test of this unity among the bishops is whether, while personally holding diverse positions on matters such as the ordination of women to the episcopate, they are committed to 'ministering unity' to the whole church. Similarly a sign of God's gift of unity to a church holding a diversity of positions on such an issue would be its willingness to receive such ministry from all its bishops.[6]

Undoubtedly there will continue to be a diversity of positions for a long time, so we will all need to learn the art of maintaining unity under such circumstances. For women who are bishops, we need to recollect continually that the sense of mistrust with which the wider church regards our ministry is not a personal mistrust but rather the consequence of where we stand at this point in history. We live with a measure of vulnerability, which is always a gift to the soul but which also places us, insofar as we are in relation to the rest of the Anglican Communion, less firmly in the centre, more on the boundary of the patterns of power. In our experience of at least partial exclusion, we are reminded, from the inside so to speak, of the feelings that are attached to that experience. It is not a common experience for bishops, and I believe it is a gift.

Unity of mission

In a world and a church of such diversity and plurality, the church finds itself spending more and more time on the resolution of its own

internal questions of structure and doctrine and less on engagement
with the mission of the church. There is, however, a critical association
between the establishment of right relations within the formal structures, and the conduct of our mission. It is not easy for us to reach out
to people with a gospel of Good News to those who are excluded,
while we continue to exclude others ourselves. It is worth noting too
that the unity of purpose which acceptance of a common mission can
bring is one reason that the Eames Commission gives for the possible
reception of women as priests and bishops within the Anglican
Communion.[7]

The establishment and maintenance of unity in the presence of such
diversity is undoubtedly not easy, and has led some to suggest that
it is an unrealizable idealism that makes the church ask this of its
bishops. John Zizioulas has said that 'the most important condition
attached to diversity is that it should not destroy unity. The (local)
Church must be structured in such a way that unity does not destroy
diversity and diversity does not destroy unity.'[8]

There is nothing wrong with idealism, indeed that is the whole
point of living by faith. The Christian faith has always pointed beyond
the obvious and the inevitable, to possibilities that can only be
visualized within the heart of God. The Christian church, if it is true,
is constantly in need of reform – *semper reformanda*; we will not reach
perfection this side of the eschaton.

This is clearly the point at which the church departs from many
secular organizations, for our dominant culture and purpose is not one
determined by outcome but rather it is one determined by the call to
nurture faith. Therefore any account of the unity that the church seeks
is best defined, not by reference to structure and order but rather to
common mission, to the call to 'gather in'. As the 1988 Lambeth Report
put it:

> The Church is the Body of Christ. We are cleansed and called into
> mission by baptism, empowered for mission and commissioned by the
> Holy Spirit. Our mission is to be the sign of the Kingdom of God to the
> world, and to 'go forth into the world, making disciples of all nations'.
> This mission is universal (catholic) and belongs to the Church at all
> times and in all places. It is in our acceptance of this mission that we
> discover and enjoy our unity.[9]

I have often heard it said that a mark of authenticity of any
expression of the Christian faith and life is its willingness to engage
with others to share faith, whether by proclamation or by gossiping
the gospel or by whatever means. This is both a broad criterion and a
narrow one, for if followed through, many of our church communities

who consider their faithfulness impeccable would be excluded, and many groups who exist on the fringe of the church would find themselves gathered in. There are many questions that surround the question of the unity that we find in the mission of the church.

The pastoral approach to unity

The church is always uneasy when it feels the need to enforce unity by means of legislation and control, and will usually seek a pastoral route to the maintenance of unity. This motivation is evident in both the appointment and the reports of the Eames Commission on women in the episcopate. In identifying this role for a bishop the final report of the Commission said:

> it will be the particular task of the bishop actively to promote that continuing respect and tolerance between persons and groups which establishes the tone and environment in which a contentious synodical decision can be taken forward. The bishop must also exercise a ministry of interpretation in and among those of differing views to enable them to listen patiently and carefully to one another. Sensitivity and care will be needed to ensure that the views and concerns of those opposed are recognised in and through appropriate practical and pastoral arrangements.[10]

It is an approach that is motivated by care for the church and love for those who are its members, whatever their position. Much good work has been done along these lines.

However, in situations of threat and challenge the deficiencies of our human capacity to trust such love become very evident. In fact, this kind of care for the institution contains all the ambiguities of the mismatch of pastoral care with structural power that were noted in an earlier chapter. It is extremely hard for care such as this to be perceived as disinterested. Where there is conflict it is difficult for the bishop, whatever he or she might think, genuinely to have the trust of both sides, and it is also unrealistic to think that there can be real debate in such a situation. It is all too easy to mistrust the way of love and pastoral care.

The difficulty lies in the fact that the way of pastoral care and of love is interpreted differently according to which side of the fence a person stands on. Women have often perceived what the church has defined as love as being coercion or exclusion, especially when the message given is 'we love and honour you, but keep out of our hair!'

The combination of love and power can be lethal to people in a position of relative oppression. So many of the discussions about power in the church seem to relate to power in the realm of organization and structure, and to lines of responsibility and accountability. It is as if there is greater safety in structural equity, where the love is open and accountable.

The history of relationships between the Maori and pakeha Tikanga (cultural strands) of the Anglican Church in New Zealand tells the same story. Here we have seen, within our own lifetime, the limitations and ultimately the failure of human love that was behind the need to make changes to give full independence and autonomy to Maori within this church. For most of our history, there was no lack of expressed love towards Maori people, but it was not experienced as love. It was founded on a perception of the church that was inherently assimilationist and denying of Maori identity and aspirations. It was also racist. When this was realized and the desire to remedy the situation was established, it was apparent that no amount of love could remedy the situation by itself; only a transfer of significant power, autonomy and resources would make a significant difference. The combination of power and love had been proved defective.

This has not been an easy process for our church, but there is much that is biblical in the solution that we adopted; for as Jesus set up no structural organization, so he eschewed quite explicitly the assumption and use of power as it is conventionally understood. The degree of difficulty we have experienced is a measure of how far short we had fallen. And there is a depressing inevitability about this, for despite all our efforts there are plenty of signs of the persistence and intractability of old power structures and the development of new ones.

Women too can be wary of love; if justice is lacking, love becomes quite suspect. Where this occurs, there is usually a move to reform the structures. And yet we seem to need structures to order our common life in a way that is more reliable and predictable than the way of love.

Women often feel the tensions of this dilemma particularly acutely. Certainly many women have felt both appreciated and honoured by their bishops in the development and recognition of their ministry, and have found nothing but care and wise guidance. But it would undoubtedly be true to say that in provinces where women have been moving into the power structures of the church, the nature of the struggle has often raised questions as to the degree to which the church can afford to rely on the love of those who lead it. It can all seem a bit too risky. It is more reliable to change the structures so that the process of any decision-making can be transparent, owned by the whole church and fully participatory.

Yet I would also say that women in ministry situations know that the structures can turn against them and against others; and so, in the conduct of their own ministry, they tend to be more trusting of the way of love and to put a greater investment into it. Even the best of structures can betray. Perhaps this not only reflects our informed suspicion of the way of power, but is also a consequence of our having inherited centuries of deep Christian spirituality that has come from the margins, away from the centre of power. Women more naturally espouse a spirituality of vulnerability; they know only too well what that vulnerability is.

A new vision of unity

Yet, in our humanity, which is so often untrusting and casting around for securities that can be seen, experienced and held on to, we structure our mission, sometimes until the Lord who called it into being is lost amid our structural quarrels. Jesus set up no organizational structure as a means of holding the church together. Neither did he make any claim to set forth an intellectual, much less a theological, statement of what was truth. But he did say 'I am the Way, the Truth and the Life', and in so doing made truth more than intellectual statements and more than structural purity.

For in Christ we find the connection between truth and love that is the elusive quality of unity; they are inexorably linked and cannot, for Christians, be separated. The direct authority which Jesus exercises holds truth and love intertwined – nothing is really true unless love is involved in it. And despite the inevitable failings of human love, the vision of love that we have in the person of Christ is the only basis for our unity. So the church, as the nurture, not the product, organization that it is, must find the basis of its unity in that love and become an accepting, loving, supportive and challenging community.

6

Ethics

━━━━━

FOR ALL YOUR BRAVE REFUTING

Evil is in me for all your brave refuting,
Your abstinence from blame
And yet my sins become by your transmuting
The lovely grace of shame.

The sun itself like the archangels' banner
Is blue, and dire, and bold.
It is our air, our sky of dewy manner,
That gentles it to gold.
                              Eileen Duggan, 'Any Sinner'

In many ways the church is held in little respect these days. It is no longer in a position to contribute as a coherent institution to the process of formulating legislation affecting either public or private morality. And yet, in a society that is increasingly ignorant of the basics of the Christian faith, the church is being increasingly regarded as a source of information and wisdom on questions of ethics and, more loosely, public and personal values.

An incident a few years back made me aware of this. I had been invited to a small lunch party hosted by the Mayor of Dunedin to hear the then Minister of Finance, the Rt. Hon. Ruth Richardson, explain her policies. Ms Richardson was a minister in the newly elected National Government which was pursuing a policy of major cuts to social welfare benefits and causing distress to those who were the most poor in our country. We introduced ourselves, had lunch talking informally, and then she spoke. As she spoke, she outlined the expediency of her policies but could not avoid the issue of the rightness of them. As she did, she got somewhat confused and turned towards me and said 'As Penny would know'. Now, I had not contributed to that discussion at all. It was simply because she knew me as a church leader that she expected me to be considering questions of the ethical value of what she was proposing. She was quite right.

That vignette showed me how strong is the public perception that the church has something of value to contribute to questions of social and personal ethics. As bishops have been called 'the conscience of the church' (see Chapter 3) so the church, however divided, is still in some mysterious though disputed sense seen as 'the conscience of the nation'. So it is frequently to bishops that people turn for ethical comment. Much as this is a topic that most bishops might seek to avoid, we cannot.

The quest for values and for clear ethical thinking is widespread. In part I feel that this is a search for security in a constantly shifting world, an attempt to avoid the shifting sand of seemingly random and heartless change; to find the solid rock on which to stand. In part I feel it is a reaction against the blatantly valueless character of the market forces which we have come to believe should rule our lives.

But it is difficult. First, it is difficult because not only is our society fragmented, but so also is the Christian venture. What do we mean when we speak of 'the church'? In New Zealand society there is no single, unified entity that can claim that name. Second, it is difficult because the search can easily get us into areas about which we are not properly informed and also get us into the realm of judgement, which is a public stance that neither accurately reflects the nature of God nor does the public face of the church any good.

Christian ethics are a natural consequence of a healthy relationship with God, and an understanding of Christian conduct, both personal and communal, stems from such. But a healthy relationship with God is a little-known commodity, and our world, if not hungry for faith, is hungry for direction and values. The search for ethical clarity and security often tries to short-circuit directness and intensity in our response to God, and places those whose relationship with God is deep and strong at the risk of making an offering that is obscure and inaccessible. 'Ethics tinged with emotion' is what we are being asked for.

Furthermore, God's engagement with this world is not only through individuals; God engaged, through the life and being of Christ, with God's people, and that engagement, that commitment in solidarity, continues. This is incarnation, and is fundamental to Anglican self-understanding. William Temple said in 1950: 'Christianity is the most materialistic of the world's religions.'[1] The contemporary Christian venture, even though fragmented, can do no less than seek to be a channel for that engagement, and to place discussions on the ethical values that inform and shape our public life into the context of that engagement. Bishops, in their perceived role as spokespeople for the church, have a significant part to play in this.

This chapter looks at some of the underlying considerations that, as a bishop, and as a woman, I bring to ethical analysis, and then turns to some specific areas in which these considerations take effect. It finishes by looking at the two general areas of social and personal ethical considerations. But 'for all your brave refuting', it does not seek to avoid the reality of our ethical choices.

Are ethics possible?

The very notion of ethics presupposes a community with a certain common understanding, history, interest and commitment to each other in the common good. But I doubt whether such a commonality exists. We have already noted the widespread fragmentation of both our society and the whole Christian venture. There are consequently multiple points of view on any possible ethical question, and a prevailing sense that there is no coherent set of principles that can guide our choices.

This fragmentation brings with it an assertion of the value of autonomy, the integrity of the individual. But that is all there is: individuals, living in isolated reality, full of personal integrity, but alone, and in that aloneness respecting and maintaining the aloneness of others. When pushed to the extreme, this existential isolation means that no one can prescribe for the good of another and no one can speak on anyone else's behalf. Perhaps the only value that we hold in common is the right of the individual to do as he or she thinks best – whether for their own interests or for other people's makes little difference.

Whereas we might deplore this as a post-modern madness, at the bottom line no ethical teaching can be effective within any span of any community, however small, however fragmented, unless it grabs the heart and the conscience of individuals. It is all too easy in discussing justice issues to 'pass the buck', to say 'They should . . . ', or more often 'The government should . . . '; it is much harder to say 'We should . . . ', and harder still to say 'I should . . . '. There is a very real and a very noticeable tendency to grab at talk of personal rights while pushing away talk of personal responsibility. Perhaps we want the best of both worlds.

So ethics is an area in which bishops, if not angels, fear to tread. Theological arguments can go so many different ways and it is hard to identify a common Christian base from which to speak. We speak into a society whose only common value is that of individualism, a value which itself makes ethical thinking quite problematical.

Making judgements

Such fragmentation leads to considerable insecurity, both personal and social. So it is not uncommon to find people seeking ready answers, clear statements of right and wrong which are universally applicable. But this is rarely possible; people, bishops, gurus of various kinds are often set up by the media or others, then promptly tumbled. We are a society shying away from any kind of ethical certainty, and the temptation to give clear-cut answers is one I have little difficulty in resisting.

There are other reasons also why I think that it ill behoves a Christian leader to adopt a judgemental stance. First, we both follow and preach a God who is infinite love, and an easy judgementalism does little to make that God accessible. Second, in participating in ethical debate we do best if we do it in a mode of dialogue and of mutual exploration, one that seeks through debate to identify the common ground for naming our ethical insights. Judgementalism is a closure on such debate. Third, we have to admit the limits of our ethical evaluations; we never know all the circumstances, for these involve the depth of the human heart which is only accessible to God, and oftentimes God writes some straight things with crooked lines.

This brings me to the major reason for eschewing judgementalism. When we as Christians do adopt such a stance, we implicitly if not explicitly claim that our views are those of God and are stamped with the authority of God. It is a position that we can never take, for when we do we usurp the position of God – which is damaging enough for our own souls, but, perhaps worse, it also conceals God from those we are trying to communicate with. It is also at root a position of faithlessness, for it is only when we do not believe that God will be God that we try to take on the attributes of God ourselves.

A Christian ethical position

An underlying presupposition of both the Christian faith and the possibility of ethical direction is that what we do matters: that our conduct has significance for ourselves, for others and for God. Therefore questions about what we do deserve to be taken seriously.

Ethical analysis, whether Christian-based or not, also presupposes that any discussion on ethical outcomes should be in terms of right and wrong, the nature of moral obligation and what might be the notion of the good life. Although posed in terms of the dualistic opposites right and wrong, the nature of ethical inquiry is more by way of debate, with issues and responses ranging along a continuum. But the poles of right and wrong are the boundary marks of such debate.

Christian ethical inquiry is very tightly associated with discernment and consequently with prayer. It seeks to place such ethical discussion within the context of spirituality and in particular in the context of our relationship with God. It derives this standpoint from an awareness of the close association between belief and action; we are what we do, and we do what we believe. It is thus a thoroughly holistic venture. It seeks to relate both to our public life as a society and to our private lives as individuals. It looks less at ethical absolutes than at the character of the ethical values by which public institutions and individuals within society are motivated and to which they appeal for legitimation. The concepts of motivation and spirituality are closely connected,[2] the first often seen as a secular version of the latter.

Emphasis on the character of our ethical values leads us to see the significance of questions of why we do what we do, how we do what we do, and what the outcomes are of what we do. These questions all relate us back to the underlying fact of God's engagement with our world, back to incarnation. That engagement was the process by which God abandoned absolute status to engage with humanity in a relationship of radical love. It was characterized by a deep regard for all who are excluded and a critical suspicion of those who effect exclusion by propounding moral absolutes. So, at both the individual and the communal levels, there can be few boundaries between ethics, theology and spirituality, and where one of these parameters shifts we can expect there to be some adjustment in the others.

The need for clear ethical analysis is thrown into sharp relief by the exigencies of public life. As a person who is habitually called upon to act publicly and in ways that clearly affect the lives of others, I am even more aware of the imperative to act intentionally and consistently. It is a fundamental condition for establishing trust. It is the imperative to be accountable – to those with whom I work, to the God whom I serve and, because I am a woman working in one of the most institutionally patriarchal structures there has ever been, I act out of an awareness of the ideals and visions of the women's movement as I have known it in this country for the last 25 years, and of the women who have shared that journey with me.

Christian feminist ethics

This leads us into consideration of what might be the particular perspective of Christian feminist ethics. In one sense, feminist ethics

begins with the realization that the ethical analysis that has hitherto
been associated with the Christian faith has all derived from a male
perspective. A cynic would say that it has indeed been formulated to
support the traditionally patriarchal structures of the church. They
would be right. Such ethical analysis does not take seriously the reality
and the particularity of women; it has habitually treated women as
objects and not as subjects. By this I mean that women have been
denied the right to be full moral agents; they have not been among
those who could 'choose life' (Deuteronomy 30.19).

Clearly, the complexities of the changes that have taken place
in western societies since the 'second wave' of feminism in the 1960s
have opened up for women the possibility of that choice, for it is only
in the context of choice that the notion of ethics has any validity. So
feminist ethics now poses the question 'Is it good for women?' or, more
minimally, 'Is it safe for women?' In this, feminist ethicists are seeking
a re-visioning of moral theory. The imperative behind feminist ethics
is, it seems to me, twofold: first is the need to claim moral autonomy,
the space and the right to make our own choices; and second is the call
to challenge the hegemony of male ethical theory and to insist that the
women's voice be heard.

The raw material for feminist ethics is the lives and the experience
of women. The process is essentially a reflective one, and as it almost
always happens in dialogue through discussion it is generally built on
a sense of shared experience. Feminist ethical discussion frequently
takes the form of critique, seeking to establish the particularity and
hence the limitations of patriarchal ethics; and, too, seeking to carve
out a space for women to explore the particularity of their own beings,
their own experience.

Feminist ethics are therefore often more relational in character than
conventional ethics. Certainly the work of Gilligan and Chodorow[3]
identifies the effects that traditional ethics have had on women, and
how they have contributed to the social and psychological oppression
of women.

Feminist ethics have also had a mutually-responsive relationship
with feminist theology. The critique of the penal substitution contained
in the doctrine of atonement as contributing to the sanctioning of child
abuse is a case in point (see Chapter 9), as also is the rejection of the
image of a transcendent, dominant and controlling God. In much
feminist spirituality, God is located within: both within the individual
and within the community.

Such shifts in theology, which are not as strong as they might seem,
but which are usually expressed as critique, contribute to a climate in
feminist ethical analysis that does not accept the possibility of right

and wrong as abstract and absolute concepts. This radically shifts the ground for a Christian grasp of a feminist ethic, in one major way. Because it is essentially critique, it is more clear about what it is *not*, than what it is. It also, as a consequence, eschews the character, the processes and the power of the institution of the church. There are times when it declares itself to be an ethic of an alternative community, also identifying as church.

It is axiomatic in the critique mounted by Christian feminists that the 'traditional' church has no monopoly on the definition of church. Nonetheless, boundary issues that are dependent for their rationale on the church's traditional power of self-definition occur as women seek to define themselves as 'in' or 'out', and as the church seeks to include or exclude. There are a lot of ill-defined issues and they will remain that way.

But there are women who identify both as being within the church and as feminists who, aware that the church has identified solidly with male leadership, seek to apply the underlying principles of feminist ethics within a Christian context. Such an ethic relies on an in-depth analysis and understanding of the dynamics of patriarchy – whether apparent or not, whether residual or not. It does not rest on an easy rhetoric of equality, but it takes seriously the often unspoken anxieties that will be experienced both by women and men, and it will not retreat when these dynamics and anxieties threaten to be destructive. Above all, this analysis holds out a vision of a new community, a New Jerusalem, in which men and women can work together without dominance and hurt, willing to include and co-operate for the common good, acting with openness and transparency. It is a holistic vision, embracing all parts of our lives, whether church-facing or world-facing, whether public or private. This is not merely a vision of some far-off country; it is near at hand and utterly possible, for it is a country in which we have our toes on the shore.

A Christian feminist ethic does not readily appeal to doctrine as a bench mark of correctness, but rather appropriates with pleasure and with gratitude all the energy and wisdom that God has to offer and uses it for the good of the whole Christian mission. It is an ethic which honours the integrity of every person's relationship with God, and it seeks to draw on the love of God. In the confidence of being held fast in that love, it can live generously and openly with others.

Social ethics

In the last decade, New Zealand along with many other countries has made a major economic and social shift from, in general terms, a social policy that promoted as a priority the welfare of its people to one based on monetarist principles. These policies have affected every area of our national life – education, health, social welfare, housing, family income levels and so on. The casualties have been most noticeable amongst the poorer people who generally find that they are disadvantaged on a number of fronts. For example, a single-parent family with several children may face a number of costs associated with their participation in education; their health may be bad and with the higher costs of medical care it may get very bad, involving the additional expenses associated with hospitalization. And all this may be against a back-ground of rapidly rising rents and the real possibility of being evicted from their home.

This is a thumbnail sketch but not an exaggeration. The problem is that while poverty, as measured by a high level of social distress, affects around 20 to 25 per cent of our population, the rest of the country is doing well and some are doing very well. The gap between rich and poor is widening as the rich get richer and the poor get poorer. This situation has been in place for some years, and while there may now be more employment opportunities there are many people who are just not in a position to take advantage of them, and their poverty persists.

Poverty does not strike evenly. The sad result of such policies is that they most often have the strongest impact on those who for social reasons are otherwise disadvantaged. Thus unemployment has increased enormously among the Maori and Pacific Island populations of New Zealand, and women often face particular disadvantage because of their commitment to their children and because of their lower earning capacities.

Increasingly we are becoming a country that is less concerned about poverty; it is all too easy for those of us who live in relative security to fail to notice the plight of the poor and therefore not to press for the political decisions that would benefit them. We become trapped not only into the communities of those with whom we share a life-style, but also by the pursuit of our own individualism and our own ends. But we are not just individuals, who succeed or who do not; we are also people who, as we have seen, may be tied into structures that disadvantage us.

There are many, many good people in our communities, among them many church people, who are deeply concerned at these consequences of social policy and who work hard to alleviate distress in their own areas of expertise and concern. But aid agencies are very fragmented, they find it difficult to maintain contact with each other and to devise strategies for working together; they are also severely underfunded and largely staffed by the voluntary labour of women. Food banks are an excellent example of this. They are effective within the narrow spheres of their operation, but they are endlessly concerned that what they are doing is patching up a bad system, being a Band-Aid, rather than transforming the system. And yet they care.

In the run-up to the 1993 general election, the leaders of ten New Zealand churches, including two women, came together to make a statement expressing their concern at the impact the economic policies of the government were having on the poorest in our country. To come together at all was quite an achievement in such a divided Christian community, and the statement they made was necessarily general. The statement only tangentially addressed the question of disadvantaged groups, but the church leaders offered the following as principles, which, they suggested, were a requirement of social policy:

That it:
- enhance the dignity and life of human beings;
- encourage good relationships within the community;
- recognise that all are called to work for the common good;
- see work as an expression of human worth and self-respect;
- recognise that the poor and the vulnerable must be a major concern in social policy.

The document was variously received. Within church circles, it was quite widely appreciated. There was real concern among Christian people at increasing levels of poverty, and real frustration at how limited our resources were to help. To address the issues at the level of public policy gave many church people a glimpse of empowerment. However, in the public press, particularly in Wellington, our capital city, and in Auckland, our largest city, the statement received quite a drubbing; it was criticized for simple-mindedness, lack of specifics and generally ineffectual meddling. The *Dominion* said in the editorial:

There is an old-world naivety in the belief that a government can wave a magic wand, increase taxes and all problems will be resolved. There is arrogance in church-leaders assuming that they have a mortgage on Christian belief and that politicians and others who do not agree are somehow undermining their faith.

But the fact that it drew such marked criticism is a sign it touched a nerve. Professor Lloyd Geering, also writing in the *Dominion*, said:

It appears that the Church leaders, with only the mildest of statements, have somehow struck a raw nerve in the body politic. They have pricked a deep-seated social conscience. Beneath the brave face being publicly presented by the decision-makers, there lurks the uneasy feeling that the malaise from which New Zealand is suffering is deeper than was thought, and is by no means a purely economic one.

The statement contributed substantially to public debate, which achieved a high profile. It was undoubtedly effective at offering a base for a substantial criticism of government policies, a critique that is also highlighted, but silently, by the high level of voluntarism in our community; much of this work is done by women who, from a position of relative powerlessness, continue to bind the wounds of the poor, and continue to advocate credibly, if relatively ineffectually, for their plight. Women are still not well listened to in the public arena and they are not well placed to advocate effectively for social justice, either on their own behalf, or on behalf of others.

Personal ethics

Structures consist of individuals who each have a personal life. From a women's perspective, there is a well-established association between social and political status and the prohibitions and constraints that are placed on women's sexual behaviour. The feminists searching for understanding have long been aware that our personal and inter-personal well-being interacts with the wider social realities that shape our experience. A clear awareness of the male myths that have defined female sexuality has enabled women to recognize the extent to which these myths have served to keep women restricted to the social function of procreation and the ordered transfer of property and status between the generations. The personal is political, as the saying goes. So now, at the level of personal emotional involvement, many women have begun to look for a sexual ethic that is deep enough to clarify the relation between our capacity for love and our ability to struggle effectively for social justice in our common life.

The loosening of social constraints on sexual behaviour which began in the 1960s has led to widespread confusion, reaction and reaction to reaction. But there has been a growing awareness that human-kind cannot live well without some social ordering of sexual conduct. So there is considerable interest in the identification of boundaries, not least within the church itself (see Chapter 7). And women within and without the church have begun to explore the relationship between its almost unchallenged male leadership and the well-established conventions within Christian sexual ethics in which men have ordered the sexual behaviour of women. The structure of the 1552 marriage service reflects this.

The church is still seen as the guardian of our sexual ethics and has conventionally been presumed to have a monopoly on opinion about correct sexual behaviour, and, like other bishops, I am often asked whether this or that view of sexual behaviour is right or wrong. In many respects the church has been back-footed on this; people who ask us to make ethical judgements are frequently looking to trip us up, treating any departure from the conventional 'celibacy without, fidelity within, marriage' position with astonished contempt. Attempts to explore the present-day reality of sexual mores, and to point to an ethic that seeks understanding of such concepts as responsibility, commitment, intimacy and love – all values which would significantly help in the ordering of our sexual lives and counter the all-too-evident tendency to destructiveness[4] – have met with thoughtless and rigid demands for a firm restatement of the conventional position. This has strangled the church in the work of developing an understanding of the desires and pressures that people experience in seeking to understand and order their own sexuality. We have let these demands isolate us with an ethic that totally fails to relate to the reality of people's lives.

For both men and women there are now fewer significant social constraints upon sexual behaviour. Feminist ethical analysis has always seen traditional sexual ethics as a barely disguised mechanism by which men control women's bodies and women's lives. A significant dynamic within feminist thought is to reclaim our bodies, and with this goes the claim to the power and right to determine with whom we will have sexual relations and under what conditions. Women have learnt that although they are vulnerable in their bodies, they are also very powerful. The advent of reliable contraception contributed dramatically to the sexual liberation of women, but has raised for women the hitherto unavailable question of the choices that they can make.

As I noted earlier, the underlying ethic of our time is the right of the individual to do as he or she pleases. This is nowhere more so than in the area of personal and particularly sexual ethics. The rationale appears to be, quite simply, that sex is a private matter and of no concern to anyone else. But is it? Sexual activity by its very nature involves someone else, and whereas it can be the source of enormous mutual pleasure, it also has the potential for damage. Sexual relations always involve vulnerability;[5] where this is mutual and not exploitative, the tender care of one partner for the other can be wonderful and open our beings to experience that has, like that of God, always defied and transcended human language.

But it is not always like this; there are times when the vulnerability is exploited and damage has been done. Undoubtedly there have always been cases of incest and child abuse, but recently we have seen a huge increase in the reporting of such abuse. It is as if a society which will effectively let almost anything go when it comes to sexual ethics is finally saying that enough is enough, and that there are boundaries which people cannot be allowed to cross (see Chapter 7).

The marked imbalance in power is clearly a factor where relationships with children are concerned. Where there is an imbalance of power within the relationship, it is not possible for meaningful consent to be given by the one in the less powerful position, and therefore there is no possibility of the relationship being truly equal. With adults the situation is less clear. The attempts by many professional bodies to establish codes of conduct that define when sexual conduct is unacceptable are founded on the premise that the professional relationship is *always* one of unequal power; they have met with many difficulties (see Chapter 7). It is not easy to define when a relationship is unequally balanced with regard to power and when it is not.

Such attempts to establish guidelines of acceptability are a further pointer to the need within our society for some boundaries. This is really only natural; there is no society on earth which has not imposed some limits on sexual behaviour. And it seems that in the public arena we are more likely to look for, if not accept, some boundaries.

Here, I am not primarily concerned with issues of abuse, or even with issues of who does what with whom and under what conditions; I am more concerned with the impact of sexual choice on the lives of individuals and the nature of our society.

I am not interested in making absolute statements about right and wrong, but there are two particular concerns I wish to address. First, I am concerned at the way in which, in the name of individual rights, so much of contemporary sexual behaviour is physically and psychologically damaging to all concerned. And yet, because it is primarily deemed to be personal business, it is not a topic that attracts much public debate. I will look at some of the very broad principles that underlie issues of personal sexual morality, in society in general and in the church in particular.

A second and closely related concern is our inclination, as a church, to pay lip service to marriage as the (only) appropriate domain for sexual relations, while failing, perhaps out of restraint or reserve, to contribute any significant understanding of all that is really good, healthy and pleasurable in that relationship, and which makes it a good, perhaps the best, sexual option. Tinged with the romanticism of a past age, with institutional rigidity and judgementalism, marriage withers. The desirability of marriage as the primary location of our sexual functioning needs more than authoritarian restatement: it needs positive affirmation.

Responsibility, love and decency

While the conduct and ordering of our sexual behaviour have moved into the private realm beyond the effective reach of ethical pronouncements by the church or anyone else, our society, especially the media, still works hard to retain the illusion that effective social control still operates. This is very strange, and quite inconsistent, for in so many dimensions of our life freedom is proclaimed as the right environment for people to accept their power as agents and exercise it responsibly, without recourse to unvarying rules. In relation to our actions as sexual beings, however, there remains a lingering fear of affirming any genuine capacity we might have as moral agents to live responsibly apart from prohibitive and restricting rules.

I believe there is a real fear on the part of church people that if there is seen to be any relaxation of the conventional stand, then all the dark and destructive potential of sexual freedom will be let loose, and the values of those who hold to the centrality of marriage will be lost. I do not believe this is so; I see among many people, including the young, a real desire to claim value in their relationships, to name those values and to be quietly proud of them. These values are closely related to those associated with marriage. The gap between the conventions of the church and current moral explorations is not always as wide as many would think. It is frustrating that this wisdom is not often articulated clearly by church leaders.

So in relationships characterized as private, there is little wisdom generally accessible about what makes for quality; and yet humankind has always craved for good, honest, trusting, intimate relationships that enable us to touch another in the depth of our being and know that we are not alone. Our preoccupations have tended to be with *either* the permissibility of relations *or* the quality; yet they are not unconnected. I have come, in the course of many years of counselling both formal and informal, to see the relevance of the values of holistic health, honesty and transparency that inform so much of the rest of my life, and I have come to appreciate the underlying wisdom of traditional morality. Much of this wisdom was so heavily overlaid with the language of prohibition and control that we could scarcely recognize it, and when the prohibitions were thrown out we lost much of the wisdom.

In what follows I need to make clear that I am not talking about whether sexual relations should exist outside of marriage or not. I am trying to tap into the underlying wisdom of the formal ethic of marriage and suggest how it might inform our understanding of sexual relations – not as decreeing what is right or wrong, but in the context of what is good for men and women and what does damage. It is not easy because much of the language of the old system of control was also phrased in terms of what is 'good' for us. I well remember my mother telling me to be careful not to 'lose my self-respect'!

At its best, the old ethic declared how infinitely precious all people were, and how important it was that they not be damaged by sexual encounters in which they were not taken seriously and in which they were not asked for much. There was a sense of timing involved, for sex was part of a formally recognized relationship that had a wider social context and was owned within that context. So people took time to get to know each other and thus avoided the situation many young people now find themselves in, of refusing to know each other by daylight.

The old ethic also emphasized that our coupling is a cause for rejoicing, and is indeed society's business. Other people have a right to know who is important to us and where our priorities lie; we protect their value when we are clear about them. That ethic also allowed for care and time in the establishing of a household before children arrived, thus giving at least some opportunity for the child to be born into a stable relationship. Children are far more dependent on parental stability than we want to acknowledge.

Because there was a certain public formality about the relationship, the people involved were less inclined to leave it, either to avoid pain or for alternative pleasure, when things went wrong. Unfortunately, because of the power imbalance with its associated economic consider-ations, in many older relationships many women were trapped in miserable marriages and had no way of insisting that the issues be addressed. But since this is now more possible we need to allow time for it to be attended to properly. These days the issue of legal marriage is less significant than the question of quality, but inherent in the notion of quality is the need for a measure of commitment.

Clergy relationships

I believe that nothing that I have said undermines marriage as we know it. In the past I have found that this conviction is quite helpful in my pastoral work generally. But as a bishop there are often more complex questions, because of the church's commitment to marriage as sacrament. This focuses particularly clearly on the ordained ministry and others in positions of leadership. I am not advocating a double standard; the commitment of the church to marriage as the right and best context for long-term committed sexual relationships is quite clear. And those of us who hold positions of leadership have both a call and a responsibility to live out these convictions in our lives. The discussion that follows identifies honesty and transparency as key qualities in such relationships and focuses on the leadership of parish priests; the questions raised apply to others in Christian leadership, whether lay or ordained.

The private behaviour of a priest who departs from that ethic of marriage, whether or not it is a matter of professional misconduct, inevitably becomes, if not the business of the parish in which they serve, certainly its interest. The notion that our private life is somehow separate from and unrelated to our public life splits us in two. We cannot live holistically and with integrity if we are two different people, or if we allow people to make assumptions about our private life that do not reflect our public life with integrity. Clergy, through their anxiety about what their parishioners – or their bishop – might think, tend to get into such equivocal situations all too easily; they may, for example, be living (or half living) with a 'partner' and it is not clear whether they are committed to each other; or they may be in a same-sex relationship and desperately trying to conceal the reality of this from the public gaze.

Now, some of the relations that they may get into are clearly exploitative; but some are quite simply sad and muddled, and made more so by the need to conceal. If there is really a liaison to be ashamed of then that needs to be dealt with, but if it is a question of assisting the necessary openness in order that a relationship might be honest, then I am willing to help. A relationship that needs to be clandestine clearly contradicts the values of integrity, transparency and respect for the other person. In a parish situation it also fails to respect the parishioners.

Same-sex relations

Whereas the church is clear about its commitment to marriage, such a course is not open to people who wish to live in same-sex relations. The church's response to people whose sexual orientation is towards their own sex is fraught with double messages which can be summed up as 'be, but don't do' or 'don't tell me if you do'! There have always been gay clergy in the church and some of them have lived in gay relationships. But at a time when the church is less secure than formerly about its place within society, and at a time too when that society is overwhelmingly permissive in its sexual practice, the discussion about sexual ethics tends to focus, as we have seen, on the church, and the consequent sense of strain for all is very great.

The situation is similar to that I noted about marriage earlier. The media, hungry for sensational headlines, place intolerable and unreal pressure on the church to 'come out' either for or against same-sex relations. This greatly oversimplifies the debate, preventing any significant discussion beyond the fact of approval or otherwise, whereas in fact the same issues of responsibility, trust, intimacy, commitment and an appropriate understanding of relationships of power are every bit as relevant in same-sex relationships as they are in heterosexual ones. This kind of pressure effectively infantilizes the discussion and is, I believe, both a consequence and a reflection of the inability of the wider society to deal with its own ambiguity about same-sex relations. There is a violence about many aspects of the debate as it is conducted in the press that is as abusive and exploitative as some people claim is the character of the behaviours that they are seeking to address.

All of this is a very difficult environment for homosexually-oriented Christian leaders to be honest and transparent about their private relationships in a way that allows these relationships to slip authentically into the background of their lives, as they do with married couples, and focus prime attention on the quality and effectiveness of their practice of priesthood and Christian leadership.

This inevitably leads to a Catch-22 situation for clergy, particularly men, who are living in a same-sex relation. Some live peaceably and privately without declaring the character of their relationship and this is undoubtedly the more prudent course; sensing hostility they conceal, which is dishonest and damages their priesthood. Others, angry at the perceived need to conceal, will go out of their way to draw attention to their private circumstances. While this would appear honest it can also damage their priesthood, because they are focusing on themselves and their own need for understanding, whereas it is unquestioningly the function of priesthood to point the way to God. In their eagerness to preach their own gospel, they may effectively neglect to preach the gospel of Jesus Christ.

The source of the difficulty lies in the current climate of ambiguity or at times open hostility towards people whose sexual orientation is towards their own sex; this makes honesty and transparency extremely unsafe. Despite the fact that it is now more than ten years since homosexual behaviour ceased to be illegal in New Zealand, there is still a climate of secrecy and fear that makes people vulnerable to malicious accusation and unable to defend without denial. This is particularly so within the church, where the debate is so often marked by the assertion of moral absolutes. As with earlier debates on the ordination of women, even to hold the debate can amount to oppression for those whose lives are the subject of debate. It is not easy even to listen to discussion about whether or not one is acceptable. A pragmatic and pastoral approach might be more prudent, but it fails itself to be transparent to the rest of the church about the call to treat everyone with respect, and as such can contribute to the underhand behaviours that are always the consequence of concealment. I believe that the pastoral integrity of the church is at stake here.

There is legitimate anxiety that the advent of more open acceptance of same-sex relations would place undue pressure on young people whose understanding of their own sexuality is still in formation. There can be no doubt that the sexual and emotional manipulation of young people, whatever the gender mix, is properly regarded as abusive. But, within New Zealand society at large, openness about same-sex relations has been both legal and increasingly acceptable for the last decade or so. The church, through direct disapproval or through ambiguous responses which create a climate of fear, makes it even harder for our young people to resist the advances of older people, men and women, because of the fear that they are somehow to blame (see Chapter 7).

Concealment always acts to protect the person who initiates unwanted sexual relations and can contribute to the exploitation of those on the receiving end, whether they be women involved in heterosexual exploitation or men or women involved in same-sex exploitation. The ethical climate of the church, in which it is difficult to own up to relationships that do not fit the traditional mould, is a climate that fosters hidden relationships – which are ones in which abuse is likely to occur.

The issues vary somewhat for women. For women in same-sex relations concealment is easier than it is for men. However, for many this is not an acceptable option, for if the maxim 'the personal is political' is carried through, concealment for lesbian women amounts to a denial of their feminist convictions. This places an ideological value on lesbianism which can become a major distraction to the practice of authentic Christian leadership, which is understandable and inevitable in our present climate of equivocation. But our church and our society are every bit as ambiguous about how they value same-sex relations between women as they are towards same-sex relations between men.

So there is a strong if tacit pressure to conceal and women are equally vulnerable to exploitation, and this is sometimes intensified by the ideological dimension.

The interactions between same-sex politics and feminism can be even more subtle. Women and same-sex oriented men share a measure of marginalization within our society and hence have often offered each other support and understanding. However, the context of continuing and persistent patriarchy can also divide, as in some places gay men have sought to protect their own privilege by excluding women. This has, in parts of the Anglican Communion, been a dynamic of arguments against the ordination of women and has been responsible for some of the most vicious statements about the appropriateness of ordaining women as priests. In part, I would guess, this is a less-than-subtle attempt to pass on to women some of the abuse that they have received as gay men. Common marginalization and common cause do not always coexist.

The key issue for all is integrity, the match between our public and our private lives. If we cannot live openly without the need to draw inappropriate attention to ourselves, then we cannot live the priest-hood to which we are called. It is my belief that the ethical interests of the church in relations that are *not* exploitative, but which support the growth of trust and commitment, should be primarily concerned with underlining the key values of integrity, transparency and respect for others, and our lives should be shaped both to promote and to display those values.

The integrity of the church is also at stake; we really want to have it both ways, but such ambiguity only continues to aid and abet decep-tion. If we cannot be clear in our acceptance of same-sex relations, we have no right to insist on honesty from the clergy or anyone else. The current ambiguity also forestalls any serious discussion about the characteristics and behaviours that make some same-sex relations abusive or otherwise unquestionably wrong. We will not be able to deal with the question of homosexual abuse until we get our own responses honest and clear.

I look for a church that is able to accept people who wish to live in same-sex relations in a matter-of-fact way that allows them to choose responsibly and freely the type of relationship they enter into without the need to defend it or to persuade others of its desirability. Such a climate would allow us to focus unequivocally on the central issues, which I see as the quality and effectiveness of priesthood and Christian leadership in general; and to make our pastoral practice, whether straight or gay, unequivocally safe. I may have to be very patient.

Reclaiming marriage

Marriage as the location of our sexual lives and identity has undergone a bad press lately. The commitment inherent in marriage is seen as being possessive and exclusive, and so all too open to exploitation, which can be masked by the language of rights and duty and by the silence which so frequently surrounds life behind the bedroom door.

I am not interested in defending destructive relations; they are indefensible. Neither do I want to address the value of marriages as places of friendship; they undoubtedly can be, but so are many other places. Nor will I be suggesting ways of dealing with relationship problems within a marriage. I am seeking rather to explore, but briefly, what are the qualities in a sexual relationship that make it endure and which can make the context of commitment a good place for living a sexual life.

Now, the social climate of New Zealand is such that no one, man or woman, has to get married; neither do they have to stay married. Marriage is always a choice, when it is made and every day thereafter. Apart from the provision of a stable and loving environment for the raising of children, why should marriage exist? The timing and management of pregnancy are reliable and predictable, so that women do not have to spend the major part of their lives in child-bearing; and with medical advances life, and marriage, now lasts longer, well beyond the parenting years. So there has been a significant shift from the functional understanding of marriage to the qualitative understanding; we have an increased appreciation of the dignity of life and a vague, ill-defined and rarely talked about sense that the quality of our sexual lives contributes to that dignity. Should we not seek to make that link more explicit? I believe that the church, if it is to proclaim the significance of marriage, needs to explore that link and to set it within an ethical context.

Explorations of the unique value of sex within a committed relationship are rare. Jack Dominian makes this contribution:

> When a married couple agree to have sex, they are assenting to a great deal more than just to unite genitally. They are making themselves totally available, body, mind and feelings and are thus indicating an enormous degree of acceptance of each other. Human beings have a whole range of possibilities with which they indicate approval of each other. People smile, shake hands, agree about things, share, co-operate, give things to each other; but the greatest donation that we have to offer is the whole of ourselves and that is precisely what happens at the moment of intercourse. Coitus demands a total surrender of ourselves to the other person and has become a symbol of total

only at its best!

physical act does not per se imply emotional intimacy.

availability of love to another person. There is nothing more of
ourselves left to offer.

People make this extremely generous donation of themselves when
they receive a signal that invites them to become the most important
person in the life of another human being. When couples make love
they signify to one another that they recognise, want and appreciate
each other as the most important person in their life. The sensual
excitation, intromission and friction leading to the orgasm are
powerful physical commitments to give the maximum significance to
the personal encounter. Spouses come to the end of intercourse with
their whole body involved in a mutual surrender which has spelt
out that they are the most significant person in each other's life.
Coitus has thus the capacity for personal affirmation of immense
proportions.

It is this affirmation which is diminished in casual intercourse
because the couple in these circumstances do not have such meaning
for each other . . .

That is not to say that such rich involvement is always present in the
life of married couples . . . What I am suggesting is that their free
consent to intercourse implies a degree of mutuality which is always
reinforced.[6]

Marriage is a relationship that has within it the potential to enable
the discovery of this mystery of love over many years. It always carries
within it the seed of hope because the full expression of sexual love
always holds out the promise of more.

Built within coitus is the wish for an extension of the joy experienced
. . . the presence of hope that our partner will continue to love us and
in this way accept us for further acts of intercourse. Thus, coitus plays
a vital part in the continuity of our acceptance as a lovable person.[7]

It holds the potential for reconciliation and it can be a place of sexual
affirmation which is increasingly significant as we grow older.

In remaining faithful to each other we not only continue to give
encouragement and meaning to the sexuality of our partner, but we go
on assuring them that we desire and need them as the most important
person in our life.[8]

This is not a commonly portrayed aspect of human sexuality; in
literature, television, movie and so on, it is the initial encounter that
makes the story and tells the wonder. But the inner richness of our
sexuality needs the environment of a committed relationship to
be revealed. The case for marriage is far stronger than the dry and
controlling ethical pronouncements that have come to be associated
with the church.

So why marriage? Not only because we need protection in this most vulnerable part of our living.[9] It is quite clear that commitment can and does exist outside of marriage. But it does so in a way that fails to acknowledge the sacred aspect of sexual relations, that is blind to the divine gift that our sexuality is and the precious way in which it opens up for us the way to intimacy and the physical reassurance that we are not alone. To claim all this without marriage is like having Christmas presents without the wrapping and without saying thank you. Marriage within the Christian tradition is a sacrament, an out-ward and visible sign of an inward and spiritual grace. When we acknowledge that most precious and private gift of God, we share that gift with others in ways that are appropriate and do not violate our intimacy. That is why marriage is a cause of thanksgiving.

Same sex marriage? — or can same sex r/ships not be sacramental?

7

The abuse of power

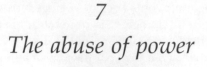

DOOMED FREEDOM

> How innocently faithful,
> Foreseeing not her tomb,
> Freedom, a Jephtha's daughter,
> Leapt forth to meet her doom.
>   From Eileen Duggan, 'Freedom'

As men and women have moved into partnership within the ministry of the church, we have become increasingly aware of the more insidious relationships of power that are so well established in our society and within our church. Here I am not talking primarily of the structural, institutional, hierarchical relationships, but of the relationship of sexual power that can so easily be exploited when it is supported by institutional authority.

Recent years have seen a significant rise in the reporting of cases of sexual abuse in all walks of life. The church has been no exception. Many of these are criminal cases involving the abuse of children by clergy and by religious authorities in whose care they were placed. By the very nature of the crimes, they remained undisclosed for many years. Undoubtedly many were never disclosed, but in a climate that is more receptive to hearing and believing that such things do happen a huge number of instances has emerged. The sheer weight of numbers makes us realize that this is not a new phenomenon but one that runs right through the silent history of the relationships between men and women – to say nothing of children – within the Christian community.

The clergy hold a highly marked position of power within the community; they are respected, they are trusted, they have responsibility for pastoral care. What they say, the compliments and attention given to vulnerable people, can victimize a trusting adult as surely as a naive child. But we are more accustomed to assigning blame to adult women than we are to children.

Sexual abuse is so totally contrary to everything that the Christian faith stands for – the care of the weak and the vulnerable, the sanctity of vows of celibacy or of marriage – that it is very, very difficult for the church, either the church official or the community of Christians who make it up, to see the problem for what it is. The strategy generally adopted until very recently was to smother episodes of abuse in silence, usually to whisk the priest concerned away to another position, and to muzzle the women concerned by putting the fear of God (*sic*) into them, blaming them for sexualizing the relationship and making them responsible. It was a strategy that was generally supported by the faithful of the church, who often had much of their own invested in the reputation of the priest, and who had no desire to see their church dragged through the mire of public scandal. It was often said that 'everyone knew, but no one said'. Thus the conspiracy of silence was very effectively maintained, and the message received and promulgated was that such behaviour was acceptable.

Times have changed. The church like other professional bodies that offer caring services is no longer willing to leave to its members the judgement on whether sexual contact with 'clients' is appropriate, but has developed clear policies regarding such contact, and criteria for assessing just what behaviours should be considered 'unprofessional' in particular circumstances. The medical profession in New Zealand has a 'zero tolerance'; so does the church. The rigidity of this position, almost neo-Puritan in tone, brings with it some resistance, among medics as well as clerics. It seems contrary to the prevailing sexual ethic; but, as we shall see, such freedom can be 'doomed' for those who become victims in an exploitative power relationship.

Freedom is doomed for both women and men. The ethics proposed apply equally to both, and women as well as men have broken such ethics and have seriously damaged those for whom they have pastoral responsibility. The discussion that follows looks particularly at the dynamics that surround the occurrence of male sexual abuse. It is still more common.

Breaking the circle of silence

Two factors at work in the last ten years or so have contributed to breaking the circle of silence within the New Zealand church. The first has undoubtedly been the higher level of publicity given to the prevalence of sexual abuse in all the 'helping' professions. Most of these, generally in response to cases of extraordinary pain and agony, have developed codes of professional ethics, so that it is possible to discipline their members when necessary. The second factor is the increase during the 1980s and 1990s in the number of ordained women. Some of those who had become aware of the scale of the problem had been ordained for some time, and they had the confidence to confront the church. In fact, in New Zealand, it was the courage and energy of ordained women that first brought this dark secret into the light; it did not happen easily. Gradually it emerged that many ordained women, and a shockingly large number of lay women, had been sitting silently on the stories of their own abuse, sometimes for many years. It was only when the ordained women, and others, realized that so many other women had also been victims that the rage became so great they had to shout.

To begin with, like any rage, it had its own internal energy that just flowed. This energy, exploding in a rush, was not organized; and since the situation was entirely new to our church, much damage was done by the total inability of those in authority to handle it. Blame was thrown, silence was commanded, the press came in on both sides; everybody was vulnerable and everybody was afraid. But the energy, the insight, the strength and the care of women, both lay and ordained, was absolutely critical in confronting the church with the full force of what had happened and what could all too easily happen again. We have learnt from it. In those early episodes we confronted the imperfections of the church, we found out – why had we ever thought otherwise? – that we are not perfect, and we began to develop codes of ethics and procedures for handling mistakes. We have learnt a lot, but there is still a very long way to go.

A new problem?

I am often asked why all this scandal, rage and exposure should be necessary, and confronted with the fact that it is a cause of shame to the church that it should be so. Indeed it is. I think there are two responses, which come from different ends of the spectrum so to speak. The first is that this is not, despite appearances to the contrary, a new problem. It has undoubtedly marred all our history, but it has been most effectively silenced. The second response relates to the marked change in personal sexual morality since the 1960s. Much has been written about this; in brief, the advent of sexual freedom that reliable contraception allowed, together with the rise of a more questioning mode of popularist Christian theology and the discussions therein on the value of situational ethics, marked the breakdown of the traditional boundaries of human sexual morality in most western societies (see Chapter 6).

With the passing of time many have welcomed this freedom; in fact most people under forty have never known it any other way. But we have also become aware of how much pain and damage casual, careless and irresponsible sexual relationships can cause, and it is as if at a sub-conscious level we are now crying 'enough'. No society has ever been totally without constraints on sexual relationships, and the persistence, despite the odds, of the popularity of marriage is some indication of this. The proliferation in recent years of codes of ethics and of pro-cedures for handling complaints of sexual abuse is an indication of a society that is trying to re-establish at least some norms, and to keep its more vulnerable and dependent members safe from those who do not know or care what damage they can do. It is a somewhat crude and elementary attempt to establish norms in a normless world.

A code of ethics

In recent years the church in this country has learnt from bitter experience that it must adopt a proactive approach to handling such misconduct. We have learnt that we must be prepared to move towards the termination of an abusing priest's licence should the case prove clearly to be one of abuse of the pastoral relationship. In this diocese the section of our Code of Ethics which deals with sexual relationships within pastoral ministry sets this out unequivocally:

(a) Clergy and lay people holding a Bishop's licence, like others involved in 'helping' professions, are required to adhere strictly to their ethical obligations. They are expected to respect the ethic of sexual fidelity within Christian marriage. They should also be aware of the deep and intense feeling that can occur within a pastoral relationship, and should uphold their strong obligation to avoid any exploitation of such a relationship.

(b) Clergy and lay people holding a Bishop's licence face certain inescapable duties. They must be competent technically and watchful to ensure that whatever happens within the pastoral relationship is in the best interests of those they minister to. In general, clergy should be aware of the need to monitor not only the emotions of those they minister to, but also their own, in the interests of the health of the pastoral relationship and for the benefit of those they minister to. This firmly excludes any exploita-tion of the person receiving ministry, sexually, emotionally, financially or in any other way.

(c) Sexual relationships outside of marriage between those ministered to on one hand and clergy and lay people holding a Bishop's licence on the other hand, are never in the interests of the one ministered to and are always an abuse of trust. Such relationships can never be acceptable, and constitute unethical behaviour. The term 'sexual relationship' is not restricted to sexual intercourse. The guideline is any form of physical contact, whether initiated by the clergyperson or the person being ministered to, which has as its purpose some form of sexual gratification or which may reasonably be construed by the person ministered to as having that purpose.

The person offering ministry bears special responsibility for the character of the relationship and should avoid any sexualization within it.

Clergy should note that these statements are issued by the Clerical Ethics Committee of the Diocese of Dunedin for their guidance in order to amplify the understanding and implications of Title D Canon II 5.4(d).[1]

This understanding of sexual relations within pastoral ministry depends heavily on an understanding of the ministry of the church as 'professional'; that is, meeting certain publicly-recognized standards and expectations. This would seem to be reasonable enough, for, like other professions, Christian ministry is a public ministry, one that offers a service to people in need, which invites vulnerable people to put their trust in the priest and which has no right to abuse that trust.

'Professional misconduct'

The concept of unequal power relations is a critical factor in establishing the rationale for regarding professional misconduct as an abuse of power. Unequal power relations are natural enough throughout human society, but within the church, as with other institutions, they have become structured. So the authority to lead and the recognition of the knowledge, skill and spiritual endowments that qualify leadership become the basis for structured relationships of power and trust within the church as elsewhere. Most obviously this analysis applies to priests, but it also clearly applies to others in positions of leadership within the church. Trust is particularly important where the leadership of young people is concerned. Hence, whereas the discussion that follows refers to priests, this should not be regarded as exclusive. It also refers primarily to abuse that occurs between men and women; the same issues and values are also significantly relevant in abuse between people of the same sex where there is an unequal power relationship.

Sexual relationships between a priest and a parishioner are never equal, and never have a basis for genuine consent to be granted and for the development of a healthy mutuality. And yet whenever an incident of clergy professional misconduct arises the Code of Ethics becomes very hard to enforce. Either the church, only too aware of the difficulties, equivocates, or becomes entangled, often against its will, in a long-drawn-out legal wrangle. Or if it does act decisively and clearly it attracts widespread misunderstanding and criticism.

It is always a temptation to offer only a minimal response to incidents of clergy sexual misconduct, for the consequences of dealing with it decisively and clearly appear to be so great. In a society that consistently diminishes the importance of sexual contact through lack of discrimination and the abandonment of all significant boundaries, it often seems like an over-reaction to end the ministry of a priest who is guilty of misconduct. In handling such issues, there are always a number of gratuitous victims, most noticeably the priest's wife and children, who have to bear the knowledge that someone they loved and trusted has let them down seriously. In addition to this, the disclosure, if it is to be honestly accomplished, will always bring unsought-for and unwanted publicity and this is frequently most unpleasant. Furthermore, the family of the priest have also, if his position is terminated, lost their home, their right to live in the community where they have been for some years, and their income. The upset is considerable, and it is easy for the anger and blame that properly rest with the priest whose actions made the termination necessary to fall upon the church authorities who acted to terminate his ministry. It is just not possible for the church to act in a way that all can see as just.

Some parallels

When a priest sexualizes a pastoral relationship, trust is destroyed throughout the whole church. Yet for healing to be possible at all, the reality of what has happened must be faced by everyone.

There are some comparisons that we can usefully point to. The church is a system, as the family is. In family situations, sex occurs normally and properly between husband and wife. But it can go wrong. For instance, one of the parents, generally the father, may become sexually attracted to and abusive of one or more of the children, often but not always a girl child. When incest occurs in a family there is always pressure on the child from the perpetrator to keep it a secret. The consequences of not keeping it a secret are spelled out only too clearly to the child: her father will be angry with her, she will lose his affection, she will lose him from the home and she, the child, will be responsible for all this. Disclosure seems impossibly difficult. And in fact the child will sometimes try to reduce her level of vulnerability to manageable proportions by behaving in what the man may construe as a sexually provocative way in order, so she thinks, to retain the affection of the one in whom she sees her security.

Often, however, it is not a secret. Other family members know what is going on. A mother may well know, and she lives with the shame and the guilt of realizing that she might well be regarded as a passive participant; disclosure would also bring the privacy of her marriage into the glare of public speculation. She feels powerless to stop the abuse herself and is unwilling to seek help, for she too knows the serious disruption to the family that will occur. Often she is just a helpless bystander, effectively colluding in the abuse of her child, and often, too, having to watch her other children coming under the terrible touch of her abusing husband.

When disclosure does come, it is all very much as predicted. There is a lot of anger. The father is removed from the family. Although both wife and children know the horror of what he has done they are sadly aware of their loss, for at one time there had been real love in that relationship. They will try to do what they can to help him. The abused child feels responsible for what has happened, and often feels that she should be punished too. She is very isolated. The ability of the child to grow into self-confident adulthood, ready to form mature sexual relationships of intimacy and trust, is seriously marred. After incest nothing is ever the same again. All are victims.

A priest, like the traditional *paterfamilias*, has structural power, a power commensurate with his position as a priest. As Neil and Thea Ormerod point out, he is used to 'running the show', to getting, or at least to expecting to get what he wants, to being the leader of the community. To this must be added the fact that he is an adult male and hence possesses a physical strength and social status greater than children and women. He may possess psychological strength or other forms of psychological invulnerability as well. Furthermore, the priest is seen as God's representative and one doesn't get more powerful than that! Priests share in a numinous power, and it is naive to think that they are not aware of this; many of them in fact enjoy it. All this can add up to a potent force and a considerable power differential between the minister and those in his pastoral care.[2]

As in the family, the sexualized pastoral relationship is a betrayal of trust of a vulnerable person by a powerful one, and the dynamics are similar. When 'Father' enters into a sexual relationship with one of the parish family, the same disharmony occurs. The woman, for whom consent is the product of emotional coercion, is enjoined to secrecy under threat of most serious consequences. She feels trapped but does not want to forgo the affection and respect of someone whom she has trusted and who is so important to her. She may, at this stage, opt for changing her dress-code and behaving in a more sexually provocative way. She is probably also feeling, quite wildly, that there is more chance of coming out of this whole if she can secure the permanent affection of 'Father'.

The wife of the priest may well know what is happening, but her own feelings of guilt, shame and confusion are often overwhelming. She senses a momentum in him that she is powerless to stop. Other parishioners may well see signs of what is going on, but it all seems so impossibly terrible that they do nothing, aware that if they did do something the results might be a major disruption in the life of the parish.

The cataclysm of disclosure

And when disclosure does occur, and the abuser resigns or is dismissed, it is every bit as cataclysmic as when incest is disclosed. People had a sense of something going on, and of not daring to guess; now they know. They have held 'Father' in high regard, often he has been instrumental in leading them to new spiritual insights, certainly he has maintained the worshipping life of the church that has meant so much to them, and they do not want to see him go. They can see his distress and that of his family and they want to do all that they can to help. They wish it would all go away. They want to forgive the offender.

The woman, the victim and often the scapegoat, can find no peace within the family. She senses that people are holding her responsible, even though they may act kind. Her sense of guilt and shame is such that she will often fumble around trying to regain favour by apologizing for what she has done. She does not feel safe. She is effectively isolated from the Christian community. As with the violated child, it is hardest for her to believe and to own that she is not responsible for what has happened to her, neither is she responsible for what has happened to the rest of the Christian community. Paradoxically, she can only begin to take responsibility for her present life precisely when she can disclaim responsibility for her past sufferings. She did not deserve them, they were not a just or divine punishment: she was a victim of abuse by another person. Often the difficulty in such a resolution is the painful realization of just how vulnerable she was and of how little control she had in the abusive relationship. It is not easy for an adult to admit to the child within.

In all of this, the wife of the priest is also feeling profoundly victimized. She has lost trust in her husband, both privately and publicly; she has lost her home, the family income, and her place within both the church community and the wider community in which the parish is situated. Her loss is enormous.

Her husband, the priest concerned, may react in a number of ways, ranging from the acceptance of his responsibility for what has happened and a willingness to work through to an understanding of the impulses within him that led him to behave in such a way; to an angry, often a furious disbelief – not at the disclosure, but that other people could see such a 'harmless' episode in such a distorted light. In his anger, he will blame everyone else: the woman concerned, parishioners, church authorities, clergy colleagues. And he may contemplate legal action. Reactions at this end of the spectrum are extremely uncomfortable to live with. The only possible response for everyone and anyone seems to be to batten down the hatches and wait for the storm to blow over.

It is so hard

Priests carry an extraordinary amount of trust. They are seen by the Christian community as people of God and are generally respected members of the broader community. They are assumed to be of a high moral standing; people trust them to be morally upright. And as is the case with all sexual abuse, the greater the trust, the greater the damage done to the victims.

The truth is that the suffering caused by the sexualization of pastoral relationships is so great that it scarcely bears confronting. Yet to confront it is to begin to face up to the evil of it. The woman concerned is unlikely to want to make a public display of what she has been through; her privacy at a most intimate level has already been invaded. And she is also unlikely to want to buy into the intensely conflictual nature of the situation by putting energy, scarce energy, into confronting the priest concerned. She needs to be believed, taken seriously, without undue repetition of her story, and she needs to know that the situation is intolerable to the church and that the ministry of the priest who abuses this sacred trust is no longer acceptable.

Because the situation is so delicate and so private, the victim becomes further abused if her story becomes the property of public debate and the raw material of rough judgement and rough justice. The wider community reacts as if astonished, concealing the fact that such 'goings-on' are well known in their private lives, and have been

well known throughout the history of human sexual relations. If we
relabel the story one of seduction, the contours of this familiar tale are
traced onto these past patterns and begin to become clear.[3] It begins,
as the Ormerods describe, when the victim gets so drawn into the web
of the priest's flattery that she can no longer see herself as a victim.
Indeed she may experience herself as 'madly in love', though it is
likely that this state was itself the product of the priest's sexual
advances, not the cause of them.[4]

But when a woman has been made a dupe in an unequal power
game, such 'love' can only be a doomed and sorry chimera. While
initially the sexual attention may have been experienced as positive
and flattering, eventually confusion, loss of self-esteem, self-doubt,
anxiety, panic attacks, shame and depression take over. These feelings
disorient the victim, leaving her unable to trust her own experience
and her own feelings. She does not want to believe that the priest was
not truly caring. She begins to grieve. Depression can take over to the
point where she can contemplate suicide and she experiences severe
grief reactions and profound feelings of guilt and shame. The damage
that can be sustained is truly bad news, the very antithesis of Christ's
love and the Christian message.

After disclosure

Because clergy sexual abuse is such a terrible experience it is extremely
hard for the Christian community to handle. Guilt flies every which
way. A not uncommon reaction is for people who have been closely
involved with either the priest or the woman concerned to feel a
measure of *post hoc* responsibility: they should have seen it coming,
they could have seen it coming, why were they so blind, so lacking in
the courage to speak out? For the priest, disclosure does not always
end the self-delusion in which he is bound. Anger at the frustration of
his sense of control over his own life (where was God?) and disbelief
that he could have been wrong prevail. For the woman, there are the
twin demons of guilt and shame. For she knows she did not say no,
yet how could she when consent was obtained under such emotive
pressure. There are no winners unless reality is faced.

One of the more serious side-effects of the difficulties experienced
in handling incidents of clergy sexual misconduct is that because
they are hard to grasp, to understand, responses very rapidly become
polarized as the case for one interpretation or the other tends to be
made more and more strongly. The need to convince becomes more
urgent and the conflict escalates. Because it is a variation, albeit not a

very subtle one, on the age-old battle of the sexes not one of us stands on neutral ground. Also, because questions of sexual relationships and sexual morality touch the lives and the experiences of each one of us, everyone has an opinion and has feelings. These feelings are often the mixed product of undigested responses to past sexual activity, some of which we might not be too comfortable with. It is always easier to throw stones at someone else, and all too often in such cases projected or transferred guilt can cause added havoc. It is quite usual for every- one to join in discussions on such episodes with great vigour. These discussions are always chaotic and painful, but are probably more therapeutic than we could possibly guess at.

Some theological contradictions

In all its official documents, in the Code of Ethics and the subscription to this which is asked of priests at the time of their ordination and at every subsequent ecclesiastical appointment, the Anglican Church makes quite clear its understanding of what constitutes professional sexual misconduct. Despite this fact, there are still many people, both within the Christian community and beyond it, who do not see the relevance of this analysis to particular cases of such misconduct. It is so easy to trivialize it, to label it as an 'affair', soon over; and to murmur sympathetically 'Isn't it good that his wife has stuck by him!' It seems as if something needs to be dealt with, but *quietly*. The conspiracy of silence lives on. More damaging is the fact that when people cannot see the reality of the power differential between the priest and the woman with whom he sexualizes a pastoral relationship, they will tend to place responsibility on the woman. It is an unarticulated revival of the old double standard; men may do as they want, but it is the responsibility of women to maintain the virtue of society.

I have wondered if this is because a constant theme of very orthodox Christian teaching is that God invariably supports those who are most poor, most weak, most vulnerable in society. It is hard therefore for any- one in Christian leadership, man or woman, to reconcile their public and private self-image of being someone particularly chosen by God, indeed ordained by the church, with the acceptance that in a human, societal sense they carry considerable power and must bear responsibility for how that power is used. At a most facile level, there is almost a theological contradiction between God's commitment to the most vulnerable and the practice of the church in ordaining its leadership. But God *does* call people to leadership within the church, and one of the realities that those of us so called have to bear is the use of our power.

Not only is it hard for the priest concerned to be fully aware of the power he wields, but it is also hard for the Christian community. The power is often very subtle. The priest lives among his people, like one of them; his children probably go to the same school. They know his humanity. It is also characteristic for a priest to operate his leadership tasks by verbal persuasion, designed to help people see things the way he sees them, and if there is a gap or a grey area they are disposed to trust him. His relationship with them gives the illusion of friendship, but it is a friendship in which the power of the priest is not acknowledged. People become accustomed to his persuasive ways, to his abilities to affirm their efforts and to win their consent for the plans he proposes. The priest is generally regarded as a 'nice guy'. And he says his prayers regularly.

The contrast between this image of the parish priest and the person who is accused of sexual abuse is too great for many people to bear. Their personal and spiritual investment is often very high, and in abandoning their image of the 'nice guy' they really do have a tremendous amount to lose. It is so much easier to trivialize the whole business as an 'affair'.

Forgiveness

There is a further internal contradiction within Christian theology that makes it difficult for us to see clergy professional misconduct as warranting the withdrawal of professional status from the priest concerned. But 'contradiction' is an oversimplification. Right at the heart of our faith, whatever understanding of the crucifixion and the resurrection of Christ one espouses, there lies the Christian commitment to forgiveness. It is so central to the practice of our faith as Anglicans that at every celebration of the Eucharist, the words of absolution are offered.

The granting of forgiveness and the experience of being forgiven is so central to the Christian life that it is important for our understanding of it not to be diminished or reduced to the recitation of a set form that in some mysterious and unspecified way wipes out the past. It is not uncommon for people facing up to the reality that their priest has sinned grievously to move very rapidly into forgiveness mode, and then be ready to continue as if nothing has happened. But the sin *has* happened, a very great deal of suffering has been inflicted, and it cannot be eradicated or healed by 'cheap grace'. Indeed, for the Christian community to show a willingness, even an insistence on acting out the formulas and behaviours of forgiveness before they acquire some real meaning, some real grace, is to collude in the abusive behaviour. Forgiveness becomes denial. It effectively says (what the priest is almost certainly saying) that it was a trivial matter, that the abuse was not significant and that it is best soon forgotten. That may not be the intention in urging forgiveness, but it may well be the consequence.

An abused conscience

The silent victim of such a strategy is the priest's own conscience. For a priest who can behave, often repeatedly, in such a way has often done so by deadening his conscience, achieving a state in which there is no longer any self-accusation, no longer any sense of self-criticism or self-reproach. What could have been an opportunity for personal growth leads instead to a further decay of conscience which can make further abusive relationships with other people more likely.

An abused woman

Cheap grace and cheap forgiveness also further victimizes the woman concerned. Not only does it disregard or trivialize the abuse that she has suffered, it also further alienates her from the Christian community which has been the context of that abuse. For, usually, when a pastoral relationship is sexualized the woman loses her faith community, because she can no longer feel safe there. Cheap forgiveness greatly increases the danger she can expect to encounter there.

An abused church

Such actions also deepen the damage done to the Christian community, for the abuse of a particular woman becomes an abuse of the whole community when it ties them into patterns of deceit and secrecy. The offer of easy forgiveness to the offending priest, which buys into this syndrome, dignifies in a quite unjustifiable way the response of deception and secrecy. It also diminishes our understanding of what God can do for us, for God can forgive the enormity of our sin: we do not need to trivialize it or resort to reductionism. It can be faced in all its gravity and it can be forgiven, without denial, at the depth of truth.

The offer of grace

It may well be that the demand for forgiveness that is cheap and quick is the natural response of people who cannot face the full horror and the tragedy of what has happened. It is a way of masking anger and the discomfort that anger brings. But it has to be faced.

Divine forgiveness can reach deeper into the soul of the abuser, for nothing can be concealed from the gaze of divine love. The forgiveness that God offers when confession derives from real self-knowledge is properly regarded as healing. It is perhaps helpful to regard healing as the appropriate theological category for the abuser, who, though aware of the wrong, is unable to get to grips with the depth of that wrong. Healing is the restoration of balance; it enables the abuser to receive forgiveness and to begin a new phase of his spiritual journey. The healing that God offers touches more than the manifestations of sickness; it is well able to reach into the whole being of the abuser, who can thus be made whole and open to the grace of God.

If we do not offer authentic grace to those who are bound into abusive patterns of living, we do not carry them firmly and rigorously into reality, inviting them into the costly and painful journey of rebirth in the Spirit. Real love is never based on protecting people from their own truths, because if we do that we hold them in their own deaths instead of enabling real growth towards spiritual maturity.

Dynamics within the church

There is a further dynamic that I have noticed that cuts deeper into the life of the church, which relates to the underlying reasons about why incidents of clergy sexual abuse should be so very hard for the church to handle.

It seems as if, when we address issues of clergy sexual misconduct by labelling them 'professional misconduct', we are somehow isolating such incidents from the rest of the life of the church. For all that it is indeed right and proper that we should regard the ministry of the church as a profession and establish codes of conduct appropriate to this self-understanding, this does, to an unacknowledged extent, fly in the face of our customary understanding of our ministry. The church has always said that in employing its priests it is not employing them just to do a job. Priesthood is not only a way of life: it is a whole character of life, as the ordination service makes quite clear. In fact, the church claims that it pays its clergy a stipend, a kind of retainer to enable them to do the job. Not a salary. The whole being of the priest is bound up in the priestly task. And too, families are closely involved. Whether or not a male priest's wife chooses to play the role of 'unpaid curate' with the other conventionalities of being a clergy spouse, the parish are always interested in what she does and what kind of person she is. And too, her children are often loved and to some extent owned by the parish.

This means that the boundaries between the private and personal lives of priests and their public roles are unavoidably and perhaps deliberately blurred. We do not expect priests' private lives to be dissonant with their public lives, which is why the church has always found 'immorality' amongst its clergy to be so shocking. But neither do we expect the priest to draw a rigid line between the public and private areas of his or her life. Parishioners want to be friends with their priest, in both light-hearted and serious ways. We expect the boundaries to be blurred. This makes the analysis of the sexualization of the pastoral relationship as 'professional misconduct' an effective contradiction of our habitual way of regarding clergy/parishioner relationships.

However, the maintaining of boundaries is critical to the establishment and maintenance of healthy pastoral relations. For there is a role distinction between clergy and parishioners. In brief, the priest is there to meet the needs of the parishioners, with care, discretion and wisdom, not buying into the fantasies of an impossible wish list as we have noted above (see Chapter 4). In meeting the needs of the people the priest will often find deep satisfaction. Not only is the priestly calling being fulfilled: there is frequently a genuine mutuality in pastoral relationships. But this obligation to meet needs, combined with the blurring of boundaries, means that it is all too easy for a priest who is unaware of his own power, and who may be dissatisfied in some way with his life, his ministry or his marriage, to rationalize the sexualization of the pastoral relationship by telling himself 'I did it for her own good'. The mixture of power and loneliness can be lethal.

There is a real way in which the description of sexualized pastoral relationships as 'professional misconduct' denies the reality of so much that we have valued in ministry. There is an urgent need to face up to these undercurrents, to the factors that shape our value judgements in the realm that is not defined as professional. It is not a problem that resides only in the visible and easily-defined area of our professionalism. It is as if there is in some way a value system operating quietly away that is in conflict with the value system of professionalism. It all comes much closer to home.

A protected patriarchy

I have come to realize that when church authorities endeavour to handle cases of clergy sexual abuse with honesty and with justice we are effectively challenging the very deep-seated patterns within the church that protect men and male leadership. These function on many levels, but always within the personal and private domain of the priest's life.

Within families, the customary perceived responsibility of the man to provide the family income has not been seriously eroded by the greater participation of women in the paid workforce. So when the behaviour of a man results in the loss of his job and of his income, and consequent suffering to his wife, this is regarded as an erosion of his area of responsibility and privilege. There is also a tendency to rerun the double standard referred to earlier. The argument runs like this: everyone knows that men's sexual desires are stronger than women's, and therefore they have a right to seek satisfaction as long as it does not do too much damage, like breaking up another marriage or fathering an unwanted child. Single women who don't get pregnant are therefore fair game. Another line acknowledges the fact that there is widespread sexual promiscuity in our society, but that what people do in their private life has no impact on or significance for their professional life. Furthermore, while no one really enjoys the suffering of another person, at least not so as they would admit, there is a very deep dislike at seeing someone who holds a position traditionally associated with male privilege brought into the arena of public censure. It would seem that the disclosure of clergy sexual abuse and any consequent termination of the priest's licence for ministry cuts at the heart of the public recognition of male leadership.

There is a particular way in which these values work within the church. Clergy have often seen themselves as having a particular and privileged pastoral relationship with their bishop. When a bishop is required to take action to terminate the licence for ministry of a priest who has abused the pastoral relationship, the bishop is seen as coming out on the side of the church and the woman, and not of the priest. Such is the essentially divisive nature of these cases. A consequence is that the pastoral ministry of the bishop to the clergy of the diocese comes under strain, for it is seen as opposed to the bishop's vocation to pastor the whole Christian community. Quite clearly, *all* – bishops, priests and laity – are the whole church.

There are very well-established traditions within our society for placing the blame on women. Traditional images of the woman as the temptress or the seductress, strong within Christianity, have supported this view. It is not uncommon for men disclaiming responsibility for the sexualization of a relationship to blame their behaviour on the clothes that the woman chose to wear. 'They excited me!'

There is also a difficulty that is probably peculiar to the church in this country. Because our church is divided into three autonomous Tikanga (cultural strands), it is at times not easy to see where the responsibility for the conduct of clergy lies. Where professional misconduct occurs across the Tikanga boundary, it is often very hard for the abused women in one culture to activate effectively the professional misconduct procedures, if they exist, of the other Tikanga to which the abuser belongs. The mutual concern of the bishops to acknowledge the mana (public respect and authority) of the other Tikanga and variations in cultural perspective can lead to a refusal to act effectively, which in the eyes of many women appears to amount to the protection that male bonding gives rise to.

All of these attitudes and values lie well outside the analysis of the sexualization of the pastoral relationship as a breach of 'professional ethics'. They are values that belong to the private domain of life; they do not belong to the professional area at all. They are values of the 'public' arena only insofar as all of them function to protect the position of men and male leadership. It may not be common now to talk of male protectionism and male privilege, but when the church engages in the 'battle of the sexes' it is alive and well.

Dealing with clergy sexual abuse

As a bishop, I have come to realize that handling incidents of clergy sexual abuse in a manner that befits the claim of the church's ministry to be regarded as a professional body is, in effect, like firing an open torpedo shot at the underlying and still very well-functioning patriarchal structure of the church. It is a formidable structure, even though largely masked these days by the presence of a number of women in the leadership of the church, and also by our claim to the neutrality of professionalism.

Some of the dynamics that I have experienced in dealing with issues of clergy sexual abuse relate particularly to the fact that not only am I the authority figure in the diocese, but I am also a woman. In these situations the conjunction of 'female' and 'bishop' can be a dangerous mix. It is not so long since the ordained ministry was an exclusively male terrain, and despite the presence of women it still retains many of the characteristics of a 'brotherhood' that will function to protect its own. When relationships between clergy and the bishop come under strain because of the handling of clergy sexual abuse, there is a sense in which clergy ask themselves whether they can still trust their bishop. In some way the undercurrents are more marked when the bishop is female.

Often the church has tended to regard its bishops as people who inhabit an area of lofty neutrality. Where the bishop is a woman, the impossibility of this neutrality is thrown into sharp relief, and hence the notion of the neutrality of all other bishops is dispelled. For patriarchy – especially covert patriarchy – to be challenged, it must be exposed.

All the other bishops that I have known, all male, who have been called upon to deal with incidents of clergy sexual misconduct have found it incredibly hard to break the bonds of brotherhood with their male colleagues and ensure a just outcome by taking steps to terminate the priest's licence for ministry. I have watched them make every excuse in the book. Some have overcome their conditioning, some have not. I would have to say that, when the unhappy occasion arose, I also found taking such action very hard. I realize that this is because I see much of the security of my ministry as a bishop in making and retaining good relationships of trust and respect with all my clergy, and since the senior clergy were all men I was well aware that in initiating termination I was risking, for a time at least, those good relations. The situation was very difficult, and it is to their credit that the good relations between us did not suffer because of the action I took.

I realized too, that when I did take action, I was not only challenging an established male solidarity, I was also consciously and deliberately siding with the victim, the woman. Because of my gender this could have been seen as a gender-related action and not one taken on principle. I felt very vulnerable – and then I realized that I was not only supporting the woman in her vulnerability, I was vulnerable with her. Not a common experience for a bishop!

I also found it very hard to initiate action because it was the first time that I had found that I could not function as a bishop in pastoral mode, which is my habitual and comfortable stance, but had to move into juridical mode, a role which I and none other could take. I remember a good friend saying to me 'You've been a very good priest. Now get on with it and be a bishop.' And that is what I did.

Issues of clergy sexual misconduct cut right to the heart of relationships between men and women in a church that is really only just beginning to learn how to share power across the gender lines. And there are times when they can place enormous strains on those relationships in a way that we scarcely know how to name. The issues arise out of an imbalance of power; and I am convinced that, left to itself, an historically patriarchal institution will never deal with them effectively. They will only be corrected by the work and energy of women, who have learnt how to stand together and can clearly and repeatedly articulate the issues. I would say too that there are healthy signs that some men are willing to share this responsibility. It is essential that these issues be dealt with. A church that cannot put an end to its own abuses of power has no place as a critic of power.

8
Authority

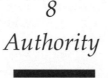

THE POWER OF BREAD

Old man, why must you keep walking
Right through the heart of the wheat,
Where it is tallest and thickest?
Have you no sense in your feet?

Do you think that wheat is like water,
Closing again where you tread?
It is life you are trampling under,
Bread and the power of bread.

Bread is today and tomorrow,
And all the yesterdays wild;
As old as the first clay oven,
As young as a newborn child.
From Eileen Duggan, 'The Wheat'

Authority always sounds very heavy. Its ecclesiastical word is oversight. It is institutional in nature and in the context of any hierarchical thinking it represents a top-down movement. But the intersection between institutional bestowal and recognition of authority and its real and effective working-out is quite intricate. This chapter looks at institutional considerations in the light of a number of personal factors, many of which are gender-related.

God and authority

Institutions are no longer fashionable. In most western societies there is a marked decline in respect for them. Analyses of the respect with which people from different professions are regarded show an increasing reluctance to invest honour in the powerful institutions of government. Ironically, as governments and the professions that seem to be pivotal to our society decline in respect, the clergy are slowly, after a long period off the bottom, entering the charts once more.

We are a very pluralistic society. The fragmented, even fractured nature of our society, the unwillingness to form alliances that are any larger than that which our personal experience gives us reason to trust, goes hand in hand with a growing sense of individualism and of the value of dependence on oneself: who else is there to trust? There is a sense of living within ever-decreasing circles, as the reference points for both our individuality and our sense of social identity move closer together. With no reference point beyond that immediacy, the norm of ambition becomes simply to live securely and happily within one's own circle.

But Christians, while searching for and finding God in their own hearts, have always reached for the sky; they have looked beyond the confines, not only of their own locale or their own social identity, but beyond the boundaries of humankind and human experience as well. We have asked such basic questions as 'Where do we come from?' and 'What is this business of living all about?' We have experienced the mystery of God and invested in the name of God our underlying trust that we were made intentionally, for our own good, and our know-ledge that we are secure despite the fearsomeness and unknowability of death, and a lot else beside. This is an existentialist understanding of God, which Tillich identified with his phrase, 'the ground of our being'.

The existentialist understanding of the nature of God has been extraordinarily influential on the development of theological thinking over the past thirty years or so. It validates human experience as data for the formulation of that understanding: whether knowingly or not, it has been taken on by many different groups with many different viewpoints who are seeking to articulate their own experience in their understanding of God. These are in turn seeking the validation of their own experience by seeing that reflected in the divine nature. This has been the praxis of feminist theology, black theology, gay theology, womanist theology and others. In fact, there is a strong tendency to use 'experience' as an existentialist notion that provides the only truly pure basis for theological exploration.

But experience is as infinitely variable as people, and it can never be verified. Thus an inevitable consequence of this approach is that truth becomes inaccessible. Furthermore, despite the rhetoric in many of these theologies, experience by its very nature is context-specific as to gender, place, time, class, age, education and so on, and is therefore open to all the questions that post-modernism has brought to the universalizing themes of more conventional theologies.

To claim divine authority

However, it is by way of comparison and contrast with our human experience of relationships that the significance of our experience of God becomes clear to us, and there is always much that remains incomprehensible about this relationship. But because it is both beyond ourselves and bigger than ourselves, and there are times when we experience it as truly awesome, we are called to give it our allegiance. This process, well attested in the literature on conversion experiences, is the source of the authority that we place in God, an authority of such magnitude that we easily see that God is there for all of humankind, whether recognized or not.

To claim God as the source of human authority is potentially enormously powerful, even dangerous; and many, many times in the course of Christian history that authority has been abused. Women have often been on the receiving end of that abuse; sadly too, some have learnt to give as good as they got. This is also clearly why issues of power are so fascinating, so significant, for they impinge on the most sacred, intimate and personal parts of our lives, where body and soul meet and are destroyed or nourished. Berdyaev put it thus: 'Bread for myself is a material question; bread for my neighbour is a spiritual question.'[1] – 'Bread, and the power of bread.'

The need for authority

Whatever form of church governance one might espouse, the church as a whole lives under the authority of God. It is simply not possible for the church to exist in faithfulness to its calling without the willingness of its members to submit themselves to the authority of its deepest convictions about God, God's purposes for the world, and the church's role in these purposes. However, these core beliefs and values which bind the church together must be articulated and interpreted in constantly changing circumstances. Conflicts must be managed; boundaries between the church and other communities must be maintained, and directions for the church's life and work must be envisioned. Hence the need for leadership structures that hold the church to God and the members of the church to each other.

So the leader is granted authority to lead because he or she is believed to be the best one to protect, interpret and represent the core values and beliefs of the group, and to contribute to their realization. While this is probably true of all organizations, it is certainly true of the church and of the authority that the church gives to its clergy and its bishops.

Leadership, and the authority to exercise that leadership, enables the community to function, to be what it is called to be. No community can function without some form of leadership. Leadership enables the community to survive and to achieve its goals. Authority, the authorization to exercise leadership, is not the enemy of the community, as we sometimes suppose. Its enemies are any form of tyranny which coerces obedience illegitimately; the various forms of authoritarianism which abuse authority; and anarchy, in which each individual is an authority to himself or herself. If there is any desire among people to form a community then there must be agreed leadership structures.

The legitimation of authority

Leadership is legitimated from within the community, and in this time of growing anti-institutionalism the demands for community legitimation, legitimation from below, are increasing. Within many church structures this process has been formalized. In an episcopal church this marks an increase in the shift towards congregationalism. In New Zealand, parish priests are now appointed by boards of nomination which, while chaired by the bishop, have equal representation from both parish and diocese. Similarly, most provinces within the Anglican Communion have a procedure for the election of their bishops by the clergy and the laity of the diocese concerned.

I am occasionally asked by people outside this country whether I am 'accepted'. It always seems to me to be a strange question, for the process of electing a bishop by electoral synod is one that is designed to maximize the ownership by the diocese of the new bishop. The people also have a stake in the authenticity of that ministry. It is a process that works equally well for women and men. Properly conducted, it is in fact the best possible start to a new episcopal ministry, and I do not envy my colleagues who became bishops through an appointment system.

Diffused authority

In an episcopal tradition no local church can, by itself, be the source of its own leadership; there must be a reference point to the wider body. To respond appropriately and effectively there is a diversity of levels on which the God-given mission of the church is carried out. So the structure of the church as a whole is a system of embedded hierarchies: parish is embedded in diocese, diocese within province, province within Communion. The cohesion of the whole is maintained by communication between people working on the same level, whose decision-making receives a measure of both input and validation from the other levels.

Because the work of Christ was in itself a reconciliation of humanity, there is evidence from the first days of the churches of concern for the unity of communities, both in their internal relationships and in their interrelationships.[2] In the life of the church now as then no one level is ever seen as simply autonomous; thus priests and lay leaders meet in a diocesan synod; bishops, priests and lay leaders from each diocese meet in General Synod; primates meet at the primates' meeting and there is some wider gathering when the Anglican Consultative Council meets. In the past and in the early days of the missionary movements, the direction of both decision-making and communication was from Canterbury out. But provinces within the Anglican Communion were soon autonomous and the Communion is now characterized by diffused authority. However they remain related by history and a measure of common doctrinal and theological understanding. The bonds have been described as 'bonds of affection'.

Within New Zealand, diffusion of authority is further evident in the decision of the 1992 General Synod to revise the constitution of our church and to give a very significant measure of autonomy to each of the three cultural strands (see Chapter 5). What we have lost in this process of diffusion we have gained in particularity.

Authority is further diffused among the seven pakeha dioceses of the New Zealand church, in that the constitution prescribes only a form of voluntary association for the maintenance and development of common practice. In fact, New Zealand dioceses are much less accountable to each other than in other provinces I know. This means that the authority of a diocesan bishop is considerable. It is, however, well restrained by a synodical form of government, and there is a good measure of informal collegiality among the bishops.

Communicating authority

While there is clearly a move to make more explicit the ownership of its leadership by church communities at all levels of the life of the church, it can sometimes, especially in times of conflict, seem a little precarious to those in leadership. There are, as one would expect, corresponding and counter-balancing moves by that leadership to declare, assert and claim authority; in effect, to make it work.

The Anglican Communion is an extraordinarily diverse gathering of churches, covering all cultures and all continents. It is held together by a primacy of honour, the office of the Archbishop of Canterbury, and there are many who would say that, despite the absence of sanctions, it is surprisingly effective. However, there is an increasing need for the Communion to articulate its doctrinal base, its perception of its relationship to that base and its self-understanding of its life, mission and ministry. The last ten years have seen an increasing number of documents issued by Lambeth Conferences and the Anglican Consultative Council that state and restate positions on this issue. Increasingly, it would seem, it is felt that the common life of the Communion is expressed in these documents, but since they are generally inaccessible to most church members, they have little impact on the parish and diocesan structures of the church. It is a good example of activity at one level being irrelevant to the conduct of ministry at another.

The links between one level of hierarchy and another are also made by people. It is the primates who maintain connection between the provinces of the Communion, and within each province it is the bishops who, primarily but by no means exclusively, are the link people between their dioceses. Similarly, within each diocese, priests and lay leaders are the link people between parishes and the diocese.

Problems of ownership

Authority therefore is often corporately exercised. Leaders, both lay and ordained, at one level come together to declare and define the nature of their relationship and to pass both their vision and their decisions on to the communities to which they are responsible. The difficulty is that this corporate authority is not one that is directly recognized by the community concerned. So while a diocese may acknowledge the legitimacy of the General Synod, as it must, it has only a fractional role in determining the outcome of any decisions that the latter makes. The movement of authority from the top down runs directly counter to the legitimation of authority by the community.

As is natural with any significant move of social and ecclesiastical change, the formal participation of women within church structures began at the level closest to the grass roots. Women first became eligible for membership on vestries and then became representatives for their parishes at diocesan synods. Within the ordained ministry women were deacons long before they were priests, and priests long before they were bishops. Thus the active numerical participation of women in the highest councils of the church, and in the formulation of the documents that those councils produce, is at present minimal and will undoubtedly remain so for a very long time. So there is, as is common with other Christian communities, a growing discontinuity between the 'culture' of the lower levels of this pyramid of embedded hierarchies and that of the upper levels. To some extent this has long existed where a British or other 'colonizing' church has come in contact with other ethnic cultures; however, although it is harder to identify, there has also been a change in culture over the last twenty years or so within those churches that have ordained women. In general, and in brief, this culture is marked by a clear commitment to legitimation from within the community.

The theology of authority

I think that there are in fact two very different theologies of the nature of authority that mark the difference between what I have identified as the culture of the top of the pyramid and that of the lower levels. This is a difficult distinction to make, because it rests on the hypothesis that each theological perspective gives different weight to different persons of the Trinity, but as such represents a tendency that has marked shifts in church history and ecclesiology throughout the centuries. So, in broad terms, and each signifying a primary emphasis on one person of the Trinity, we have had Deism, the Jesus People, and the Charismatic Movement. It is, however, also true that they intersect with each other and none of them would exclude the others.

Essentially, I believe those at the upper levels tend to see their authority as coming primarily from the first person of the Trinity, as a given. The 1988 Lambeth Report, while acknowledging that 'In any human society, of whatever sort, authority has its basis in the shared life of the community',[3] says 'In the case of the Christian community and fellowship, the life which its members share does not derive from itself but is rooted in that of the crucified and risen Christ and is conferred by God through the working of the Holy Spirit'.[4] The primary emphasis within the trinitarian spectrum is on the originating work of God, so the Creator comes into focus, hence the shift towards the first person of the Trinity.

Elaine Pagels in her study of the Gnostic Gospels suggests that the association between monotheism and the power of the bishop originates from the second-century struggle that Irenaeus had with the Gnostics. It was a time when the need to establish doctrinal orthodoxy went together with the need to establish the authority of the church – hence the association of 'one God, one bishop'.[5] There is thus an early and a clear association between the authority attributed to God the Creator, and the exercise of authority within the church.

By contrast, the theological emphasis within the lower levels of the embedded hierarchy tends to be on the incarnation of Christ and on the work of the Holy Spirit. It sees God as the God of the gathering, of the community, God in our midst; and the Holy Spirit as the creative and relational force within the community. God is therefore embedded within the life of the community, and is certainly not identifiable with one person. This perspective takes seriously the biblical account of the gift of the Spirit to the church at Pentecost.

It is an oversimplification to see these perspectives as two distinct approaches; they are certainly not opposed to each other, for both find their being within the life of the Trinity. And both see authority within the Christian community as bestowed by God. Rather it is a question of emphasis, of where, within the life of the Trinity, we locate God. And the answer is clearly 'everywhere' – but the simplifying processes of Christian theological thought tend to separate out the persons of the Trinity and to identify with the different characteristics of each.

It is not surprising that the ministry of women finds a theological place within both the incarnation and the life of the Holy Spirit. A woman has a central role in the incarnation; the concept of Immanuel, 'God with us', has always related to women's concern with the intimate details of human living. And, too, the ministry of women as priests and bishops is still new within the life of the church; little wonder that the creative and renewing powers of the Spirit are particularly appreciated in that context.

The recognition of authority

With the general decline in respect for institutions, however, the granting and the holding of institutional authority does not necessarily ensure either that leadership will be effective or that it will be honoured. There are two other axes on which the authority of the clergy effectively rests. The leader must adequately represent the sacred, and he or she must have the ordinary worldly competence to handle the nuts and bolts of the job.

For Christian leaders, the authority of the sacred is largely assumed. In episcopal churches the gift of the Holy Spirit at ordination is regarded as both sealing and institutionalizing faith: sealing it because the laying on of hands follows the ordinand's declaration of faith; and institution- alizing it because his or her public and to an extent private practice of faith is thereafter deemed secure by virtue of the ordination.

Priests and bishops generally operate sacramentally in ways that are both accepted and anticipated. They are 'ordered', as the term 'ordination' suggests. And while nothing can take away their orders, and traditional sacramental theology affirms that the validity of the sacrament is not negated by the unworthiness of the ordained person, if priests and bishops fail to act within that order then people begin to question the validity of their ordination. For their authority as priests or bishops to be honoured people need to be sure of their willingness to be bearers of the sacred in public liturgical functioning.

The relationship between a priest's public, liturgical function and the practice and growth in personal faith is an elusive one. This is an age that increasingly recognizes that God can be found without the church, and there are large numbers of spiritually attuned people who do not need the church to enable them to identify the presence of God. This can present real questions for clergy, for whom the anchor point of their job is the liturgy of the church. And they are not helped, I believe, by much of what is currently on offer as spiritual direction, which tends to focus on the relationship of the individual to God, disconnected from community. There are some significant spiritual questions here which I shall take up later.

Priestly ministry is not all show, in any case. If public liturgical functioning is not backed up with the practice of a real and genuine private faith and piety then it becomes hollow. I believe that this is in fact the dilemma that a number of clergy find themselves in. The significance of private piety has grown in recent years, both with the decline of institutional respect and with the rise of individualism. A personal and authentic piety is essential to the practice of Christian ministry. It is cruel to ordain without it: I have seen lives deeply hurt.

The existence of a strong personal piety is not always evident, indeed it is necessarily a personal and private matter, but there is a sense in which its presence reassures the Christian community in which priesthood is practised. Whether intentionally or unintentionally, some clergy cultivate a mystique of distance which is well aided by the established custom of putting clergy on a pedestal. This distancing operates particularly effectively for bishops. Before I was ordained to the episcopate, a wise old priest suggested that bishops should find ways of sharing their faith authentically, deeply and personally, without ostentation and without intrusion.

The intersection of personal faith and public competence is a mark of effectiveness in ministry, and is necessary if their authority for leadership is to be validated. Clergy may have the experience and the qualifications, but if they do not have the demonstrated competence and a personally disciplined and spiritually sound approach that validation will not be forthcoming.

In practice, effective ministry is a combination of all these factors, held in a flowing balance. If we have authority as clergy, it is because laity perceive us to be reliable interpreters of the power and purposes of God in the context of contemporary society. And this involves both spirituality and expertise, not one without the other.

The challenge to institutional piety has also come from the many movements around the world for the ordination of women, for the claim of women to be ordained has largely rested on the claim to personal piety, on the call that God makes to women apart from and despite the institutional church.

Cultural acceptance

The ordination of women has also raised the question of cultural acceptance, acceptance that depends neither upon call nor upon competence but which acquires some validity, not, I would contend, from the requirement that the conscience of each member of the community be respected, but from the identification of the community as the locus for the legitimation of authority. The work of the Eames Commission on Women in the Episcopate[6] has stressed that the ordination of women as both priests and bishops is subject to a process of 'reception' within the church, and that the result of that process cannot be presumed upon.

In my experience, both as a priest and a bishop, women are not unaware of the necessity for them to be accepted by the people whom they would serve in God's name. It is not uncommon for women, as they present themselves as candidates for ordination, to stress how well they have been 'accepted' by people who have begun to see the signs of vocation within their lives. This is associated with the general tendency that women have to emphasize the relationships they have with others, the support they have received from other people and the regard in which they are held.

The reasons for this can be found within the wider structures of society, and the place of women relative to men. History, tradition and current practice give women little reason to believe that institutional acceptance will be as readily forthcoming for them as it is for men. There is no ready-made job slot for them to fit into, and women are not the ready and familiar carriers of the symbols of power that men are. So they tend to be insecure, and this social insecurity also reflects the general sense of personal insecurity and lack of self-worth that is often characteristic of women. This has been reinforced by the wide use of the key word 'acceptance' by people who are on the outside of a community in which the ministry of women is in place and who seek to make inquiries. This usage seems likely to continue for some time yet in New Zealand.

But the concept of 'acceptance' can be distorting. I see a danger in this, in that too great an emphasis on acceptance could lead women – or men for that matter, but women are more vulnerable to this – to shape their ministry according to the practices that they believe will earn that acceptance. Where the emphasis on acceptance is too strong, the significance of the call of Christ is lessened, and so is any prophetic thrust. While few women would identify with the imagery in the words of our Lord, 'I am come not to bring peace but a sword' (Matthew 10.34), the underlying truth is that the function of the gospel is not to confirm our prejudices and limitations, but to bring us to the foot of the cross. Gospel values are not those of secular society, and a clearly claimed Christian identity is an essential mark of call. I would not like to see the ministry of women hamstrung by an over-dependence on acceptance at the expense of clarity about the Christ they serve.

Where women, or men, anticipate a negative reception, they will generally place more emphasis on their sense of the sacred, on their personal piety and the strength of their relationship with God; it has been so throughout Christian experience in women as widely different as Teresa of Avila and Rebecca Jackson, the black American evangelist of the last century. Closer to home for me is the Methodist lay preacher Mrs Joan Scott, who came to live in New Zealand in 1863. She was a very effective preacher, but not authorized by the Methodist church in any way. It was said of her that 'Though not allowed the honour of being Conference Evangelist, she certainly is God's evangelist'.[7] The women in the Anglican Church in New Zealand who were earliest in line for ordination, especially those who were deacons for a good many years, have this mark about them very clearly. God is a powerful ally when you are daring to challenge the church to break with the pattern of centuries.

When I hear women, or men, who come to tell me of the first stirrings of vocation within them speaking of the 'acceptance' that they have received from others, I hear them beginning to claim the authority of God within them. I have seen them, as the authority is recognized and given space to move, growing in confidence and in their ability to talk convincingly about God. Sometimes this becomes for them a powerful symbol of personal liberation, and they are free to move beyond acceptance and into a more challenging and prophetic relationship with the church, and also with society. It can be an isolated and lonely position, for such people and such messages are not always welcome, but it can truly be said of some that I have known, as it was said of Mrs Joan Scott in relation to the Methodist Church, that they are certainly God's evangelists.

Relational authority

Authority is not only given to Christians by God through due process of the church, it must also be received. The process of receiving this authority, the route by which it becomes both authentic for the individual concerned and able to function in mutuality with the community that has called, can be quite long and tortuous. Celia Hahn[8] categorized four types of authority that we can experience as we move through our lives, which for some can be usefully regarded as stages of the journey: that is from 'received' authority through 'autonomous' and 'assertive' authority to 'integrated' authority.

For Jesus the route was much shorter. When Jesus was baptized he received authority from God; that baptism marked the beginning of his ministry. It was not too long before he began to speak as one with authority of his own: 'But *I* say to you . . . ' (Matthew 5.29). The authority of God had become, as it were, internalized, owned and able to be expressed with conviction; it had moved towards integration.

The church uses many symbolic ways of liturgically enabling those on whom authority is bestowed to demonstrate their acceptance of that authority. The service of ordination for a bishop allows for the giving of a number of gifts. The only one that is mandatory is the giving of the Scriptures with the injunction 'Here are the Holy Scriptures; learn from them, teach them, live by them, and proclaim Christ, the living Word'. The new bishop's acceptance of the Scriptures is a clear indication of his or her acceptance of episcopal authority. After this, other gifts are given, and in recent years their number appears to be growing. All are symbols of office and all are given by different communities and sub-communities that either are or will be in relationship with the new bishop. The acceptance of these gifts is a visible and strong symbol of the new bishop's acceptance of the authority that has been bestowed on him or her through the laying on of hands, and of her, or his, willingness to enter into this episcopal relationship. Some of these communities are sub-groups of that community for whom she or he will be bishop, some are communities with whom he or she will enter into a relationship of collegiality. The impact of the ordination service is so tremendous and so strong that its initial impression is of divinely bestowed authority firmly anchored within the community of the church. It is given, it is received, but it is yet to be owned.

Hahn calls the first perception of authority as given by the community 'received authority'. It is there when authority is very raw, very new, and it is characterized by a noticeable dependence on and respect for the authority structures of the community. At this stage in my life as a bishop I well remember spending hours trying to master the canons and statutes of our church so that I would exercise the kind of authority the church had made very clear that it expected its bishops to exercise. When a person is operating out of received authority, they are clearly aware that the source of their authority is beyond themselves, most frequently seen as being located within the institution. Received authority is in some ways very safe – until, that is, one discovers that a pedantic adherence to the rules and regulations can frequently violate both common sense and one's personal conscience.

The step to a fully owned authority is not quite straightforward for there are two possibilities en route, autonomous authority and assertive authority, which, depending on personality and gender, people may pass through, pass by or get stuck in. In practice, most people holding any kind of authority tend to move between them according to the demands of circumstances.

Autonomous authority is characterized by a move from dependence on the authority of others to confidence in our own internal authority. For my own part I found myself pushed very quickly into this mode, and I would have to say it was almost a defensive reaction. In the early days of my ordination as a bishop I found myself piled high with the expectations of others, all of which contained images of how I should use my authority. All this was strongly interwoven with the powerful sense of the sacred which had been so public and apparent at the time of my ordination that it seemed as if I was being iconized. The rule books were quickly found to be inadequate and I pulled a ring around myself, metaphorically speaking, turned the icon face to the wall, and began to explore and to exploit my own authority. I began effectively to define my own reality instead of letting other people do it for me. By placing boundaries around myself I began to see myself as I thought I was, and not according to the multiple images that were being projected upon me. But it was a very lonely time, and I was undoubtedly unbearable to live and work with.

At this time, and clearly overlapping, I was exercising what Hahn would describe as assertive authority. This was a sense of taking responsibility, and while I was ready enough to do so, there was a certain randomness and unreliability, for both myself and others, about the way I did it. As yet I had little security in where I was placed in my relationships with others. Because I was so isolated at that time I was very vulnerable and I experienced any questioning of anything that I did as profoundly and personally threatening. It was an extraordinarily painful time.

But it was not long before I began to seek allies and to draw other people into the confused conversations that were going on in my head. In the process of doing this I began to be aware much more solidly of the bonds that held me with the people who had put me in that position, and mutuality began to grow in our relationships. I had begun to experience what Hahn called 'integrated' authority. While I now – as Hahn would predict and any perceptive human wisdom would assume – still move from one experience of authority to another, I am most certainly much more at ease with it than when I began.

Gender differences

Feminist analyses of authority structures and the way that they are worked out in the lives and modes of functioning of individuals who hold authority very strongly contrast the more confident and dominating style that men are perceived as having with the more diffident and inclusive style that women tend to have.

The basis for such an analysis rests on the structural difference between the roles that men and women customarily play within our society. There is clear evidence from my own experience, both of myself and of other women, that there does tend to be a diffidence and even anxiety within many women about assuming authority. Women presenting themselves as candidates for ordination will repeatedly stress that they seek this in order to serve, that they do not seek power. Yet it is also clear to me that one of the reasons why more women are seeking ordination is that they feel they need the authorization, the 'received' authority that the institution can bestow, in order to function effectively. It is frequently hard for women to move from their gratitude at being granted authority by the institution to a clearer sense of who they are, and to the authority that comes from being who they are. When this point is reached it is a real and genuine personal awakening. It has concerned me that within the church, ordination for women has frequently served as a jumping-off point into more owned experiences of authority. I would like to see more lay women claiming that authority without benefit of ordination.

Men, in general, tend not to need or to seek this authorization. Their expectations fit them more appropriately for taking on leadership positions; it is expected of them and they expect it of themselves. However, their assumption of authority is not without its difficulties. As women find it difficult to move into an owned 'autonomous' authority, I have frequently noticed that men can struggle to move out of an owned and 'assertive' experience of authority and into a style that is more mutual and more relational. But when the switch happens, for both men and women, the result is truly effective leadership.

I believe that it is because men assume leadership roles more naturally and more readily that we are seeing fewer men presenting themselves for ordination. They simply do not need the authorization of the church to exercise leadership; some built-in antennae tell them that they are always welcome, as they are. The contemporary challenge to both men and women is to develop patterns of mutuality in leadership that will strengthen the whole Christian community.

By established social convention, men are accustomed to a measure of authority in relationships. Frequently this manifests itself as a bias towards independence, to seeking some control in a relationship. I notice this in small ways: for example, if I am driving around a parish, the vicar (male) will almost always express a preference for driving me in his car. It worries me not, but a friend pointed out to me that the action was, whether intentionally or unintentionally, a way of establishing his male authority and that it in a small way diminished mine. For my part, I was more easy about any pattern of behaviour that established relationships that could move away from the formalities and become real; I was interested in establishing connections.[9] This observation and many others that support this analysis are a sharp reminder to me that when it comes to questions of authority and relationships it is not uncommon for men and women to view the world in and from 'different frames'.[10] It is clearly an issue when attempting to establish mutuality in relationships with those over whom I hold formal authority.

Mutuality in the use of authority

Clearly authority gives the person the power to control who is consulted and who not. As bishop I have a very strong say in who participates in the formal structures of the church, and consequently who is excluded. I have access to the flow of information within the diocese and to the resources that enable my ministry of oversight to function, and I have the responsibility for licensing the clergy or not. These are resources given to me by the community that has asked me to serve them in that role.

The process of developing a pattern of 'integrated' mutual ministry involves learning to be more relaxed about who might offer to serve on a committee, to become less hands-on about access to the flow of information and also more generous with the use of resources. It is all part of learning to forgo the need to control and of sharing the responsibility with others. It is a very important part of community-building. When I first became bishop I found there was a very high expectation that all these means of control would stay in my hands. 'After all', I was told by one of the senior clergy in the diocese, 'we elected *you* to be bishop and not the Archdeacons.' There was a lot of the church's need for security invested in my keeping the reins tightly in my own hands. It took a while for enough trust to build up for people to trust me when I trusted others. Other people had some learning to do too. But I have discovered how empowering it is to relinquish control – and not only for others, for I too have gained.

Leadership

Any institution needs an authority structure that enables it to achieve the purposes for which it exists, which keeps it faithful to its core beliefs, and which initiates trouble-shooting when necessary. The church is no exception. However, the core beliefs and values which bind the church together must be articulated and interpreted in constantly changing circumstances. At the same time, authority rests in a person as much as in a structure, and people cannot be neatly divided into functional parts. There are many images attached to Christian leadership: servant, lord, father, priest, watchman, shepherd, president; and some that invite the imagination to consider the possibilities that are opened up by women's leadership: mother, midwife, nurturer and so on. However, there are three particular functions of authority within the church that I want to address. These are to shape the future, to deal with conflict and to maintain boundaries. This is leadership.

'Leadership', like 'power', gets a bad press these days, but because it seems to be perennially necessary it is as well to consider carefully what it is there for. For leaders too can overstep boundaries. Hans Küng has pointed out that many of the functions we ascribe to leaders are not exclusive to them. But if leaders do not in practice concern themselves with these functions, either directly or indirectly, then nothing will happen. No one else has been given the gift or the commission to make sure that things get done.[11]

However, Jim Cotter has pointed out that leadership like any other ministry is a *gift*, a *charism*, always to be exercised as a service, a *diakonia*. All such gifts are given for the purpose of building up the whole Body, for *koinonia*, for fellowship, community, communion.[12] The functions of authority that I am considering here must, if they are to constitute authentic leadership, serve these purposes.

In short, leadership is sacrament.

Women and leadership

Women often find questions of leadership particularly difficult to deal with, undoubtedly because these are so readily associated with power. Women tend to stress the servant role of leadership, feeling more at ease with a serving use of their authority than with one of power. I think that this is a form of denial of the power that they do have, but it is also, more insidiously, a way of making the power that they hold acceptable to men; for the Christian tradition, essentially paternalistic, has always honoured the serving role of women and this honour is now generally seen as an ill-disguised but effective way of keeping them in their place.

'Service' is also sometimes more acceptable to women for the wrong reasons: it is all too often a soft cover for feelings of worthlessness. Women, whose self-image is shaped by their mothering role and who are hungry for the care and affirmation that they are not receiving elsewhere in their lives, will seek through no fault of their own to fill the void by taking care of others. Much good has been done through such actions, but if need is not acknowledged there is no real choice involved and little sense of responding freely to a call. Anyone, man or woman, needs to be able to say No before her Yes is truly free. It is only after a woman has both claimed and rejoiced in all she is meant to have and to be that she is free to 'give' herself appropriately and to serve the needs of others and not her own needs badly disguised; and to form relationships that are strong and free with those whom she serves. Then such a service has a good chance of being both liberating and empowering.

The context of leadership

Christian leadership never operates in a vacuum or in isolation. Because it arises out of and in the midst of a network of relationships, it can never be the function only of the ordained. Representative ministry and the community represented are inseparable. Ministers may represent the community to the wider world and may represent the wider church to the local church, but they are not set either above or over against the community. As *Baptism, Eucharist and Ministry* put it:

> All members of the believing community, ordained and lay, are interrelated. On the one hand the community needs ordained ministers. Their presence reminds the community of the divine initiative, and of the dependence of the Church on Jesus Christ, who is

the source of its mission and the foundation of its unity. They serve to
build up the community in Christ and to strengthen its witness. In
them the Church sees an example of holiness and loving concern. On
the other hand, the ordained ministry has no existence apart from the
community. They cannot dispense with the recognition, the support,
and the encouragement of the community.[13]

I wish to pay particular attention to the three functions of leadership
mentioned earlier, for they are necessary to any community, however its leadership is structured. These functions are, once again, the
shaping of the future, the maintaining of boundaries and the managing
of conflict.

Shaping the future

If this was a book about management this section would be headed
'Setting goals'. Recent years have seen many instances of parishes and
other church communities holding consultative gatherings for just this
purpose. To an extent, this is a formalized reflection of the contemporary concern of the church for consultation, but it is also a reflection
of current insecurity. To define goals is to find a sense of certainty
about where we are going and to reduce anxiety about the future. In
the process, a form of corporate leadership is exercised.

In my experience however, such processes, while often helpful,
can run contrary to the nature of the church, and for three reasons.
First, there is a sense of trying to pre-empt God's future. If we try to
determine the direction of the church for the next five to ten years then
we are leaving little reason or scope for the continuing process of
prayer and the discernment of God's will. Second, it seems as if God
always wins anyway; the church just simply is not in control of its
life. It is in fact extraordinarily vulnerable to changes in society, in
demography, in the economic climate, in the distribution of personnel,
to say nothing of the response of the people of God to the gospel of
Jesus Christ. Efforts at setting and realizing goals frequently lead to a
profound sense of failure. Third, setting goals can both distort and
limit our achievements; if for example we decide to aim for twenty
baptisms in a year and achieve that in the first four months, what do
we do next? And even worse, our methods of achieving such baptisms
might be quite inappropriate.

Leadership as sacrament

Christian leadership is less specific than this, and that can be frustrating for some people. It attempts to define the place of the local Christian community within the purposes of God, within the church and the community of other Christians, and also within secular society. It seeks to relate the major questions of life to faith in Christ. It endeavours to give the local Christian community a sense of its identity within the complex spectrum of communities alongside which it exists. It inspires in the Christian community a sense of confidence in being, and it offers direction, suggesting practical and possible ways in both liturgy and life which enable this confidence in place and being to grow. When this happens, communities grow in faithfulness and in numbers.

The gift of leadership I am trying to define here depends critically on the quality of the relationships that the leader has with the community. He or she must be able to listen very carefully to God and to the people, to find where the deepest, often unarticulated longings of the community are placed, where its members have hurt and where they are afraid to move for fear of hurting themselves or others again. It is out of this closeness that true leadership is born. For it then knows, from the particular situation in which it is placed, how to respond to people's yearnings to make sense of their lives, how to attend to the tasks that the community exists to perform and how to interpret the symbols of the tradition that overarch them all. Leadership is the outward and visible sign of the inward and spiritual grace of the Christian community. Again, it is sacrament.

To claim that leadership is sacrament is to relate our practice of leadership to the sacrament of ordination. Ordination is always a public sacrament; the ordinand is questioned, and replies in the presence of the whole church, bishops, clergy and laity. The public nature of ordination reflects the fact that the character and gifts of each of the three orders of ministry are each present in the body of Christ, but that some members of the body are called to be both sign and agent of these gifts. So *diakonia*, service, is there very noticeably, for Christian communities are full of good and loving people: deacons, perhaps especially vocational deacons, highlight this. The fact that we have so few – none in this diocese – is a sorry sign of how little we regard this gift. Priesthood too is there in the Christian community, which gives flesh and reality to God's redeeming presence in this world and forms the body of Christ; priests act *alter Christus*, as the signs and agents of God's action in Christ, giving human shape to the connection between God and God's people. So also oversight is present within the Christian community. I know only too well the deep care that all members of the

Body of Christ have for the welfare of the whole body, and I know too that God always shows me those people who will, very practically, share that care with me on specific issues. The bishop is simply the sign and the agent of that care. This is the theological context in which it can be claimed that leadership is sacrament.

Styles of leadership

There are a number of ready-made styles of leadership on offer these days. At one extreme, there is the strong charismatic leader who offers an awesome view of the power and the majesty of God; and there is the leader from the more Catholic end of the spectrum whose style of leadership suggests the overwhelming authority of God. Both can operate well within a context of good relationships, but the powerful and prevailing images of these styles mean that they frequently do not. It is all too easy for leaders, both men and women, operating within these images to lose touch with the people they serve, and not even know that it is happening.

Most of the New Zealand church cannot be defined by either of these images, so while the qualities of leadership that I would point to can easily operate within either of them, in fact most of the New Zealand church is 'broad' church, in which the leadership style depends more critically on the style of the individual who holds leadership. This makes leaders terribly vulnerable, for it becomes all too easy to hold them personally responsible in the event of failure.

I have found that some women are particularly skilled at exercising a relational style of leadership. I have observed women, through the quality of these relationships, giving a church a strong sense of its worth and a strong affirmation of its being. In so doing they impart a vision of a community that is generous hearted, because the God they know and love, and who they know loves them, is so generous hearted. They are inclusive and open in their relations, and find it a privilege to welcome into their number people who are misfits elsewhere in society. These leaders are skilled at recognizing and affirming the gifts that God has given and they encourage their use, knowing the point at which delegation is possible. They co-ordinate the community, ensuring that all are working together and that the efforts of each person contribute effectively to the whole. At its best, such leadership is an enormously satisfying calling. It is a style that is not and need not be confined to women; it is a model for all of us.

This model of leadership works well in parish life; I have found it more difficult to put into practice as a bishop. The primary reason for this is the fact that the community I lead is in fact a community of communities, and as such is very diffuse. The Diocese of Dunedin is large geographically, the largest in New Zealand, and the church communities that make it up are very scattered and often very small. For each of them, their primary community is quite naturally their local one. I have also found that the nature of a bishop's ministry is that I am spread very thin. I visit the parishes regularly, once a year or more, but find that this is insufficient to get to know people well and in depth. But I do my best and there are some whom I work with more frequently and have become quite close to. I really appreciate their friendship.

This 'thin spread' has led me to explore different ways of exercising leadership; there is no single community with which I can function in every aspect of my ministry. So I find that I have had to develop a number of different ways of working, in particular a number of different groups with whom I work on particular issues. It can be time-consuming, both for me and for them, and I need to be alert and responsive to when people are moving into overload. But it is worthwhile. It is possible, with a group of people, both to explore and to capture a vision of the way we are going, and through them to begin to communicate this to the wider group.

For, primarily, the style of leadership that I am exploring and suggesting relies on modelling for the communication of its essence. It self-destructs with an excessively authoritative style, and it often depends on hints and humour for its effectiveness. It is essentially about the nature of the Christian community, about its culture; and it relies on a measure of personal closeness.

Maintaining boundaries

Leaders of a Christian community are called to focus and to embody the unity and the continuity of the people of God. As I discussed at length in Chapter 5, this is in fact one of the particular responsibilities with which a bishop is charged. It is apparent that leadership, whether by bishop, priest or lay minister, needs to be authentically and recognizably Christian leadership. Clergy are under enormous pressure in these days of multiple spiritualities and values. When I was a parish priest I was frequently asked to take a service, generally a wedding, that was 'not too religious, not too Christian'. My answer was always that I was very sorry, but I only knew how to take a Christian service. Our ordination services specify the creeds of the church as the basis of our understanding of the definition and boundaries of the Christian faith. These form a sound base as long as they are not slavishly followed. It is the responsibility of the Christian leader to develop ways of articulating the reality and excitement of the faith in a huge variety of contexts of meaning. It is not easy in this pluralist society, but it is very necessary, for the central authenticity of our faith must be maintained.

A leader is essentially someone who holds together the life of the community. In a Christian community this is primarily done by living the love of God so that it informs and shapes all aspects of the life of the community. In so doing, the leader in a way defines the life of the community, so that its members know why they belong, and also offers a measure of security, but security firmly set in the context of dependence on God. As such, a significant function of leadership is to maintain the boundaries between what is the community and what is not.

So leadership within the Anglican Church will be recognizable, within a very broad band of acceptability, as Anglican. People who come to worship at an Anglican church expect to continue to be able to see their church as a legitimate and integral part of the wider Anglican Communion. Christian communities are always vulnerable to the fanatic and the one-sided, and it is the responsibility of leadership to fend them off. I have found that some of our smallest communities which have difficulty in providing their own leadership are particularly vulnerable to such people.

When authority is primarily seen as the function of maintaining boundaries it can be very negative, mainly associated with stopping things happening, preventing violations of the rules and regulations. It is very strongly associated with controlling. To counter this tendency, the questions I was soon asking myself when I was first a bishop were: how can I make things happen? how can I enable people to effect the ministry that God has called them to? can I give permission for them to break the rules in a way that is sustainable and fits the common life of the diocese?

This negative and inhibiting aspect of authority is particularly noticeable among our Co-operating Parishes. These are Anglican parishes that have entered into a formal agreement of co-operation with Christians from other denominations (like Local Ecumenical Projects in England) with the result that they become subject to a complicated series of rules that reflect and honour the identities of each of the denominations involved. Charting a way through them can be extraordinarily dispiriting for a co-operating church that is seeking to respond creatively to the difficulties it is facing. It is a time to be as relaxed about formality as possible.

Boundaries are not maintained by adopting a ghetto-like and superior stance. So a good leader will form good relationships with other Christian denominations. Sometimes I have noticed that parish priests can feel quite threatened by the presence of Christians from other traditions, but if the people are confident of their identity and know who they are and what they are, then they can only experience the joy of both giving and receiving.

Managing conflict

Conflict within a community always hurts, and the hurt within a Christian community is particularly marked. Christian churches are supposed to be places of peace and harmony where people come together to worship God, to pursue the cause of God's justice and to be the Body of Christ in the world. Conflict tears that body, re-crucifies Christ.

In his book *The Once and Future Church*, Loren Mead outlines the many changes that are occurring within society and that are affecting the Christian churches whether we recognize it or not. A consequence of these is an increase in the stress that is affecting churches as they become more vulnerable. Mead predicted a big increase in conflict within the church and in the workload of bishops and other church leaders as they respond to the needs that local communities have for help in resolving their conflict.

Leaders, particularly bishops, are supposed to focus and embody the unity of the people of God. When that unity is fractured, it clearly fractures the heart of a bishop. I certainly have found that in my time as a bishop when I have had to deal with conflict. Frequently the conflict that arises in parishes can be attributed to past successes: the more impact a particular style of worship has had in the past, the greater the controversy that will be generated when change is proposed. And, too, the more a parish has failed in the past to move gently with the times, the greater is the stake that those who remain have in the continuation of things as they are. Generally the most substantial groups that remain in a parish in such strife are those who are resistant to change; others have drifted away.

Conflict is often marked by the formation of coalitions within a parish and then people taking sides. Personal attacks increase and are substituted for efforts to identify the problems. As the sense of threat and anger increases, highly emotional appeals are made as a substitute for rational or kindly thought, and each faction assumes that it knows what the other is thinking and what they should do. In such circumstances no one is willing to make peace overtures. Struggles often seek a scapegoat, and all too easily it is the vicar who is chosen for this role. Some fight back, some cave in; all are extremely unhappy when they find themselves in this position.

There are many techniques and processes available for assisting communities caught in conflict. I have found that it is essential that I am prepared to initiate such a process; it is usually impossible for those concerned to do so by themselves. I have also found that it is an essential part of my role to offer reassurance, prayer and hope while a parish is going through the painful process of working through their difficulties. Optimism, the optimism of God, is one of the best gifts that I can bring.

There is, then, a clear association between the holding of authority and the willingness to engage in the resolution of conflict. In fact, it is in times of conflict that appeals to authority are most often made. At such times these can feel like a very raw need. The report of the last Lambeth Conference saw very clearly the connection between conflict and authority:

> The operation of authority in the Church involves conflict and disagreement. Indeed it would probably be true to say that authority in the Church works primarily *through* rather than in spite of disagreement. Its primary function is not, then, to provide ahead of time answers to all possible questions, but to assure that when disagreement occurs it is settled in accord with the principles according to which Christians normally discern the mind of Christ for them: that the solution is rooted in Scripture, consonant with the mind of the Church, and 'reasonable' in the sense that it speaks a language the world can understand – that it makes 'good sense' even if the sense it makes is unexpected. At this level, authority in the Church refers not so much to an absolute right to decide, vested in some particular individual or group, as it does to a right to orchestrate argument and consultation with a view to guaranteeing that what emerges from disagreement will be an understanding that grows out of the authentic sources of the Church's life.[14]

It is most humiliating, but also salutary, to acknowledge that our human inability to resolve conflict is one of the most pragmatic reasons why we have authority structures.

9

Searching

CLIMBING BEANSTICKS

Spirit, spirit, come feed from my hand:
Be not so trembling, so anxious to fly.
At least I can school you to understand
What bean climbs up to the sky from our land . . .
From Robin Hyde, 'Among Neighbours'

The environment in which our churches find themselves has changed enormously in the years since the flourishing times of the 1940s and the 1950s. We are no longer the natural focus for community identity and values, we cannot expect people to turn to us as they did in the past. Indeed, there are many who scarcely know we exist. Our stance towards those who are not of us and not amongst us needs to be much more engaged, much more open, much more obvious. Such a stance is not only a necessity for survival, it is also essential if the church is to be faithful to the God who has called it into being, and if the practice of our faith is to be authentic. The words of the prophet Amos come to mind: 'I hate, I despise your religious feasts; I cannot stand your assemblies. Even though you bring me burnt offerings and grain offerings, I will not accept them . . . but let justice roll on like a river, righteousness like a never failing stream' (Amos 6.21–24).

I have in the last year or so been closely involved with one of our parishes which has for many years offered fine worship to God. A city parish, in the 1940s and the 1950s it was one of the largest parishes in this diocese. In the 1960s the tide began to turn, just gently. However the past was strong enough for the parishioners to feel sufficient security in one another's company and each other's commitment so that they could afford not to notice that their services were enabling the worship of fewer and fewer people.

As the size of the congregation dwindled, so did its life, the general sense of fellowship, of contact with the real issues of our society, the sense of out-goingness. It became a gathered congregation, to which people came from all over town for the particularity and the excellence of the worship that was offered there – and they were very committed to that worship. They turned increasingly in on themselves and became strongly defensive when any change or addition to their worshipping pattern was proposed. They took on many of the characteristics of a holy ghetto; they so valued what they had, and themselves, that they came to despise those who did not worship with them, and worse than that they began to tell those whose anxieties and insights led them to suggest change that they should leave.

This is not the story of all of our parishes, but in varying ways it is the story of more than one, and there are a number of parishes who could identify with this story. In part it is a product, as I have indicated, of a church that became stuck quite selfishly in its own ways; but it is also a victim of its own success. Any Christian community that lives only for itself is dead, and such death usually comes lingeringly and slowly. It is incredibly painful. The natural direction, the natural reach for living the Christian life is outwards, with eyes and hearts of love and compassion turned out onto the world that God created and that God loves. When that direction becomes reversed, when that reach withers, there is nothing there.

This is not the whole story; there are parishes that are willing to be less protective of their specialties and which turn out openly, generously and welcomingly to others. I am thinking of one in particular that has had a significant ministry with children, to the extent that the children really own the church and the Christian gospel as their own. This in turn is reaching wider into the community.

I cannot pretend that as bishop I know what makes some parishes dare to share their faith and their life, or what there is that I can do to promote such attitudes. When parishes do get turned in on themselves in the way I have described, they easily see suggestions or direction as attack; and it is all too easy for me to get caught in the same self-righteous defensiveness from which I am trying to move them on. I know no other way than through the love and engagement that I have with them, and my willingness to stay with them no matter how much they hurt themselves and others; but I do this without compromising my own questions which come through in many of my dealings with them, as also in the sub-texts of my preaching.

Beyond the church

I also try to model my vision of the outgoing face of faithfulness in the stance that I take to the community beyond the church, in the choices that I make in my own ministry, and the people and the parishes that I affirm. As a bishop I have a very high public profile and I am consequently asked to engage in any number of issues of community concern. To some extent this profile is a consequence of the extraordinary circumstances that brought me to Dunedin. The publicity that surrounded my ordination was such that there was a strong sense that I belonged to Dunedin and not just the Anglican Church. I have been glad to trade on that publicity, for it is a privilege to be given the opportunity to engage, in the name of Christ, beyond the community that bears his name.

It is undoubtedly always easier for us to stay in the environment and the company with which we are familiar and which shares the values that we hold, and it is always a pleasure to be with people with whom we share faith and whose spirits reach out towards God. To move beyond those circles, especially with the commission to engage at depth and with due regard to the realities and the imperatives of our faith, always involves for me a sense of stretch and a sense of search. It entails a stretching because it requires that the embrace of my heart widen to include so many others – not just abstractly, but as particular people: individuals whom God made and whom God loves, but who do not share my central preoccupation with the things of God, and indeed quite often are suspicious of those. It involves searching because it requires me to find, with as much precision as possible, the common area of understanding so that together we may journey for a while on a path which is of God.

All this is for me the underside of moving towards an understanding of the role of the bishop in the mission of the church. Not in terms of the ideal, but in terms of the possible and beyond. This chapter looks at some of the issues I have had to face up to as I have both endeavoured to shape an outward-looking stance for the church and as I have myself moved beyond the Christian community in the course of my own ministry. It is a quest, a searching; and, if not flying, it is 'climbing beansticks'.

Mission

'Mission' is a much overused word these days, having been hijacked by contemporary management theory to describe the particular goals of an institution, as in 'mission statement'. Its meaning is very clear, it is a statement of where the organization is going. But many of our churches who have owned the word since the time of the Great Commission do not know what it means, for them, here, now.

The real confusion happened with the missionary expansion of Christendom that began in the eighteenth century and went hand in hand with colonization. Those of us who are on the receiving end of the faith that was imparted through colonization are often all too aware of the unfortunate association between the proclamation of the Good News of Christ and the process of subduing indigenous peoples. So there is a measure of suspicion about overseas mission that is the inheritor of this movement.

Mission as we know it in New Zealand, for this land was on the receiving end of the endeavours of the missionary societies, is mission in the sense of 'sending out' and is peculiarly a product of the nineteenth-century patriarchal church. Indeed, it has been suggested that this is a concept that relates in imagery and energy to male physiology. By contrast, an image that has been used to describe the way women share the gospel is that of a web. This is an image that draws attention to the capacity that is associated with women of drawing people in, and places firm emphasis on quality relationships. Both images have their limitations.

More problematic is the vision of mission that came into being at that time, which was essentially to separate it off from the worshipping congregation. It became the work of people with a special dedication, a special calling, if not indeed of professionals; and the home parishes were invited to support them by prayer and by financial giving. Mission became someone else's job, and less clearly recognized as the calling of all who are baptized. Meanwhile, like the parish whose withering I described above, the world around the home bases was becoming much less attuned to the Christian message, and frequently quite ignorant of it.

The contemporary mission field is on and within our own doorstep, and it involves engaging in such dialogue with our neighbour as might mark us off from them. Vincent Donovan's memorable phrase that he uses to describe missionaries is 'social martyr' in that they are people who are cut off from their social and cultural roots, and who are strangers in their own land.[1]

Many Christians these days find it extraordinarily difficult to make connections between the practice of their faith, their church life, and their community life. The divide is often very great. Given this situation, churches will move in one or other direction; either they will move into a ghetto of their own making and clearly distinguish themselves from all who will not join them, or they will be at such pains to identify with the issues and problems of the community beyond the church that they will, apart from the preservation of some quaint rituals, come to identify with it completely and therefore become scarcely distinguishable.

We badly need to rediscover the connection between our churches and the communities in which they stand, to re-find the gift of 'gossiping the gospel', to know to what we are committed and to stand firm to it without compromise, but without judgement of those who cannot join us. We need constantly to turn with loving eyes onto God's world, ready to engage at depth with the longing for significance and meaning in life that is the lot of all of humankind. As Jim Cotter puts it:

> The apostle, the missionary, the evangelist of today, the pioneer for God, has to become the crucible out of which flow burning words and deeds that will convict and convince. They may be heard and seen in public. But there will also be the lonelier ones, the artists who are compelled to be creators before their time of images that will speak of God in the future.[2]

But because God's creation, while infinitely diverse, is also all of one piece, and also because authentic Christianity has always sought to engage with the society of which it is a part, it is not possible for the line between the Christian community and what lies beyond to be totally distinct. It might be obvious what is clearly part of it, and what is clearly not, but there will always be a grey area. This is the matrix of much confusion. Sometimes, as indicated above, assimilation can be thorough to the point of indistinguishability. The fragmentation of the whole Christian venture, outlined in Chapter 1, has led to quite marked variety in understanding of the Christian gospel and in interpretation of its implications for particular questions and problems. Hence the challenge to the faith of the church comes as much from those who identify as being within it as from those who identify as being outside.

I see in this a new kind of mission necessity. It is one that has to begin with an indefatigable love for all of God's people. This is a calling that directly challenges our own secularity and it is one that I do not glibly reiterate, because in a world in which Christian security stands at such a high premium, who would not feel fearful or threatened by the exposition of ideas about faith that run counter to those on which we base our lives? This calling can come so close to all that we hold dear, to our self-understanding of the identity of our being as followers of Christ; it can be extraordinarily painful. For Christians who deeply understand the pressure and problems of our time and demonstrate compassion for these can often be misunderstood by Christians who remain protected within their ghettoized communities; the centrality of their Christian conviction can be obscured and the response of more sheltered Christians can be one of scorn. This is where the church has used the language of heresy; it is the stuff of schism, of exodus communities, of war. It is the story, the history, of the whole Christian venture.

The issues over which such differences arise are too numerous to list. They include just about every ethical question you could think of, ranging from social justice to personal and sexual morality, and include questions concerning the structure of the Christian story and its implications for human behaviour and values for women and for men. Such questions clearly present as challenges to established doctrine, and a facile and closed response reinforces the view that doctrine is irrelevant to the questions that our contemporaries are asking.

But explication of doctrine, whether by way of declaration or by challenge, is always an inadequate representation of the reality of God's love for God's people. God will be God, whatever. The function of doctrine within the Christian community is not primarily juridical or legalistic. The primary function of church teaching or doctrine, in all the forms it takes – teaching, liturgy, church pronouncements, the work of theologians, of artists, the lives of holy women and men – is to enable each person to appropriate, to internalize, the meaning for the world that God has revealed in Christ; in short, to enable faith to be caught. This meaning is dynamic and is understood in relation to the particular concrete circumstances of one's life. Such a task is never-ending. The final word has not been said, nor will be until the end of history. The searching goes on.

Teaching, interpretation and encouragement

I have always found that the traditional image of a bishop as one who sits *in cathedra* and teaches people is not an image that I wear easily. Nor is it a very realistic one in the society in which I live and work.

I find such an image an uneasy fit because it claims for the wisdom of the bishop a kind of disembodied and non-relational authority that I do not have and do not seek. It rests upon a declamatory, almost pontifical style of teaching which presupposes little interaction, little engagement with those who are taught. It implies that the role of such teaching is to fill up empty vessels and to guide lost souls. I have found that it is both unhelpful and quite frankly wrong to begin any interchange with assumptions that imply so little respect for those with whom I am dealing.

This approach is also not realistic, because it derives from a culture in which the church and consequently the bishop held an authoritative place. That is no longer the case. The church is accorded residual respect as the carrier of the values on which western culture was founded, but these are fragmented, questioned and ignored. It seems to me to be unhelpful to adopt a stance that declares publicly that the church has not noticed that things have changed, and that it still expects the world to come and sit at the bishop's feet. There is little respect for bishops who act in such a way.

These reservations have led me to think through carefully the teaching role of the bishop as I relate to the church and to communities beyond the church. In each case I seek to listen, to engage and to interact, to learn from them as well as to share my insights. This may well seem like a loss of perceived authority to others, but I have found it is the only effective way that I can live in obedience to the call to teach the faith.

I have found that when this call is directed towards the church, the primary function of what I say is generally to place the church, in all its width, its depth and its complexities, in the context of the world that we are called to serve in God's name; to turn the face of the church outwards in challenge and in love. It is in many ways a ministry of interpretation, mediating the church to the world and the world to the church, weaving the threads of understanding between the church and the secular world. It involves enabling and encouraging people to name the real difficulties with which the contemporary mission of Christ is engaging, not in order to find excuses for our failures, still less to find someone else to blame, but rather that these difficulties might be honestly, courageously and prayerfully faced.

There are a number of our churches which, like the one I described above, have failed over many generations to hear that call, so that they move rapidly into denial; or if they do hear, they become paralysed with guilt because the task seems too great for them. Somehow, by the grace of God, I need to find ways to stay alongside such parishes, holding out to them a vision of the possibility of a vibrant, authentic and contemporary faith; for some this is a vision of 'another country'. I need also to keep on gently and lovingly nudging them, establishing a climate in which they can safely admit to their failures, which is surely a fundamental characteristic of a Christian community, and in which they have less need to be defensive and can brave more for the sake of the Lord that they love.

Defining priorities

My ministry beyond the church is primarily responsive, inasmuch as it depends upon the invitations that I get to speak to different groups or to engage in discussion on particular issues. There are always a lot of these, far more than I can accept, and so the ways in which I define my priorities have become a way of defining my ministry beyond the church.

Some diocesan priorities

For the first months of my ministry, the priorities were obvious: I needed to get to know the people, the places and the problems. And I focused on these, somewhat haphazardly and with little prioritizing. But beside that there were a large number of requests to address gatherings of all sorts of people beyond the church, both ecumenically and outside the Christian community, within the diocese and elsewhere.

I quickly realized that I should make it a priority to accept as many as possible of the invitations that come to me from groups and communities within the diocese, no matter how small or isolated they might be and no matter what their priorities. This has taken me into an extraordinary variety of situations, from school trustees, nurses, university women, police community education and so on, to Country Women's Institutes, Rural Women Support Days, school prize-givings and any number of clubs that exist solely so that their membership might have the opportunity to hear visiting speakers.

It is always good to meet people from beyond the church communities which are the focus of my ministry, and I have frequently found that the contacts I have made have been most enriching. It is not unusual for me to find that after such a gathering there are people with personal issues they wish to talk to me about. I find these gatherings a constant challenge. They always attract a good deal of interest among the community of the local church, who are proud that I am talking at a non-church function, and therefore their friends will have a chance to meet me without stepping onto holy ground! For them such an occasion is often seen as a bridge-building opportunity, between the lives they live as part of the local church and the lives they live as part of the local community.

I try to make sure that I address issues and concerns that are real to the people who are there, but I also need to make sure that I do it in a way that is true to what I am, a Christian woman. Such events are clearly not occasions for preaching, for a sermon presupposes a common purpose that is not present in such gatherings. But there are other places of common ground. There is in our society a very widespread concern for Christian values; and, more personally for individuals, there is an interest in the spiritual quest. I find that I can generally presume on these and address them in ways that are implicitly, though not outspokenly, Christian. Quite often I centre my address on one of the major themes that attach themselves to particular years, such as Suffrage Year, International Year of the Family, Maori Language Year and so on.

Some national priorities

I am less responsive to invitations to address meetings beyond the diocese; time and travel make it impossible to accept many such invitations. The ones that I do accept are invariably to speak to gatherings that would not normally ask someone from within the church to address them. Because of the high profile of my position as bishop and the image that I bear in the popular mind as a woman of power, I am often asked onto territory that is not usually open to bishops of the church. Some examples are a Women in Management Seminar, an address on feminist ethics, addresses to gatherings concerned with Christian social justice, a University Extension address for women on the inner journey, entitled 'The Open Womb – is any space sacred for women?', and so on. A common theme that runs through such invitations is the continuing fascination in all sectors of society with issues of women and power, and a search for what might be the face and the nature of the leadership that women have to offer. I am part of that community of exploration and I enjoy playing my part in it.

The challenge of such opportunities is to engage with a section of the intellectual community and the community of ideas within our country that would not themselves otherwise interact with someone from an explicitly Christian perspective. It is for me both a social and an intellectual challenge; I find it extremely stimulating to wrestle with Christian issues on other people's turf, where they define the environment and the agenda.

Some overseas priorities

Like so many people who start a new job, I soon found that there was a need to establish some priorities. The high public profile made this more difficult. But also, I had a huge range of invitations to speak to gatherings of all sorts and in all kinds of places. I was even invited, before I was ordained, to be the after-dinner speaker at a fund-raising function in San Francisco! San Francisco is a very long way to go for dinner, from Dunedin.

One of the first priorities that I set was that I would not travel beyond New Zealand for the first two years of my episcopacy. There was just too much to do and too much to get to know at home. It was an absolute decision; I debated no issue; it was easy.

Since then, I have been overseas several times, to Australia, Canada, the United States and England and Scotland. I have, naturally enough, tried to pace these travels so that they do not inconvenience my diocese. The reasons that I am invited vary, but they all rely heavily on the high novelty value that I carry within the Anglican Communion as the first woman to be a diocesan bishop. I felt some companionship when Mary Adelia McLeod was elected as diocesan Bishop of Vermont. The ways in which people regard my novelty value and their often unarticulated vision of what I might be able to do for them vary considerably, but there are basically three types of visit that I am asked to consider.

The first is pastoral: that is, pastoral care for people, generally women, who have been wounded by the clumsy and difficult journeys that their churches are making or have made towards the ordination of women as priests. In this sense I am regarded as, and become for a short time, a bishop for those women. I have found this to be enormously rewarding, for the process towards the ordination of women in New Zealand was so long ago (the first women were ordained to the priesthood at the end of 1977) and, in marked contrast to so many other places, so comparatively easy that it is a real privilege to be invited to share that pain at such depth, and to minister to these women. For the tragedy of such pain is that it can displace love, drown out vocation and refocus the individual onto her own suffering and the case for her own rights. All of this is a terrible noise which makes it very hard for these women to continue to hear the still small voice of God. So deafened, they may hold onto their vocation with grim rigidity, for a lot of hurt pride is involved in letting it go; but such barriers of pride and pain are very excluding of God. Or they can become overwhelmed by the politics, the debate and the public expressions of hate that come their way and under such pressure it becomes impossible for them to discern protest from injustice.

In such situations my ministry, both public and private, is primarily one of enabling a refocusing back onto the God who calls, who loves, who wills us no damage and who can be trusted through thick and thin. In all of this I am doing no more than passing on to others the insights and strengths that my own struggles in ministry, albeit under different circumstances, have taught me. I also have a ministry of encouragement: to women so placed, my whole life story, without my ever opening my mouth, speaks of both the possibility and the inevitability of women's ministry in western cultures. Quite simply, by what I am I show the broad sweep of the direction in which God is moving. In this regard, people often say they see me as a role model, but I think the issue is both more complex and more simple than that, for, since I come from a different country, and the contact is so brief, the opportunities for modelling are scarce. This is a great relief to me. They really only need me to affirm that, in the midst of the hostility they are experiencing, there is a place for women within the ordained ministry of the church.

However, whenever I am in a country or a diocese that does not ordain women as priests, then I inevitably, and very openly, take on the exclusion that is the lot of the local women. By this, I mean that I accept that I am not permitted to celebrate the Eucharist. This is a real contrast for me, because one of the major functions of my life as a bishop is to ordain others to celebrate the Eucharist in their communities. In accepting this restriction, I draw attention to the exclusion of the local women and I identify with it, and in so doing revive my own memories of exclusion. It is a painful privilege.

Where women are ordained as priests, but not as bishops, the excluding behaviours of the local church leaders are less marked. Functioning as a bishop outside of one's own diocese is more a matter of honour received than of sacramental tasks performed. I find, however, that there is frequently· an awkwardness, which can range from some rather petty acts of exclusion, like a nervousness about my wearing a mitre, or what I might do with my hands, to some outright attempts at insult. I simply take no notice, but neither do I offer such behaviour the protection of secrecy. It is not directed at me personally, but at what God and the church have called me to be; and I know that local church leaders who indulge in such acts of petty oppression are more wounded by their oppression than I am.

The pastoral theme, with a different slant, occurred when I was in the Diocese of Toronto in Canada in 1993. The Canadian church was among the first to ordain women as priests, a year or so before New Zealand. But they had not elected a woman as a bishop, and they were wondering why. I had a strong sense that in spending a day with the clergy of that diocese I was ministering pastorally, not to individuals, but to the church in that place. I scarcely talked about the reality of being a woman bishop; but, since they were about to hold an electoral synod to elect two new assistant bishops, focused rather on the role of a bishop and the expectations that the church placed on its bishops. I had a sense that it was not what I said that was significant, it was quite simply that in being there and in talking as a bishop with them the possibility of a woman being bishop became more real. It was a delight to hear that they had subsequently elected Victoria Matthews to be one of their assistant bishops.

The second of the reasons that I am asked to go overseas is related precisely to who I am and what I am at this point in the history of the

Anglican Communion. In 1988 the Lambeth Conference passed a permissive but cautious motion giving the go-ahead to the ordination of women as bishops, and this was followed within a few months by the election and ordination of Barbara Harris as Assistant Bishop in the Diocese of Massachusetts in the USA. Since then, the Anglican Communion has been slowly working out what it means to be part of this new reality. Following Lambeth 1988, the Archbishop of Canterbury established a commission on Women in the Episcopate which was chaired by the Archbishop of Armagh, Robin Eames. I was invited to join them as an observer for their meeting which was held in London in December 1993.

There were many who thought that the Commission had seriously damaged their credibility in leaving it so long before they invited one of the women bishops to join them. And before I went I numbered myself among such people. But I would have to say that I felt that the value of any contribution I could make depended not on what I said but, once again, on who and what I was. The simple fact of my presence spoke of the inevitability of women becoming bishops, so the questions that the Commission addressed focused not on *should* there be a woman bishop and *if* there is a woman bishop; but rather on *how* do we maintain communion within the diverse range of churches that comprise the Anglican Communion, in the light of the reality that there *are* bishops who are women? I felt again that the symbolic impact of my presence was high.

There is a third reason or set of reasons why I am asked to go overseas which I find less easy to define, and about which I would have to say I am less comfortable, but ambiguously so. In many places, particularly in North America, there is considerable interest in me and in the job that I am doing as a woman who is a diocesan bishop at this point in the history of the Anglican Communion. But in many senses the interest is superficial and goes little beyond the pleasure of meeting. I can feel that I am little more than a symbol that reinforces their established commitment to the ordination of women as both priests and bishops. Their commitment is not in doubt, and does not need reinforcing. So, in such circumstances, I try to avoid the assumption that I will talk directly about my experience as a woman bishop, for that would mean focusing intolerably on myself. I would rather talk about the New Zealand church, and in particular about the ways in which we are trying to address issues of justice for the indigenous people of our country within the life of the church. In this way I am talking about something real. I always find such situations much more convincing when I am invited to engage in some dialogue at depth, and when the time can become a mutual learning experience.

Stretching

When the new wave of the women's movement began in the 1970s, women, myself among them, felt some urgency about making the structures of the church more just for women through the acceptance of women's ordination. Our thinking was that we would in this way make the church we knew and loved more acceptable to our sisters who were outside the church. The motivation was a profound combination of feminist insight interweaving with a desire that the sheer thrill of contact with spiritual reality and empowerment which we had found within the church would become accessible to more people, to more women.

But we were seriously mistaken. The rapid secularization of our society in the last twenty years has made it much harder for anyone, man or woman, to respond to the call of Christ. In the last twenty years or so the gulf has widened between the cutting edge of feminist thinking and the structural, personal and theological reality of the church, which has really changed very little. Yes, there are a lot more ordained women and our language is much more inclusive, but the undertow of patriarchy has scarcely been checked.[3]

Meanwhile the feminist critique of Christianity has deepened. At a general level this is associated with the feminist critique of power and of institutions of power, and the church cannot expect to be spared. Associated with the critique of power is the difficulty that feminist thinking has in coping with the concept of God, let alone the concept of a transcendent God who is external to our being. It simply is not perceived as supportive or encouraging of the identity and aspirations of women, which is seen as the primary validation for any theology that would speak to women. We are here revisiting the feminist essentialist issue that I discussed in Chapter 1. The question is really very simple: is the God that we know through conventional Christian faith and worship large enough to embrace the identity and aspirations of women? I firmly believe that this God is, that God is all magnitude and mystery and utterly unable to be hijacked by either gender. But it is the experience of women that this is a God that men have made 'in their own image'. These then are the reservations expressed by women out of the pain they have experienced.

The issue goes far beyond questions of the language that we use about God, or even about the gender of God. Quite simply, the conventional notion of an all-powerful, all-knowing, all-seeing being who claims to have made us and to have an on-going claim on our life is a nonsense, if not an anathema, to women seeking their own empowerment. No matter how much Christian feminist theology explores the evidence for the female attributes of God, the insights of the Wisdom tradition, the relational mutuality of the Trinity and so on, the fact is that the overwhelming image remains of God as a vengeful, mirthless, dominating male deity. It seems that there is nothing we can do to displace that.

The problem deepens when we come to consider Christology, for there the dominant image of the crucified Christ is profoundly unacceptable in much feminist thinking. This God, this male deity, is one who demands payment for the fact that he has been disobeyed, and sentences his only son to a violent death. Concepts like expiation, blood-sacrifice, condemnation and guilt-offering have led writers such as the post-Christian feminist theologian Mary Daly to dismiss the 'gospel' as sado-masochistic. Her spine-chilling summary of Christianity as 'a necrophilic religion centring around a dead man hanging on a cross'[4] finds solemn echo in the writings of many more women.

The critique deepens and really bites when the parallel is drawn between the sacrificial and expiatory interpretation of the crucifixion and the reality of child abuse that is the experience of so many women. The concept of justice that becomes normative through this view of the cross is in fact highly distorted, and is notoriously unsuccessful in creating true equality or real justice. It supports a system of domination and uses the name of justice to keep the powerful on top and prevent the oppressed from speaking out. It has been labelled 'divine child abuse' because it suggests that God the Father has the *right* to require such a sacrifice from God the Son, however willing the son is claimed to be, and thus it sanctions a patriarchal model of parental power, in which child abuse frequently occurs.

It makes no difference to point out that God is a God of love and that such an understanding of the cross makes no sense from that standpoint. The sad reality is that this view of the atonement has supported a dominant, violent and excluding patriarchal power in family, society and church. Children have been viciously punished by fathers 'for their own good', and women have been beaten mercilessly and not infrequently in the name of a 'righteous' God. The record of clergy in dealing with such abuse is more a record of collusion, in the name of maintaining the marriage or the parental relationship.

It is just impossible to deny that this interpretation of the cross is a significant strand in Christian social theology and practice. Christian feminist theologians may weep at being the inheritors of such a history, and they seek to find and to write about many other understandings of the cross – and fortunately there are many of these – but none of this makes any impact on a feminism concerned at the continuing evidence of child abuse, and angry at anything that appears to sanction it.

Such a critique is itself enormously powerful. In the energy of anger and of mockery it cannot see the God who weeps too, and who suffers with and when anyone suffers; the God who can be united with us in our suffering and transform the death experience into a birth experience. Any such understanding as this caves in under the anger, and itself enters into a hole of suffering, for, if its adherents are to be at all true to the God of love with whom they want to keep faith, they cannot retaliate with anger, or even with theological reason, and neither would they wish to belittle the reality of the abuse inflicted by patriarchal structures.

The anger kindled by the 'divine child abuse' interpretation of the cross has left many Christian feminists who still identify with church structures feeling very isolated and very stranded. For we, in our life, our work and our commitments, contribute to the life and the health of the very church that has been responsible for sanctioning such behaviour. It has been a humiliating experience; we have had to realize that, despite our commitments, the church is still extraordinarily patriarchal and that we are not able to save it: only God can do that. We have wept to find ourselves caught up in an institution with such a vile history, and we have wept at the loss of our friends who have found our continuing association with it quite incomprehensible. To maintain relationships, communication has at times been an intolerably stretching experience.

But, somewhere in the midst of all this pain, we have re-found and been re-found by the God who hung with us in all the pain of humankind, the God who was stretched and in that stretching found birth.

10

Relationships

═══════

EXORCIZING ABEL

In a dream not long sped,
I stood on the sands, in the glassy-shattering reach of the waves,
Quarrelling with my sister,
And caught her arm, as in their first furious childish quarrel
Cain caught at Abel's sleeve.

From Robin Hyde, 'Sisters'

The personal and social impact upon me of becoming a bishop was such that every single one of my relationships shifted: my family, my friends, my working relationships. The extraordinary novelty of what was happening was personally highly disruptive.

This chapter seeks to explore the nature of this disruption, and both the process of re-forming relationships that ensued and the character of those relationships. It was such a difficult time that I found myself, sometimes rather blindly, holding onto the truth that I was still a human being and I still had a right to relate to others in ways that reflected, stretched and consoled my humanity. Even bishops, as a kindly stranger told me, have a right to be happy.

It is essentially a case study in what happens when an individual comes up against an enormously demanding structure; it is the intersection of the personal and the political.

Transition

One of the most pleasant things about that time was that a number of old friends and associates with whom I had lost touch took the opportunity that the publicity afforded of renewing our acquaintance. In the mass of mail that followed there were some real gems, and I am profoundly grateful for that.

For my family, there was first and foremost the question of how they were to react to the fact that the election had happened, and that the change in my relationship to the church and the world beyond would undoubtedly affect them, each in different ways. And each one, for different reasons but also in collusion with each other, decided that it was all right by them.

Next was the need to come to grips with the fact that we would have to shift to Dunedin. We had lived in Wellington for all our family life and had only a passing knowledge of the southern city. We realized that all the friendships we would make in Dunedin would be new friends who had only known us in that new job. It was indeed a wrench to be leaving Wellington; in some ways, and in retrospect, the farewell party that my women friends put on for me was like being present at one's own funeral. Not that there were speeches, and the focus was far more on the excitement of the future than at a real funeral, but I was still amazed that there was such a gathering and that so many people had a stake in what I was doing.

That was even more evident when the ordination came round. It was highly significant for me that so many of my friends travelled south and took part in the service, offering, after all the symbols of ministry had been given, the Celtic blessing 'May the road rise before you'. And too so many women both within and outside the church had contributed to the making of my cope and mitre. It was quickly clear from the excitement that accompanied my ordination as a bishop that, at least at the beginning of my ministry, I was bishop not just for the people of the Diocese of Dunedin but also for a much wider gathering.

Settling

It was all quite impossible. But I was amazed at the way the hype and the excitement were so empowering of other women. The suggestive power of novelty can be very exciting; and for a while, a short while, I thought I could do anything. How wrong I was. Fortunately, novelty fades inevitably with the passing of time. Gradually the width and the depth of the expectations that had been laid upon me began to take on more realistic proportions.

They adjusted most rapidly among the people who came to know me best. For the first two years that I was in the job, I did no travel overseas and the minimal amount within our New Zealand church. I had everything to learn and I wanted to get to know these people who had called me to be their bishop. I wanted to listen to them, to learn their hopes, their fears, what they were easy telling me and what they hoped no one else would tell me. I knew that the only place that God could teach me how to be a bishop was among the people for whom I was called to be bishop.

I also needed to get to know the provinces of Otago and Southland, parts of New Zealand I knew next to nothing about; what of their history, their stories, their values, their loyalties? It was all there for me to discover and it was just wonderful that so many people were so willing so rapidly to share their lives with us. It was a long process of grafting our story onto their story, and although I have now well and truly put down roots it still goes on. I am profoundly grateful to these good people.

I did indeed have an enormous amount to learn. These were all people to whom at my ordination I had expressed a primary commitment, and I intended to give primary expression to that by engaging seriously in the people and places and processes with which I was newly involved. It took a lot of concentrated time, and there is still a way to go. But it has got to the delicious stage of sensing that I will never know it all, because God has made people of a fascinating and constantly evolving complexity. The excitement and privilege of such engagement grows no less with time. I praise God for that.

In addition, like the whole world, I was aware that God was doing a 'new thing', but also like the whole world I could not yet see the shape of it; it was a promise with no form. I needed to be with the people for whom I was bishop in order to find out what it meant to be a bishop. This way I would, in part, be doing my theology in a way I have come to regard as authentic: in action and reflection and in dialogue with the Christian Scriptures and tradition. How could I possibly have anything of any integrity to say about episcopacy, about women in episcopacy, without that experience? Indeed, at the time of my ordination I was asked what I began to feel were a distressing number of questions along these lines and could only repeat, in a way that failed to satisfy my questioners, 'I can only keep praying and see where God leads me'.

I am still human

I scarcely knew myself during those first few months, years even, and neither did other people. I began to be called by titles and names that sat awkwardly with me. This diocese had been accustomed to calling its bishop 'Bishop' on all occasions. To me, the title designated a measure of formality, and it took a while before people realized that it was quite acceptable to call me by my first name. And too I began to be called by the full version of my name, Penelope. I wondered if 'Penny', the name that had served me well hitherto, was good enough for the job, for these people. It became hard to recognize myself at times. This came to me in particular incidents which acted as vignettes on how others saw me. One most startling occurred when I met a lay person in the supermarket: 'Do bishops have to shop too?' Another was when I was waiting for a blood test and a cathedral parishioner said to me 'Et tu, bishop!' My very humanity seemed to be in question.

All this alerted me to just how difficult it would be to form real relationships with people, to get to know them at some depth and to let them get to know me. For a while it seemed as if few people wanted to do that; they preferred to see me in role. Celia Hahn notes that those who look at authority figures from the outside are not well positioned to distinguish person and role, and find it natural to focus on the role.[1] But from the vantage point of knowing myself from the inside I realized that I was both more than the role and less than the role. I remain profoundly grateful to those people who saw what was happening and took the initiative themselves to develop friendship with us.

I found the role of bishop so limiting in the early days that I was at times severely tempted to throw it over as I tried to resist being defined by my role in all my relationships. Yet there was a tension, for, like it or not, I was bishop, and that fact was bound to affect all my contacts with others. It took a while before I learnt what the mix was and how to hold its elements in tension.

Friendships

Although I had moved to a new city, the life of a bishop is very mobile and I rejoiced in being able to keep up with my friends outside of Dunedin when they were kind enough to have me to stay when I attended meetings in Wellington or other cities. They were very necessary to me, especially in the early years. They remain pure gold.

In Dunedin I found it difficult to make friendships that were simply enjoyable. Most pragmatically, and most regrettably, I found I had very little time to give to such relationships. In time I realized that some of the life of my spirit would wither if I did not do that. But for some potential friends it was too late and they gave me up as lost.

I found too, quite early on, that it was not wise to mix business and pleasure; there is so much that happens in my work which I am not free to share and that can give a very misleading impression in a general conversation. Since talking shop is one of the major ways in which clergy get on with each other, that cut out quite a bit of talk. But there were other people. I also learnt not to overload a friendship with my own personal needs and problems. The confusing life of my first years made this very tempting but it invariably stressed out a friendship. There was still plenty left of me, that was not needy, to share.

Working relationships

While the big stage of liturgy is the context of public ministry, it is not the stage for the formation of working relationships. The setting for these is the detail of the job, frequently operating in one-to-one situations, where I was trying, and learning as I went, to establish a style of working that was predictable and consistent. I endeavoured to move carefully and slowly, taking time to listen to all perspectives and to filter them through my prayer life. And I endeavoured to set up situations where not only did I listen to others, and they to me, but also where they were enabled to listen to each other. In time, I found it was possible to reach decisions that could have a wide measure of acceptability.

I put a high priority in setting the groundwork for trust to develop. I was fortunate in that the diocese was well staffed and there were a lot of wonderful people among both the office staff and the clergy. It was a privilege to be working with them; and from where I am placed to evaluate that process, it seems to me that it went well.

It is never easy to know how to understand the difficulties that arise in forming working relationships. As I look back on the difficulties that I experienced, I can see that some of them are clearly related to personality and some to gender and structural factors.

It was in a way strange that the Diocese of Dunedin had elected a woman to be their bishop, for at the time of my ordination there were only four ordained women in the diocese, two of whom were well established and well respected. But the senior clergy and administration were all men, a situation that has largely continued. Conversely, the women, who were testing the water about how they would relate to me, were on the margins of the church. The dynamics in each case were quite different.

Some of the women had high expectations of me, quite unrealistic expectations, and I could only disappoint them. In some cases their expectations amounted to a ready-made blueprint of the sort of person I should be and a ready-set agenda which I had to carry out. I could do neither. A number of men also had such well-formed expectations, but, together with most of the women, they persisted with the relationship and in time we came to accept each other. But there were some who could not. And a particular dynamic at work where some women were concerned, that of a sense of mutual betrayal, gave the situation with women a highly emotively charged character that was not there with men. I took some comfort from the fact that it was only a very few who moved themselves out of the reach of any ongoing relationship.

I realized that these women saw me, in my resistance to doing and being all that they wished me to do and to be, as buying into a style of authority that they identified as top-down and male. They saw it as a very negative model and, as I struggled to find a workable style that was exactly the opposite of that, I was very hurt to find I had so failed them. Women who identify as feminist often have a very high expectation of friendship; 'sisterhood' is sacred as well as powerful. In reality women are a diverse bunch and it is to be expected that some will not choose to be friends with others. It is still disappointing. A further bind came when I realized that although this strategy allowed them to steal an illusion of independence, their picture was in fact like a photographic negative; the fact that their ideal was defined as 'not me' meant that it was still my image that was printing their analysis. There was no escape from the power of my position, either for myself or for them. 'How can we exorcize Abel?'

With men, the situation was very different: I had for some time, both in my professional life in educational research and in my life in the church, worked with numerous men in authority positions. Their visions and viewpoints, their hang-ups and their strengths were well familiar to me and I knew how to relate to them with respect but with the clear expectation that they would respect me. I thought that I would have no unforeseen problems. But what I had not reckoned on was that a number of them would have had little experience of working with a woman in a leadership position, certainly not in the church: we are rare beings. And after a while I began to understand that there were gender-related reasons why they found it difficult. Sometimes these involved their strong sense that I did not really know what I was doing and that things would run more smoothly if they were to run them for me; sometimes it involved sheer disbelief that I could believe what I did believe, propose what I did propose, and work in the style that I was seeking to develop. In fact, there were several times near the beginning when some took advantage of my more slow-moving and consultative style, and seized the high ground. I found myself thoroughly detesting the competitive mode that this moved us into, and with considerable difficulty holding on to the values and style that I was endeavouring to communicate. More than once, the demands of integrity meant that I conceded victory in a struggle.

I also found that a dynamic with some men was that they were projecting maternal images onto me. In one case I found this meant that I was supposed to be sweet and gentle and to let this man take care of all my problems. When he found that was not how I saw the relationship and that I intended to do the job myself, he was very disappointed; it took a long time to build something more productive.

A new style

In time I realized that my tendency to act slowly was surprising people. One of the younger clergy said to me when I was about six months into the job that people had learnt that if I was pushed, I would probably say no; but that if I was given time I would probably find good reason, based also on the reactions of others, to agree to a particular position. Despite the huge number of pressures that were on me, I acquired a reputation for not panicking when things went wrong, but for slowly praying and working through them until a resolution was found. Some people found this very frustrating and their own anxiety levels could not cope; others found it reassuring.

It is not uncommon for clergy, whether priests or bishops, to find that the administrative load of their office weighs heavily upon them, and for it to be the downside of the job. I certainly do not enjoy shuffling paper, but I have been richly blessed with an excellent personal assistant who helps me to do it much more quickly than I would do it by myself. When I was an assistant curate my vicar used to tell me repeatedly that it was not possible to run a parish from behind a desk, and I am sure that the same is true of a diocese. I know that I need to be out and about and with people in order to be effective. And that is what I enjoy doing.

However, I have learnt to see the implications of the fact that the heart of the word 'administration' is 'ministry' and that behind every piece of paper, every letter that passes across my desk, is a person; and these people, even though they may be quite distant from me, are as important and as precious as ever were any of my parishioners who were much closer to me. So my prayer has become very closely related to those pieces of paper and I endeavour to respond to them with care. I have also come to realize that proper administration provides people with a sense of security, of place and affirmation of the value of the contribution that they are prepared to make. All these are quite proper expectations for people to hold of those who are in authority in the church.

Contradictions

However, it does not always fit together so easily. The ministry of a bishop is all too often full of contradictions, and all too often these contradictions are gender related. I have often found myself musing on how I can both model and operate a consultative and inclusive style of leadership, one that is open to the integrity and the viewpoints of others, and at the same time, by the space that I leave, prevent others from filling it with doctrinaire and restrictive decisions.

Essentially I have come to learn when I need to let something go and when I need to reclaim it for the good of the whole. The basis of this comes back to the quality of my relationships, my love for those I am dealing with, both those on hand and those who will be affected by the outcome of the decisions. In this I have been profoundly influenced by a saying of Dietrich Bonhoeffer which I keep, in large print and with the appropriate changes of pronoun, on my study wall, to keep me on track:

> She who loves her dream of the Christian community more than the Christian community itself becomes a destroyer of the latter, even though her personal intentions may be ever so honest and earnest and sacrificial.
> God hates visionary dreaming; it makes the dreamer proud and pretentious.

Relationships without love, that are there merely to meet an agenda, frequently fall apart under stress. God asks more than utilitarianism of the relationships that we form to enable us to do God's work.

The power of power: pastoral questions

Any comment on the work of a bishop will point to the tension between the pastoral role and the juridical role, when the bishop is required to operate by the rule book in a way that conflicts with the interest of someone with whom they are in a pastoral relationship. There is a real difficulty in maintaining the balance between the two. There are some[2] who will say that because the juridical function is so heavily apparent in the office of a bishop, it is impossible for a bishop to act pastorally. There are others who point out that if a bishop comes too close to any community or individual within the diocese then they cease to have any impact on the situation; they cease, in effect, to be bishop for them.

I personally found this ambiguity of distance to be a considerable loss. As a parish priest I had been privileged to be close to people in their need, their pain, their hopes and their yearnings, and I was also close to the community who had asked me to lead them. As a bishop it was very different. With individuals, it is not easy for me to function as both priest and bishop, but not impossible. With some people this works, and I am able to get reasonably close to them and be of some personal use; with others it is more difficult.

In part these difficulties can be traced to personality. It is not uncommon in discussions of women's ministry to claim that women are more effective pastorally than men. Many are, but in my experience this is not necessarily true; there are men who are fine pastors and women who are extraordinarily careless. The raw fact of the matter is that in my ministry, as in that of most other people, there are some for whom I am effective and some for whom I am not. Such limitations are an inevitable consequence of being human. Certainly, one of the dynamics that makes it difficult as a bishop is the perception that some people have of the power of a bishop, which for them totally overshadows any ability to look for pastoral care from that quarter. They are unwilling to expose their vulnerability. It takes time and a good deal of trust for people to learn that I too am vulnerable, that I too make mistakes – often.

It is only possible for me to act pastorally for people when they trust me, and the degree to which I am effective is a measure of that trust. I have found that lay people, who perhaps do not see my juridical role so clearly, are more open to that trust and I am able to function as their spiritual director, whether formally or informally, and also to be their confessor. This is less easy for clergy, but not impossible. When it happens there is a real sense of doing, at depth, what I am called to do, and I thank God.

Positional authority can impede my pastoral effectiveness in other situations. In all my dealings with people I seek to have real relationships which are fundamentally honest, even if it means that I sometimes have to blow people's expectations in order that they will see beyond what they want to see and what they think they see. When I am working with someone who sees my authority as primarily a function of role, it is all too easy for me to feel alienated and separated; real communication is very difficult under such circumstances. So I try to establish a very human relationship with them, so that any authority I have comes from the quality of my engagement with them and with the issue at hand.

But the term 'pastoral' does not apply only to one-to-one relationships. A bishop is bishop for the whole church, both clergy and laity, so the health of the whole church is a prime focus. So much of the work is involved with wider church issues – administration, helping to plan the shape of ministry in a particular parish and so on. I have found here that it is important to develop the expectation that I will approach each one of these situations from a pastoral perspective. When people come to me and ask me to make a decision along lines that they propose, I will take the time to work through the issues with them; and too, I expect them to work through the issues with all the other people concerned.

It is not uncommon for some people or groups of people to attempt to hijack my authority; to tell me what I should do in a way that effectively asserts that authority over others. Appealing to a higher level of authority is not an uncommon tactic and is known throughout the church as it is in other hierarchical structures.

However, there are times when it is necessary for me to act out of the juridical role that a bishop has. Inevitably this means that there is a conflict between the need to maintain order and discipline within the church, and the welfare and happiness of some people. Despite the perception that so many people have of the power of a bishop, it always seems to come as a shock when I have to act in that way. This is certainly so when the matter in hand involves the disciplining of the clergy, for the clergy are accustomed to the expectation that the bishop is there to be their pastor and not their judge, and they can be very hurt. These are occasions when the interests of clergy and laity do not run together; it is in conflict that both the need for and the effect of authority is most noticeable.

There are gender issues here as well; people simply do not expect that a woman will act in a juridical manner, and there is surprise, resentment even, when it happens. There are a lot of contradictions in this, for the negative reactions to the exercise of authority by women are invariably strong, and yet there is the continuing need for the security that the proper use of authority guarantees.

That pedestal

An underlying theme that runs through all this discussion is the inevitable tendency that many people have to place me on a pedestal, and to feel that it is somehow unwise or unfair of them to engage in honest discourse. I find that this is both very distancing and strangely contradictory, for it is overwhelmingly the expectation that people have of those in Christian leadership that they will be able to get close to people. I found that it was really quite easy to break down these barriers when I was in parish ministry, but the sheer size of my ministry as a bishop makes this much harder. There are times when I find this very frustrating.

It is also limiting in ways that are not of my choosing, for it means that, unless I have taken initiative and worked hard at the relationship, I can but rarely find people who will risk robust dialogue with me and I must continually be aware that the feedback I receive may be motivated, albeit unintentionally, by flattery. When I was ordained someone told me that I would never want for a meal and I would never be told the truth. It was a frightening prospect.

The pedestal effect means that I both have to and wish to work hard at establishing relationships that will lead to honesty and reality. It means that not only do I have to be aware of the positional power that I hold, but I also need to avoid the somewhat diminishing if fashionable talk of empowering others, because such talk simply reinforces the notion that I have power and others do not. They do, and I respect that.

The pedestal effect can be quite damaging. It can be hard for people to say no to me, yet the value of what they have to give is only as good as the genuineness of their commitment, and there is nothing worse than reluctant volunteers who effectively prevent a job from being done. I find that I have to work hard to overcome the sense of insecurity that my positional power can give to people, and make it safe for them to say no, and still stay in relationship with me and with the church.

The pedestal effect is also a factor to be reckoned with in my relationships with the Christian community at large, not just with individuals. Just as it is not always easy for me to create an environment where people can, and will, take responsibility for their own actions, so it is not easy for me to enable the church, specifically that part of the church for whom I am bishop, to take responsibility for its ministry and mission, working in partnership with me as I seek to create the wider environment in which that ministry can flourish. There is within all such relations of authority a tendency towards dependency rather than mutuality, and dependency is essentially passive and disempowering. The challenge to me, and it is one that I am constantly working on, is how to get the Christian community to know and to claim the power that God has already given it, and to run with it strongly.[3]

Our hierarchical structures are frequently so destructively divisive; division, however subtly it takes shape, does not reflect the unity we have in the heart of God and is not conducive to good mission. The issues raised here indicate a challenge to me to offer and receive solidarity; it is also a challenge to the church to offer and receive solidarity. Strong and healthy relationships within the body of Christ are the sinews that bind the body, and are very precious.

Did Abel have a sister?

Women who move into powerful positions that were established by a male system of power are often aware that they can be displayed and used as a token. I am very aware that this happens, but because the circumstances of my election were so genuine it is hard for people to recognize or admit. However, there are some subtleties of interaction through which my position as a bishop can reinforce the patriarchal structures in ways that are by themselves not significant but can have a cumulative effect.

One of the ways in which this happens is when senior positions are vacant in the diocese, and the opinion is expressed that because the bishop is a woman the appointment in this case should be a man. The same line has been taken with regard to the continuous and long-standing debate over whether or not Dunedin's cathedral choir, which is all-male, should admit women. There are two implications here: first, that it would not be wise to have too many women in positions of leadership; and second, that because the diocese has a woman as a bishop it has proved its commitment to gender equality once for all.

A similar dynamic occurs within our national church, where people seeking to get other women ordained to the episcopate have been told 'You already have one'. This line of thinking makes me acutely aware of the persistently patriarchal bias of the church. What I hear is that if I do not draw attention to the fact that I am a woman, and do not ask too much for women from the church, then I am acceptable. But do not, I hear, expect too much. The effect is to make me feel silenced, which is the effect patriarchal structures have always had on women; I certainly need to be careful and wise about when I break silence. From my position on the other side of the patriarchal bar, so to speak, this is extraordinarily constricting and very isolating.

Responses

When I began this job, I was naive enough and arrogant enough to think that I could please everyone. After all, that was the expectation that was running high at the time of my ordination. I very quickly learnt the impossibility of this, but it was not a lesson that was easy to learn. My difficulties were those that I have found to be common among women in ministry; they stem from the fact that most women are pre-programmed to please people, and find it very hard to say no. This is a quick route to burn-out, but it also results in a ministry that is only reactive, that never has the time and energy to initiate action.

In many ways it is a very secure ministry because one always has immediate feedback that what one is doing is acceptable. But as a strategy for choosing priorities, it leaves little room for God to act.

For my own part, I found that it was not until I learnt to take control over what went into my diary that I could begin to have some sense that God and I were working together on the job. I had to say no, but I was able to take a shortcut, because my excellent personal assistant often did it for me!

There is a real seductiveness about pleasing people that goes deeper than simply responding to requests; it is the seductiveness of seeking approval, seeking to be liked, seeking to have one's wisdom, insight and skill admired. Again I think this is a trap for women, who seek, and need to seek, the security of knowing that they are on the right track. But inappropriate admiration spells danger for those of us in ministry; we need to sit loose on the judgements of this world, to trust our own ability to discern God's way. When Christian leaders unquestioningly accept the admiration seductively laid out before them, they have forfeited their authenticity.[4]

Beneath all these questions of the relationships that form between a bishop and the community that he or she serves is the underlying question of where the bishop is located within the community. The clearest image deriving from the hierarchical structure of the church is that of 'oversight', of one set over, but bishops have been struggling against this since the time of Augustine: 'For you I am a bishop, but with you I am a Christian . . . As then I am more pleased to be redeemed with you than I am to be set over you, I shall, as the Lord commanded, be more completely your servant.'[5]

Bishops also need redemption and also belong with the people of God. For my own part, I have tried when appropriate to identify with the people, to take my stand with them before God. As a bishop I have more opportunity to worship from the pews than ever I did as a parish priest, and I am grateful for that. I have acquired the custom, when presiding at the Eucharist, of using 'we' in giving the absolution.

The traditional symbol of a bishop is that of a shepherd's crook, the sign of Christ, the good shepherd who laid down his life for his sheep. Another symbol, one which comes from South America and which also refers to shepherding, suggests that the ministry of a bishop can be likened to a llama who lives among the sheep, grazes with them, sleeps with them, but when they are in danger, becomes as fierce and as wild as any beast and drives the danger away.[6]

11
Praying

THE SPIRIT FUGITIVE

Oh break the walls of sense apart
And let the spirit fugitive
The light engendered of itself
Is not a light by which to live.
From Eileen Duggan, 'Untitled Poem'

I reckon that I have always been a person who prays, from right back to the time of my earliest memories when my greatest delight was to go for long walks by myself, for there, it seemed, I was able to grasp a sense of who I was in relation to the sheer size of God's creation. I knew then that I was a 'natural', but in those early years the delight in being alone was mingled with a desire to escape. As I grew up and became familiar with the Christian tradition, I began to make the links between the deepest parts of my being and the day-to-day questions with which both I and all of humankind were confronted.

At the time when I became a bishop, I was well settled in my prayer life. I had been a priest for some seven and a half years, not long if the history of most bishops is anything to go by, but long enough to get established; and longer, I noted, than St Augustine had been before they made him a bishop.

Episcopacy threw my spiritual life, my relationship with God, into considerable disarray. As in my relationships with people, I scarcely knew who I was or how simply to be in relationship. But God was persistent even if I was not; and in the lengthy process of re-establishing that relationship, I learnt more about myself and about God than I had in the whole of my life. But first some history.

Some history

In every way, religiously speaking, mine was not a politically correct childhood. It could not possibly have been; it was so profoundly mixed. The school I attended from the age of seven through to fifteen had been founded by the Sisters of St Mary the Virgin at Wantage. The sisters were only residually there when I was a pupil, but their influence was still very strong. It was very high church, and totally uncompromising in its Christian commitment and witness. As was common in that part of the church, faith was not drawn out of us, it was assumed – but very strongly and very confidently; and there was no avoiding the challenge to live strong and committed lives. The worship was magnificent; I grew to love darkened chapels, candlelight, early Eucharist and singing *Jerusalem* at least once a year. I am by no means the only product of that environment, which knew that women had souls and minds as well as bodies, but which never dreamt of ordaining women or of their seeking ordination.

We studied the Scriptures, but it was called 'Divinity'. I was taught about the great tradition of which I was an inheritor, stretching back – and this is the part I remember very clearly – to the crossing of the Red Sea and the escape from Egypt. Great stuff, that! There was no biblical criticism in it, either explicit or implied. It was all the great story of our faith. I revelled in it, quite unquestioningly, but it was not the faith itself that was taught; in that environment it was all mind. But faith was *caught*, very thoroughly.

It was in the worship that both my imagination and my heart were stretched: I began to see that here was a vision of humanity that embraced the longings of my isolated heart, the enormity of the universe that I knew God had created. And also, in all the fascinating stories about Jesus, especially in his death and resurrection, which in worship always had such a high emotional charge, I knew that God was present in all the muddle that was in between the magnificence and the mess, the muddle from which I had sought to escape.

There was another strand to my life, another input from the world of religion, the parish church that I attended with my family. It ran exactly parallel to my life at school, because that was a day school. The parish church was one of a string of churches around southern England that had been founded in the early years of the Victorian era by the Simeon Trust, set up by the eighteenth-century evangelical Charles Simeon. It was very strong evangelically, and I responded warmly to the more explicit challenges it threw out to me. In fact I chose, against the grain I might say, to be confirmed from that church rather than from the school, and I taught Sunday school there for many years. The biblical challenge was strong, straightforward and often repeated. I attended many a mission there; the late Bryan Green was a frequent missioner. I often gave my life to Christ, but I could not understand why no one seemed to believe that that was where my life had been for as long as I could remember.

Despite the realities of the present-day church, I never felt any conflict or lack of harmony between these two traditions. They both clearly told the same story and spoke to the experience that I knew in the depth of my being. There was an urgency and a sense of commitment about them both and both made strong claims on me. But the claim that they made was to the call of Christ and not to a particular way of being church. From this blending of two traditions, which took place so peacefully in me and which I only now recognize were regarded by others as being totally separate, I learnt that God was far bigger than any one expression of our commitment or our worship. From the confidence of each of those persuasions I learnt that God was knowable, and that there was even – and this is not a contradiction – a knowable quality about God's unknowability and about the mystery of the God that I had known so well since my early days. The limitations of my humanity were something I learnt about much later.

When I left school I wanted to be a nun; I even spoke with one of the sisters from Wantage, but was persuaded that it would be advisable to wait a few years. This was a wise response, not only for the general reason that I was young, but also because, in seeking a life of contemplative prayer, I was acting out of my earliest impulses which had contained a strong element of escapism. I had learnt too that God was part of all the living that I and anyone else was engaged in. So I went off to university, and there I refound the God in the middle – between immensity and minutiae. This was how I had come to think of God with the intellectual part of my being. I also had my view widened to embrace far more of the world and the affairs of human beings than ever the constricted and very safe arena of my childhood could show me.

I went to Edinburgh University, where the Presbyterian Church flourished and the student chaplaincy nurtured a very evangelical Student Christian Movement. I continued to satisfy my by then deeply instinctual need for worship within the more select bounds of the Anglican chaplaincy, but the world of intellectual excitement was beginning to draw me and I was finding it hard to make the connection between that world and my Christian life. The event that did furnish a link – and this may well surprise in the light of subsequent developments – was the publication of John Robinson's book *Honest to God*. I knew nothing of the controversy. The scandal of a bishop authoring such a book was something I learnt about much later: the license it was purported to give to all sorts of dubious morality, and so on. I quite simply found in it, for the first time, someone writing from the inside of the faith I knew so well, in a way that demanded and stretched my intelligence, that connected the young woman who was thoroughly enjoying her studies with the young woman who could not stop worshipping God if she tried.

It was also while I was at university that the wider concerns of the time began to impinge upon me. The early 1960s was the time the Cold War was still expanding and nuclear weapons were being deployed. The Polaris missile bases were being established in Scotland and there was apprehension and anger among the Scottish people. Within the SCM we debated this endlessly, but we also went marching in protest. I well remember the anguish that gripped me the first time that I walked down the middle of a street with a lot of other people shouting and waving placards, knowing fine how my parents would have disapproved. But I learnt that God was there too, and in all the concerns, the longings and the pain of God's people. I knew then that I could never go back to that convent – and I was pleased too that I had learnt to march, to stand publicly, if not fearlessly, for what I believed to be right.

Vocation

It was out of this initial sense of vocation, expanded and humanized by more years of living, and in particular by the rearing of a family, that my vocation to ordination as a priest crystallized.

Some years later, after marriage and the birth of children, I discovered, again along with many contemporaries, the feminist critique of Christianity. To cut a very long story short it was another turbulent time. I was involved with a group of women in questioning absolutely everything. It was a life-changing experience for us all; some of us left the church for ever, some of us were drawn further into it; and pulled by the urge to link body and spirit, I read avidly in Christian feminism. When I came to study theology straight, so to speak, it was like putting the cake under the icing. For I found it took me right back to the fervour of my childhood. This was a world, a world of the mind, where God and the practice of faith really mattered. In my study of the Scriptures, I came to realize that these were written from the inside of faith: here were people who had wrestled with all the questions I did. Who was this Jesus? Why did different people have different experiences of him? Something of the old evangelical love of the Scriptures and the ability to take them seriously had stayed with me, and I revelled in it all.

I began my study of theology a few years before our General Synod passed the canon permitting the ordination of women as priests, but in those days I had nothing to do with the affairs of the church and I still wonder at my confidence. Cause became call to some extent, as I brought my new-found theological skills to bear on the question, and I addressed a number of meetings about the ordination of women. They were all somewhat marginal gatherings and not the sort of place where church leaders would be present. I well remember the realization that there was a huge gap between the reality of my life, my experience of church, and the institution of the church. I was about to tread some very new territory.

To cut another long story short, the first time I applied for ordination, the bishop was horrified. Not only was I a woman, but I was married; as he saw it, my marriage should be my exclusive pre-occupation. After a number of years I was ordained; I went as a curate to St James' in Lower Hutt, and then I was parish priest at St Philip's in Karori West for just under five years. It was from there that I was elected to be Bishop of Dunedin.

Priest and bishop – some differences

I thoroughly enjoyed being a parish priest. It was for me a very integrated life: parish, family and prayer all interwove very happily. Above all, it was a very rhythmical life. I was regularly praying the round of the liturgy of the church, and I was in the same place with the same people every Sunday. I grew to know and to love them within the context of the lived and experienced love of God. Those were good years.

There was quite naturally a lot of grief in me when I left. In part I was prepared for that, but I still relished their notes, the stories about how their children were getting on and the progress that the parish was making in the building of a new church. As a bishop, pastoral relations are very different.

But I was not prepared for the loss of the rhythm of public prayer. The prayer life of a priest is very robustly supported by the regular, public and externalized worship of the parish. The worshipping life of a bishop is not so supported and frequently becomes more internalized. Now I am in a different place every Sunday, with different people, using a different lectionary; and each parish has their particularities in celebrating the liturgy. I found myself living entirely by my diary, and the sense of the predictability and security of the rhythm of parish life was lost to me. I grieved very deeply.

It was some time before I realized that the rhythm was not weekly or even monthly, but it was a yearly round. I was grateful to the presiding Bishop of the Anglican Church in Canada, who visited us some six months into the job, for pointing this out to me, and I waited in confidence for that moment of realization to come to me. But of course, being such a protracted spin, it took me several years to experience this myself, and it is really only just taking root in my being.

My sense of liturgical rhythm has also shifted. In parish life the celebrations of the major festivals of the church's year are wonderful parish family occasions and require considerable work from the priest and others to prepare well for them. They are worth every ounce of energy. They become milestones in the annual round. I find that is less marked now; it is not my job to prepare with others for the festivals of the liturgical year, and I find myself internally and spiritually less aware of the impact of the seasons of preparation and penance, Advent and Lent. I have as a consequence come to a deeper appreciation of the smaller rhythm of the daily office which is very noticeably cyclic and reflective in form. The incarnational structure of the office speaks very clearly to me of God with us. I often say this with others, but I often say it by myself and I am grateful for the opportunity it gives me to link my prayer with the whole Body of Christ as I seek to express not only my own prayer but the prayer of the whole church.

It is not always a liturgical round, although that is there as a sub-theme of my spiritual life. It is rather more a pastoral round: the pleasure of visiting and revisiting parishes and of building a shared experience of having worked through problems together. It depends in part on my making it clear that I am willing to be with them for ordinary occasions as well as the special celebrations. I thoroughly enjoy those celebrations, but it is wearying to have a party every week. That is not the kind of rhythm that I am looking for. As the years move round and familiarity grows, I find that my praying in preparation for these visits becomes much sharper.

In part, the annual round is administrative; meeting schedules have a relentless predictability. When I first realized this I groaned, because I have always been clear that I was not ordained to attend meetings. However, their very predictability can focus my prayer, and I have learnt to integrate the business of those meetings and my participation in them into my prayer life. When I am able to do this, I am much more open to both the presence and the participation of God in the structure and process of meetings and in the people who take part in them with me.

Praying the liturgy

It is always a challenge to those of us who lead worship to really pray the worship that we lead. If we care about the liturgy, some of our attention will go on to that. I have found that such personal and prayerful identification is the critical point of linkage between the church and myself. It is a gift that comes with the familiarity that is possible as a parish priest, and not a gift that is given to a bishop. It is not only a question of attention; if priest and people are accustomed to being together in the presence of God, then there is an ease that allows the mind to wander prayerfully and to take delight in seeing someone who has been absent for a while, in being proud and happy when a young person takes part in the liturgy and does it well, in sensing the grief of the recently widowed and in being open to the unexpected. Such praying the liturgy, priest and people together, is rarely possible as a bishop where there is so often the sense of being a visitor and being on show, and at the same time trying to be alert to the idiosyncrasies of each parish.

In my early years as a bishop there was a marked discontinuity between the person I was in public and the person I was before God; some of this I can trace to discontinuity that I was experiencing between liturgy and prayer and the difficulty I had in praying the liturgy. It was essentially the gap between my exterior life and my interior life, which always leaves one feeling fractured, because God created us to be whole people.

I came to value those occasions when I could pray the liturgy. I enjoy the times I am with a parish for some weeks in succession; and I truly appreciate the little church of St Andrew's at Maheno, in North Otago, near which we have a seaside crib (weekend cottage), and where I am often in the pews and sometimes take services for the vicar when he is on holiday.

But the most regular round for me is the early morning weekday Eucharists at the cathedral, on at least three days of the week, and if I am in town it is my turn to celebrate on Fridays. It is a precious opportunity for me to keep in touch with the liturgical rhythm and routine of the church. I have come truly to value those times, for they are the opportunity for me to 'pray with the church' as I undertook to do when I was ordained as a bishop; and I am profoundly grateful to the people who are regularly and faithfully 'the whole church' for me.

Praying the seasons

The itinerant life-style that as a bishop I inevitably lead has not been without its compensations. As the natural rhythms of the church's year have receded from the forefront of my spiritual consciousness, I have found increasing support in the natural rhythms of the annual cycle of the seasons. Such a cycle is of course intimately connected to the cycle of the church's year: Christmas at mid-winter, the light shining in the darkness; Easter with the arrival of new life; and the long green days of summer, when the brilliant green of the trees found a silent echo in the liturgical green that adorned the altars. But for me those associations belong to my childhood, a long time ago.

However, that awareness did teach me that the links that prayer makes reach well beyond the Christian community; they tie us in with the very breath of God's creation. It is the mystical and poetic aspect of incarnation, of God's solidarity with all creation and it is an awareness that has never left me, but which resurfaced in significance as I seek to find the basic rhythms on which my life is based.

When, at the age of 22, I made the transition from the northern hemisphere to the southern, like so many others I was faced with the transition from an easy synchronicity between the movements of the seasons and the movements of the church's year. So much of the accumulated understanding that the people of God have acquired about the significance of God's engagement with creation finds a ready image in the fecundity and promise of the natural world. But these are images and parallels that relate only to the northern cycle of seasons, and thus are partial.

The picture of this engagement is filled out in the southern hemisphere where all is reversed. This reversal makes me even more aware that God acts both with and independently of the seasons. For here there is no seasonal match with the Christian tradition, and yet Christ still is born amongst us at Christmas time and the celebration of his resurrection is real enough. I sometimes think our southern sequence saves us from too easy an identification of Christmas with the incarnation or of the resurrection of Jesus with seasonal rebirth. Yet the experience and the rhythm of the seasons has expanded my perception of the workings of God.

Our Christmas basks in the warmth and the brilliance of the mid-summer sun. 'Christ, the light of the world' takes on a new significance. And the red flowering pohutakawa tree that is such a vivid mark of Christmas in North Island coastal towns makes a magnificently simple Christmas tree, with its red on green colouring. There is a growing collection of Christmas carols that celebrate the delights of a New Zealand Christmas.

In the south, Lent and Easter is at the dying time of year, when all is becoming, slowly but surely, colder and darker. Ashes are the burning of the fallen leaves, Palm Sunday is the last shout of gold from trees that are awash with autumn brilliance. On Good Friday, the bare winter wood seems stark with death. The growing coldness and blackness, the shortening days and the wind that blows sharper make us very aware of the grief of Good Friday, and the newly exposed wood on the trees hangs like grieving crosses all round our cities and countryside. A recurring Easter image for me is the sight of a dying, just-on-dead tomato plant holding brilliant red fruit, bursting with seeds that will grow more fruit; death and the promise of life seem to hang together.

Into all this bursts the new life of Christ, defiant of the grave, defiant of the seasonal ordering of God's world, proclaiming the defeat of death, proclaiming redemption. It is the miraculous and utterly gratuitous gift of the resurrection. So Easter, the resurrection of our Lord, cuts right across all seasonal expectations. It is truly an astonishing event, defiant of all expectations and of all that has gone before. We notice the incongruences, but find that the divine mystery is thrown into sharp relief by them. And we have found that the resurrection is a splendid way to begin winter.

As I seek to trace the finger of God on the wandering movements of my life, I am aware of so much that is gift. As my appreciation of the width and depth of this gift has expanded with my life's journey across the world, so my sense of the value of what is given has deepened.

Contemplative prayer

This sense of gift has expanded into my life of prayer. Because I am not as close as I was to the mighty movements of the church's year, I was for a time, until my pattern of worship at the cathedral became established, quite rootless. And this was a time when, having so recently moved south from Wellington to Dunedin, the rest of my life was in severe upheaval. It was then that I began to find myself drawn repeatedly to my old longing for and practice of contemplative prayer. It had never really left me, but the routine of the priestly life had been so satisfying that I had not felt the need for it.

In my experience there are a lot of people who in their habitual mode of praying are contemplatives, but who from shyness or humility would not claim that they are drawn to 'the prayer of contemplation'. We have a lot to learn from the great spiritual teachers on prayer and many of us have rejoiced that their teachings have become more accessible in recent years. But as we wonder at the greatness of what they have to teach us, our own practice of prayer can fall into insignificance and possible misuse.

When I became a bishop, I was so hectically busy; and when I let up, all the 'deeds undone' flooded into my consciousness. I kept rigidly to the discipline of the daily office and of the Eucharist when possible, and that was very sustaining, but it was part of my working life, part of what I had to do. I felt again the pull of contemplative prayer, but did not see how God could call me to be both a contemplative and a bishop. I am profoundly grateful to the friend who saw my dilemma, encouraged me to give contemplation a go again, and pointed me back, with some tentativeness, towards the natural roots of my prayer life.

For me the prayer of contemplation takes time, is still and is without words. I am a visual person and I am greatly helped by both a candle and a crucifix. The candle acts as a focus; and such prayer is primarily a sense of being in the presence of divine love. I find it extraordinarily nurturing and attractive. It is both restful and yet full of surprises. 'Love whose cause is God is like a spring welling up from the depths: its flow never abates, for God also is that spring of love whose supply never fails.'[1]

My thoughts may well wander for a while but I am happy to let them. I find that I am gently, and without direction from me, opening up all the many issues that concern me to the love and the guidance of God. In the light of the candle, I turn them over and around and inside out and let the light of God in on all the shadowy places. I do not seek answers to the questions that trouble me, but as I place these problems and people into the presence of God, I also open myself, and my senses become sharpened to the presence of God.

The daily liturgical round in which I am also engaged feeds into this, so that, even though I do not always make the connection, the particularities of the seasons of the church's year, together with my own intercessory prayer, are the food with which this prayer is nourished. And they do seem to be connected, for at the times when through travel, pressure of work or sheer disaffectedness, I let that daily discipline drop, I find that I become less open to God in the prayer of contemplation, and all too often then my prayer can become very woolly.

I find it quite understandable that those who have become the great teachers of prayer are those who have had a vocation to contemplative prayer and have followed it exclusively. The pull is very strong and it can be quite addictive. Isaac the Syriac was aware of this when he said 'The person who hungers and thirsts for God's sake, God will make drunk with his good things, with the wine whose inebriation never leaves those who drink it'.[2] However, I am equally convinced that such prayer is part of the mix of ways that God has given us to live with the mystery of God's being, and, because it never quite leaves me when I blow out my candle, something of the divine whiff lingers and is there alongside me, like someone praying for me, when my heart and my mind must necessarily engage on other issues which are equally the call of God on my life.

The longing for contemplative prayer as a full-time occupation can set up a sense of either/or, and then I find that I am approaching the escapist tendency of my youthful prayer. When I am tired, frazzled and stressed-out my sense of constant prayer fades and I long to get back deeply into the prayer of contemplation. In part this is a way of escaping difficulties, but it is also God calling me back, and when I do indulge my need for such prayer, it is not long before I begin again to let God's love work on my stressed-out life, and I begin to see once more where the points of connection are between the problems I am wrestling with and the God in whose name I am called to wrestle with them.

This tension between the desire for withdrawal and the call to engagement and compassion is by no means new in the life of a bishop. St Gregory, in his *Pastoral Care*, pointed to the need for a bishop to preserve quietude, yet he (*sic*) may not thus refuse to be of service to others, but must follow the example of Christ who 'came forth from the bosom of His Father into our midst, that He might benefit many'.[3]

Contemplation can also be dangerous. The writer of the Epistle to the Hebrews says 'It is a dreadful thing to fall into the hands of the living God' (Hebrews 10.31). Contemplative prayer is a space, a place of real transformation and of real risk. Anyone who rests with a disarmed self in the presence of God experiences vulnerability. And vulnerability is a concept that women are wary of; too much damage has been done to women from sexual and physical abuse, and some of it has occurred within Christian families and churches. The legitimation of vulnerability as a virtue of the spiritual life is rightfully suspect.

Contemplative vulnerability is always intentional and always sought; it is chosen vulnerability and it is not easy. There is a long literature of advice to the would-be contemplative and reading books is much easier than, but no substitute for, the doing. I am never sure whether I or others are attracted by the desire for vulnerability or the desire for transforming engagement with God. I think both, for vulnerability and transformation go together: while undoubtedly risky, contemplative prayer, placing oneself intentionally close to God, is paradoxically and profoundly transformative. It is a resting, a staying in the presence of Christ, a yielding to divine power, a self-effacement that draws the contemplative into the pattern of the cross and resurrection. It is silence, but not silencing, for from its depths prophetic voices have shrieked. It is the choice to 'practise the presence of God', a God who gently moves into our being, soothing and challenging in an inimitable mix. The emptied self is not a negated self but a self that is open to and ready for the transformation that grows from this expansion into God. While the risk of real vulnerability must be genuinely entered into, the prayer of contemplation is anything but passive.

Above all, contemplative prayer is the prayer that lets God be God. As such it is the best possible antidote to any illusions of grandeur that I might have. It supports, encourages and draws me into a more trusting stance, one that has less need to be controlling, and hence when it is necessary that I act strongly it is there to sustain me. When I light my candle and place myself in the presence of God, I am at one with the rest of humankind in knowing my need of God.

Contemplation and poetry

Notwithstanding my attraction to silence, I am a person of words, and spinning the words of faith is for me nearly a contemplative activity as I seek to find the spaces between the words, the meaning that eludes the obvious, drawing connections that illuminate and discover. At its best it is an experience of touching the place where mystery and meaning meet.

Writing a poem is a creative act, drawing this barely-accessible meaning into a shape that will be a gift to whoever has the grace to receive it. It is a gift created to be wondered at, not least by the creator. As such it may not communicate either effectively or accurately; it moves into the affective areas of communication, drawing the reader into fresh areas of experience.

Writing poetry is for me an act of participating in the divine act of communication, when the Word became flesh:

> There's a poem in the air,
> Hanging out of reach,
> But full of promise.
>
> People come in poems,
> Wrapped up in gently hinting
> Words, that image their particularity
> Into the eternity of humankind.
>
> And I reach out to grasp;
> Transmuting the promise into black and white,
> Teasing to find the Flesh made Word,
> Daring to try to capture,
> The Christ in each one of them.

Both the discovery and the formation is deeply satisfying. Something of the discovery often underlies the process by which my sermons come into being, but there the words are more strung out, less compact and have to live without the support of form. For, at root, both are the search for connections, and making connections is a radical understanding of the incarnation.

The possibility of connections is there all the time: it is there in all my interactions with people, processes and prayer; but in this regard it is particularly sparked off by words. So it is there every time I read the Scriptures, the Word of God, and it can often take me by surprise as when I read the Scriptures aloud in the Sunday service and become aware of sparks in those texts that I had missed in preparing my sermon, and find another one taking shape. It is a wonderful experience for a poet to have, as it says much about the power of words continually to astonish and invigorate us, and even to surpass human understanding.

I thank God for the gift of words, for the Word made flesh, who lives in me.

Contemplation in the life of a jet-setter

I also make and hold within my being connections that cross the world. I am one of many New Zealanders who have known two countries at opposite sides of the world as home. For myself, my belonging is now clearly in New Zealand, but my upbringing, my formation as a person was in England. So, like others, I find identity in more than one place and I know well the all but unconscious phenomenon of looking over my shoulder.

There is a sense in which this has become more marked in recent years as I have had more opportunity to travel and the isolation of New Zealand has, for me, been broken. On one level it has been a wonderful opportunity to reconnect with the country of my upbringing and with the members of my family who still live there. But such travel also brings with it a sense of uprooting, a sense of reality being nowhere in particular but located primarily in the world of ideas. It can, and I have seen it happen in others as well as myself, bring a diminished response to the particularities of place. It is exciting but spiritually dangerous.

For New Zealand is a very particular place, with its own story and character. There is much to enjoy in this country and much to tell about it, but nevertheless, many New Zealanders who travel overseas have a strong sense that this is a country that compares unfavourably with all that they find overseas. This is a small society and many comparisons show us up in a poor light. There was a time when the most obvious characteristic of a New Zealander overseas was an inferiority complex!

So looking back, making comparisons that reveal (if not help us to understand) our limitations is not only an unconscious pastime for New Zealanders who have migrated during their lifetime, it is also bred by travel. It is not uncommon for these comparisons to breed discontent. But there are possibilities in New Zealand's very limitedness that invite us to reach beyond comparisons and the tendency to discontent and appreciate our uniqueness.

For myself, in the writings of the desert fathers, I have found a way to deepen this appreciation, to discover the spiritual gift that I know is here for me. Not that New Zealand is a desert. The point of the desert that St Anthony stumbled into in the fourth century, in an intentional move to escape the distractions of the city, is that it was a place that did not have the attractions that drew people to the city. It was a search for an unencumbered relationship to God, one that was not driven by the all-too-human tendency to desire more and more of what gives us instant and easy pleasure. It was a search for contentment.

And herein lies the wisdom. It is a basic truth of asceticism that it is not necessarily a denigration of the body, though it has often been misapplied for that purpose. Rather, it is a way of surrendering to reduced circumstances, or that which because of our restless tendency to compare appears as reduced, in a manner that enhances the whole person. This is a radical way of knowing who, what and where we are in defiance of those powerful pressures in contemporary society – the attraction of being at the frontier of 'new' learnings and discoveries, to say nothing of the analgesics of alcohol, drugs, television, shopping malls and so on that aim to make us forget. It is knowing our place in the heart of God; it is contentment.

I am reminded of the insight of the fourth-century monk Evagrius, that in the desert most of one's troubles come from 'distracting thoughts of one's former life' that do not allow us to live in the present. This reflects what I regard as the basic principle of 'desert' survival: not only to know where you are but also to love what you find there.

There is a kind of silence in this. Not the absolute silence of the lips, but the silence that does not always seek to be in the forefront of debate that is happening elsewhere, that can rest content and present with the people and issues that are where God has called us to be, and can eschew the larger stage. Silence is an attitude of the heart, an attentiveness to the present.

There is a strange mystery about this, the paradox of the desert reworked in the face of the contradictions of jet-set travel. But silence is the best response to mystery. Perhaps the real miracle is that when this brand of asceticism is lived at depth it can breed a deep love for this country that reflects but does not ignore its shortcomings. This reflects a truth Thomas Merton once related about his life as a Trappist monk: 'It is in deep solitude and silence that I find the gentleness with which I can truly love my brother and sister.'

For many New Zealanders whose history and practice of life inevitably leads us to make comparison, the decision to live here is a deliberate decision to choose life in the slow lane, comparatively speaking, and as such it has a contemplative reality. Despite the pressures that afflict the minutiae of my life, the deep waters, those closest to the earth, flow gently and slowly; the undercurrents are smooth. Paradoxically, as with St Anthony when he moved from the city to the desert, I am open to its awareness because I know what life in the fast lane is like.

So I have learnt to seek intentionally a selective silence, a silence that goes beyond the holding of confidence but which can pick up the rhythm and the undercurrents of the flow, and which seeks only God in the search for the right way. I have learnt to trust the slower pace, not to seek the answer to my questions by reading the latest book or consulting the latest guru, for if I did that, it would be all that I did. I have learnt to trust the processes that take time, to value change that is not sudden or ill-considered but grows out of experience well grounded in a contented reality. I have found God in this slow lane.

Reflective spirituality

There are consequences to being in leadership. One of the earliest that I became aware of was that people took much more notice of what I said than they had ever done before, and consequently they took me much more seriously. I had to learn new techniques for reining in my tongue, for I also realized that the consequences of speaking or acting carelessly were much more far-reaching than they had been; I could do much more damage and some of it would be irreparable. I also realized that when this happened I was essentially wounding the church, the Body of Christ that I had been called to serve.

I was profoundly grateful to an excellent soul friend who said, quite briefly, that God would look after the church, but who also took my concerns seriously and enabled me to embark on a journey of self-knowledge and self-awareness. There was just so much to learn about how I was responding to this new call, what the baggage was that I was carrying and that I was tripping over – often quite badly. So I learnt much about my strengths and my weaknesses; some of the latter I shed, some I took with me, continually aware of and appreciative of God's mercy and grace.

I learnt to reflect, honestly and openly before God, on both the person that I was, whom God had called, and how I was interacting in the situation in which God had placed me. Reflection, as I understand it, is an effort to estimate the significance of what we perceive and what we know. Reflection steps back to ponder how these mesh together and with other things. Reflection is then concerned with coherence and with likelihood. It wants to know how a new singer harmonizes with the chorus already begun. It asks whether a given proposal is likely to promote a fuller disclosure of the truth or a fuller sense of obedience. It finds its energy and inspiration from the life of the Holy Spirit of God which draws the whole of creation into God's reconciling love.

A reflective spirituality enables one to dig deep into a situation, to look carefully and self-critically at one's own responses and conduct and, because it is done in the presence of God's unreserved love for us, to be unafraid of what we might find and to make the personal turn-arounds that are necessary if changes are to be made. As a bishop, this also means that on occasion I need to be quite open with people about this process of discovery and discernment. For others as for myself, it is all right to make mistakes; God's mercy has no boundaries. I would like to think that this enables others to explore a more reflective spirituality.

A reflective process such as this is never-ending. Its tendency is to begin spinning, from inside a given question, the web of connections necessary to place that question in a more fully adequate context. But the strands can, at times, get into a terrible tangle. Moreover, the more Christian a reflective process is, the more it reckons with the divine mystery. The ends of the thread pass out of our sight. The more complicated the reflective process becomes, in fidelity to the seemingly infinite complexity of human nature, the greater becomes my desire to pivot and move below reflection into the silence of divinity itself. When this happens, I turn once more to contemplative prayer as a necessary antidote to endless reflection, as well as a more profound response to the mystery of God.

Prayer and pastoral practice

I have long felt the need and the delight in the call to hold God's people before God in intercessory prayer. Effectively, I do this in a number of different ways. I do it formally with the church at prayer through the many prayer lists that occupy our prayer desks; then I have my own list which, while it has some regularity, is constantly changing according to circumstances and need; and too, where people rest more heavily on me, I find myself holding them in the light of the love of God in my more informal prayer times. But there are so many, and the longer that I am in this job, the more I get close to people, the more I feel my heart stretching so that a constant theme of my prayer is 'Oh Lord, enlarge my heart'.

For prayer not only strengthens my ministry, it also informs my ministry. It is there that I begin to understand how the great themes of our Christian faith relate to the nitty-gritty of all that I am involved with. So that, by the grace of God, I find the way to trace the parallel between the movement of God within my own soul and the movement of God within the Christian community that I lead. For the great Christian themes that I know so well, like grace, trust, mercy, justice, healing, obedience and so on, are just as applicable to whole communities as they are to individuals.

I feel that it is important that I can with others be ready, as we go about the business of church affairs and administration, to articulate such questions as: where do we find grace? how can it be acknowledged? and mercy? It is so much harder for a community than for an individual to come to the point of turn-around, of coming to grips with wrong and making a new start. And yet there are times when this is necessary, and it always involves, first, a turn-around in my own heart, because I am integrally part of the Christian community I lead. All too often I find myself faced with a conflict between forgiveness and justice.

Soul friends

An essential ingredient of the spiritual life is the willingness to place oneself in utter honesty before God. We can never deceive God about what is going on inside of us. If we attempt to deceive ourselves and bring a sanitized version of ourselves into God's presence, we not only place limits on what God can do for us, but we can, if we are not careful, subvert the action of God in our lives, by hijacking God and the power of God for purposes that have nothing to do with the being and the work of God.

For me, a soul friend is not an exclusive relationship with just one person. I have found that God works through the networks of people that I know. In many of them I can share at depth and also receive back, and in so doing perceive something of the workings of God. I have valued very deeply those people who, over the years, have been soul friends to me. People to whom I can talk with real and deep honesty, and who will share my joys and my sorrows and stay with me whatever. A soul friend is also someone who will both accept and challenge what I say, and will hold it sacred and deep in their own prayers, thus reinforcing, by the resilience of their faith, my own faith when it might be at a point of faltering.

A soul friend also needs to be someone who will not let what I might say affect any other relationship in their lives. This has been particularly important for me in the years since I became a bishop, for I have found that there are some people who wish me well to such an extent that, when they sense that relationships are going wrong for me, they try to put them right and frequently make things worse.

A soul friend is someone who can, at least for a while, be there for me and for my needs. I have so often found that the general impression the role of a bishop imparts is of someone who has no needs and who is only there for others. This is a by-product of the difficulty that people who see me in role have in seeing me as a human being. But I do have a need for relationships in which I can be both honest and real myself.

A soul friend needs to be someone who trusts God, and trusts that, whatever the distress I might be experiencing, there is no need for panic; and that given time and prayer the good that God wills will prevail. If a soul friend moves into panic mode they belie their trust in God, and that trust is the greatest gift that a soul friend can offer.

I remain also profoundly appreciative of those who without any expectation of intimacy or openly expressed honesty are ready and willing to pray with me, to minister to me, explicitly in the power of the Holy Spirit. I have learnt very visibly, physically even, what it is to abandon myself to God. I have been blessed.

An appropriate spirituality of strength

For me, and for other women seeking to exercise authentic Christian leadership, a central question is the necessity of coming to terms with power, to acknowledge the power that I hold and to use it openly and responsibly. This is balanced, held in tension by the power that we do not hold, the power that rightly belongs to God, for it is God I am here to serve, by pointing in all that I say and do, in every detail of the conduct of my ministry, to the immensity, the majesty and the mystery of God.

For the truth about the power of God is that there is more than enough power to go round. It is like the bread in the gospel story of the loaves and the fishes, multiplied to provide excessively, extravagantly for the crowd. The power that God holds, the power that God gives is infinite. 'The point is, one will never get to the end of it, never get to the bottom of it, never, never, never. And never, never, never is what you must take for your shield and your most glorious promise.'[4] Our God is generous beyond imagination and calls us to generous ministry.

God empowers us by drawing close to us, by relating to us in ways that draw out our honesty and our energy (see Chapter 1). When we, in our turn, empowered by the love of God, draw near to others to empower them, open the way for God's power to work through them, we are in a way diminishing our own power. The real challenge is to trust that the power of God in others will be used by God through them for the good of God's people and to reveal the truth about God.

Our spirituality, our experience of God, our awareness of what it is to trust God and to relinquish control in our personal lives, means little unless it finds expression in the practice and conduct of ministry. We are not, as Foucault would have it, 'isolated atoms of power', but people living in community, enmeshed in the lives of those with whom we share community, and our experience of interdependence receives vision and validation from the experience of God in Trinity.

This is the mandate and the motivation, theological and ethical, to seek justice, passionately, both within the Body of Christ and in the world that does not know Christ. Justice-making moves us from a personal spirituality to a spirituality of community, of the church. In accepting this mandate, the church agrees to become a gracious place, a place of hospitality and safety, wombspace, where all of God's people can experience and delight in loving and being loved.

There is real hope that the insights of women's theological reflection will sharpen our awareness of God's otherness, and transcendence. Women have always had to move outwards; we have had to understand and relate to the culture in order to survive. Herein lies, I believe, the key to transcendence, because we must transcend what *is* in order to *be*. I am quietly optimistic.

All institutionalization represents some loss of vision. I do believe that the church throughout the ages has genuinely wished to be a place of hospitality and safety for all of God's people, but the entrenched and unobserved structures and habits of power within the institution have set limits to hospitality. These limitations are now being questioned from a number of different perspectives, and, I believe, the hospitality of the heart of God is becoming more evident and appreciated within our life. Like the mystery that is God its full meaning is not accessible to us but we can sense what Emily Dickinson called 'a dim capacity for wings',[5] and be thankful.

Transfiguration is always possible, with God.

Notes

Introduction

1 Quoted by Rowan Williams, 'Direct contact, and accountability, in a small church', *Cambridge*, XXXV (1994–95), pp. 23–5 (p. 25).
2 The Rt Revd Sir Edward Norman died in 1986.
3 Brian Davis, *The Way Ahead: Anglican Change and Prospect in New Zealand* (Christchurch: Caxton Press, 1995), p. 76.
4 Muriel Porter, 'The Christian origins of feminism' in *Freedom and Entrapment: Women Thinking Theology*, ed. Maryanne Confoy and Dorothy A. Lee (Blackburn, Vic.: HarperCollins, 1995), pp. 208–24.
5 Penelope A. B. Jamieson, 'The bridge too wide: women in Christian leadership', the 1992 Caroline Chisholm Lecture, La Trobe University, Melbourne, Australia.
6 The indigenous people of New Zealand are the Maori, the *tangata whenua*, the 'people of the land'.

1 The context of power

1 This loosely woven collection of theological positions takes its starting point from the Conference of Medellín, Colombia, in 1968.
2 Sometimes referred to as 'Brown theology' in New Zealand.
3 A comment reported by Nancy Hartsock, in 'Foucault on power' in *Feminism and Postmodernism*, ed. Linda J. Nicholson (New York: Routledge, 1990).
4 Michel Foucault, 'Body/Power' in *Power/Knowledge: Selected Interviews and Other Writings 1972–1977*, ed. Colin Gordon (New York: Pantheon Books, 1980), p. 57.
5 Michel Foucault, 'Truth and power' in *Power/Knowledge*, ed. Gordon, p. 119.
6 Linda Alcoff, 'Feminism and Foucault: the limits to a collaboration' in *Crises in Continental Philosophy*, ed. Arlene Dallery and Charles Scott (New York: State University of New York Press, 1990), pp. 69–86.
7 Ranjini Rabera explored both the persistence and the attraction of male structures of power in a paper 'Feminism and changing images of power', given in New Zealand in 1994.

8 Patricia Brennan, 'Loosed and bound: women's reform and the question of God' in *Freedom and Entrapment: Women Thinking Theology*, ed. Maryanne Confoy and Dorothy A. Lee (Blackburn, Vic.: HarperCollins, 1995), pp. 78–99. She quotes S. Gunew and A. Yeatman (eds), *Feminism and the Politics of Difference* (Sydney: Allen and Unwin, 1993).

9 Betsan Martin, 'Luce Irigaray, feminine divinity and Women-Church: a philosophical exploration of feminism, theology and education', MA thesis, University of Auckland, 1993. I am greatly indebted to Betsan for introducing me to the work of Luce Irigaray.

10 Luce Irigaray, *Sexes and Genealogies* (New York: Columbia University Press, 1993), p. 61.

11 Irigaray, *Sexes and Genealogies*, p. 62.

12 I have been unable to trace the author.

13 Dietrich Bonhoeffer, *Letters and Papers from Prison* (London: SCM Press, 1971), p. 360.

14 Augustine, Sermon 340.

15 *Church Times*, Leader (14 October 1994).

16 Edward W. Scott, 'The authority of love' in *Authority in the Anglican Communion*, ed. Stephen W. Sykes (Toronto: Anglican Book Centre, 1987).

2 Power in the church

1 See for example: Anne Patel-Gray, 'Not yet Tiddas: an Aboriginal womanist critique of Australian church feminism' in *Freedom and Entrapment*, ed. Confoy and Lee, pp. 165–92; and Jacquelyn Grant, *White Woman's Christ and Black Woman's Jesus: Feminist Christology and Black Womanist Response* (Atlanta, GA: Scholars Press, 1989), American Academy of Religion Academy Series, 64.

2 Andrea Dworkin, *Women Hating* (New York: New American Library, 1974), p. 24.

3 John Howe, *Highways and Hedges: A Study of Developments in the Anglican Communion* (London: CIO, 1985), p. 198.

4 Elizabeth Bettenhausen, 'The feminist movement' in Miriam Therese Winter, Adair Lummis, Allison Stokes, *Defecting in Place: Women Claiming Responsibility for Their Own Lives* (New York: Crossroad, 1994), p. 207.

3 Discerning

1 St Gregory the Great, *Pastoral Care*, ed. H. D. Davis (Westminster, MD: The Newman Press, 1950), Part 1, para. 11, p. 41.

2 *The Truth Shall Make You Free* (The Lambeth Conference, 1988), para. 150, p. 61.

3 Roger Pym, 'Crumbs from the mitre: a comparison of the ministry experiences of ordained women and men in the Church of the Province of New Zealand', MA thesis, University of Auckland, 1992.

4 Carole Grahame, 'Re-membering the past . . . reshaping the future', MTh thesis, Vancouver School of Theology, 1994.
5 Isabel Carter Heyward, *A Priest Forever* (San Francisco: Harper and Row, 1976), p. 3.

5 Holding

1 *The Truth Shall Make You Free*, para. 144, p. 60.
2 Elaine Pagels, *The Gnostic Gospels* (London: Penguin Books, 1979), pp. 55ff.
3 Cf. Thomas Nagel, *The View from Nowhere* (Oxford: Oxford University Press, 1986).
4 Gunew and Yeatman (eds), *Feminism and the Politics of Difference*, p. xiv.
5 *The Truth Shall Make You Free*, para. 141, p. 60.
6 *The Eames Commission: The Official Reports* (Toronto: The Anglican Consultative Council, 1994), p. 75.
7 *The Eames Commission: The Official Reports*, p. 83.
8 John Zizioulas, 'The Church as Communion', presentation to the Fifth World Conference of Faith and Order, Santiago de Compostella, 1993.
9 *The Truth Shall Make You Free*, para. 135, p. 59.
10 *The Eames Commission: The Official Reports*, p. 82.

6 Ethics

1 I have been unable to trace the source of this.
2 Note the rise of motivators hired by organizations to generate energy.
3 Carol Gilligan, *In a Different Voice: Psychological Theory and Women's Development* (Cambridge, MA: Harvard University Press, 1982); Nancy Chodorow, *The Reproduction of Mothering: Psychoanalysis and the Sociology of Gender* (Berkeley: University of California Press, 1978).
4 Church of England Board for Social Responsibility, *Something to Celebrate: Valuing Families in Church and Society* (London: Church House Publishing, 1995).
5 Karen Lebacqz, 'Appropriate vulnerability' in *Sexuality and the Sacred: Sources for Theological Reflection*, ed. James B. Nelson and Sandra P. Longfellow (London: Mowbray, 1994), pp. 256–61.
6 Jack Dominian, 'Sex within marriage' in *Sexuality and the Sacred*, ed. Nelson and Longfellow, pp. 264–76 (p. 267).
7 Dominian, 'Sex within marriage', p. 269.
8 Dominian, 'Sex within marriage', p. 269.
9 Lebacqz, 'Appropriate vulnerability'.

7 The abuse of power

1 Title D is the discipline canon of our church.
2 Neil and Thea Ormerod, *When Ministers Sin: Sexual Abuse in the Churches* (NSW: Millennium, 1995), p. xiii.
3 Rose Macaulay's novel *They Were Defeated* is a powerful illustration of 'ecclesiastical seduction'.
4 Ormerod and Ormerod, *When Ministers Sin*, p. 5.

8 Authority

1 Nikolai Berdyaev, *The Fate of Man in the Modern World* (London: SCM Press, 1934), p. 124.
2 Inter Anglican Theological and Doctrinal Commission, The Anglican Communion, *The Virginia Report*, in preparation.
3 *The Truth Shall Make You Free*, para. 70, p. 99.
4 *The Truth Shall Make You Free*, para. 71, p. 99.
5 Pagels, *The Gnostic Gospels*, pp. 59ff.
6 *The Eames Commission: The Official Reports*, p. 83.
7 Ruth Fry, '"Prim" preachers to ordained ministers' in *Out of the Silence: Methodist Women of Aotearoa 1822–1985* (Christchurch: Methodist Publishing, 1987), pp. 209–19 (p. 210).
8 Celia Allison Hahn, *Growing in Authority, Relinquishing Control: A New Approach to Faithful Leadership* (New York: The Alban Institute, 1994).
9 Deborah Tannen, *You Just Don't Understand: Women and Men in Conversation* (New York: Ballantyne Books, 1991, p. 36.
10 Tannen, *You Just Don't Understand*, p. 33.
11 Hans Küng, *Why Priests?*, quoted in Jim Cotter, *Yes, Minister* (Sheffield: Cairns Publications, 1992), p. 58.
12 Cotter, *Yes, Minister*, p. 63.
13 *Baptism, Eucharist and Ministry* (Geneva: World Council of Churches, 1982), Faith and Order Paper no. 111, para. 12, p. 21.
14 *The Truth Shall Make You Free*, pp. 104–5.

9 Searching

1 Vincent Donovan, *Christianity Rediscovered* (London: SCM Press, 1984).
2 Cotter, *Yes, Minister*.
3 Beverly Harrison refers to the difficulty that she as a Christian woman experiences as the struggle to 'know what it means simultaneously to "keep faith" and to keep my integrity': Beverly Wildung Harrison, 'Keeping faith in a sexist Church' in *Making the Connections: Essays in Feminist Social Ethics*, ed. B. W. Harrison and C. S. Robb (Boston: Beacon Press, 1985), p. 206.
4 Mary Daly, *Gyn/Ecology* (Boston: Beacon Press, 1978), pp. 79ff.

10 Relationships

1   Celia Hahn, *Growing in Authority*, p. 59.
2   Cf. Gary Bouma, 'Who cares for the carers? Organisational constraints on providing pastoral care for clergy', *St Mark's Review*, no. 143 (Spring 1990), pp. 2–5.
3   I have recently begun exploring Open Space Technology. It has the potential to release considerable energy from within a group. Cf. Harrison Owen, *Open Space Technology: A User's Guide* (Potomac, MD: Abbot Publishing, 1992).
4   Cf. Celia Hahn, *Growing in Authority*, p. 68.
5   Augustine, Sermon 340.
6   I am grateful to Maggie Ross for this insight.

11 Praying

1   *The Ascetical Homilies of Isaac the Syriac*, tr. Dana Millier, 268. In A. M. Allchin (ed.), *Heart of Compassion: Daily Reading with St Isaac of Syria*, no. 6.
2   *Ascetical Homilies*, tr. Millier, 50; Allchin, no. 4.
3   St Gregory the Great, *Pastoral Care*, Part 1, para. 5.
4   Iris Murdoch, *Henry and Cato* (New York: Viking Press, 1977), p. 270.
5   Emily Dickinson, *Final Harvest: Emily Dickinson's Poems*, sel. and intro. by Thomas H. Johnson (Boston: Little Brown and Co., 1961), p. 245.